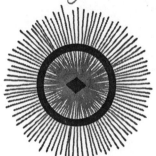

At a Journal Workshop

The basic text and guide for using the Intensive Journal

by
Ira Progoff

*guiding people to meaningful places
and look around for themselves*

DIALOGUE HOUSE LIBRARY | NEW YORK, N.Y.

Published by
Dialogue House Library
80 East Eleventh Street
New York, New York 10003

Library of Congress Catalog Card Number:
75-13932
ISBN 87941-003-5
Paperback ISBN 0-87941-006-X

First paperback edition published 1977

Printed in the United States of America

Foreword
to the Paperback Edition

The *Intensive Journal Process* with its varied techniques has become an active part of a great many lives since it was first described in book form a year ago. Before that, the *Intensive Journal Method* was available only to those who could attend a Dialogue House workshop conducted either by myself or by persons studying with me. Using this guidebook, however, many people have been able to carry out the Journal exercises in their own privacy, thus setting into motion in their lives the self-balancing process by which this method achieves its dynamic effects. With this paperback edition it is my hope that many more people will be able to use the *Intensive Journal* as an instrument for self-guidance, to crystallize the decisions they need to make, to identify their goals, and to find the meaning of their own unique life.

There are a few things to be said at the outset that can make your use of this book and its method more productive. In the first place you should bear in mind that, while we use a personal journal in this work, we are not engaged in journal or diary keeping in the usual sense. We use a specially structured format in order to feed life data into our journal process where it cumulatively generates energy and builds a momentum for our lives. This active process is called *Journal Feedback*, and you will gradually become familiar with its procedures and possibilities as you work with each of the exercises.

Since it carries a process of continuous life experience, this is not a book to be read through at a sitting or two but to be worked with a step at a time. When you have carried out all the exercises, allowing them to stretch over as long a period as they require, an exciting awareness like the breaking of dawn will come to you. It will be the cumulative impact both of seeing your life set itself in perspective and recognizing the elusive process by which your *Journal Feedback* exercises have been working for you.

The experience of recognition that will come to you then will be very much like learning to play a musical instrument. After slow and stumbling beginnings, you suddenly realize that you now comprehend not only the keyboard as a whole but the infinite possibilities for combining the keys creatively. From that point onwards, the instrument is accessible to you with all its potentials.

The same is true of learning to use the *Intensive Journal*. First you must begin slowly, even arduously, to learn the nature of the instrument and its techniques. Once you have learned how to use it, however, the *Intensive Journal* will always be available to you. You can then call upon it as you need it, not only to help you through the crises that may recur in the cycles of your life, but also to give you access to depths of creative resources within yourself.

You will perceive as you work with it that this is not a book of pat answers nor advice for quick success. It does not espouse any particular doctrine or belief. It does, however, describe a method that persons of all ages and levels of education coming from the most diverse cultures have been able to use effectively in clarifying their lives and developing their own beliefs.

You may glean some of my personal philosophy as you read, but the purpose of this book is not to set forth any beliefs. It is to explain a method of working privately at the inner levels of our life. You may agree with my personal philosophy, or you may not. That will not matter. What *is* important is that you use these techniques to help you become your own person and find a way of living that will validate itself to you both in terms of your inner sense of truth and the actualities of your outer experience.

IRA PROGOFF

Table of Contents

Preface

This book goes to press almost a decade after the first steps were taken toward the development of the *Intensive Journal* and the *Journal Feedback* method. After a series of books, notably *The Symbolic and the Real*, had laid the foundation for it, the essential principles were formulated and published in a paper delivered at the Eranos Conference in Switzerland in 1965. The *Intensive Journal* could then be designed with its operational structure as well as the techniques for using it in groups and in privacy. That was done during 1966.

During that same year, Dialogue House was established as the organizational vehicle for making the Journal Feedback approach available at various levels of society. The first step was to publish the *Intensive Journal*. With this as the instrument, it was possible to proceed experimentally and systematically in developing a program for the growth of individuals that could be used effectively by the diverse groups in modern society regardless of social level or educational background.

Since its publication*, the *Intensive Journal* has been used in hundreds of workshops led by myself and others, with several thousand persons

---

* The registered *Intensive Journal* is reprinted in the Appendix of this volume, p. 298 in the format that is currently used at Journal Workshops.

7

taking part. Of particular significance is the fact that these participants have come from all age levels, religious, social, economic, and educational backgrounds; a large percentage of them continue to work with the *Intensive Journal* after their basic Journal Workshop experience, using it both in their own privacy and in subsequent workshops.

As an outcome of this varied and continued usage, a core of principles and methodology has crystallized, with ample opportunity over the years for being tested, revised, and validated by repeated experience. It is this refined core of concept and technique that I am now undertaking to present in a series of volumes, beginning here with the fundamental life-integration experience of an *Intensive Journal Workshop*.

This first volume is intended as a practical guidebook and basic reference both for those who are meeting the *Intensive Journal* for the first time and those who have already participated in one or more Journal Workshops. In the course of this book we shall have an opportunity to work with the main exercises in all the sections of the *Intensive Journal*. It contains a full introductory experience of a basic *Intensive Journal Workshop*. In addition it provides the guidelines and directions for using the *Journal Feedback* procedures continuously in an ongoing, open-ended program of personal growth.

This program for the development of persons has been applied by Dialogue House in numerous social contexts over the past several years. The present volume presents the basic Journal Workshop experience. Companion volumes in this series which are now being prepared deal with the larger structure of thought and specialized applications of the *Intensive Journal* approach in such areas as creativity, spiritual experience, the transitions of aging, psychotherapy, education, and social change. The volume on *Process Meditation* presents a supportive procedure that is increasingly used in conjunction with the *Intensive Journal* to deepen the level of the work. Here, however, we begin with the basic experience of the *Intensive Journal* for drawing an individual life into focus, since this is the foundation of its advanced techniques and extended uses.

Chapter 1

The Intensive Journal as
an Instrument for Life

The *Intensive Journal* plays an active role in reconstructing a life, but it does so without imposing any external categories or interpretations or theories on the individual's experience. It remains neutral and open-ended so as to maintain the integrity of each person's development, while drawing him further along the road of his own life process. It does this by specific procedures which give vitality to many factors that are lying dormant in the depth of the self, drawing them into the movement of the person's life by means of the self-balancing principle that operates through the Journal Feedback process.

As it has evolved in practice since 1965, the *Intensive Journal* has become the instrument for a wide variety of techniques which progressively draw each person's life toward wholeness at its own tempo. It has been spoken of as a method that is *beyond psychotherapy* because it takes a *transpsychological* approach to what had been thought of as psychological problems. Here the word *transpsychological* means that it brings about therapeutic effects not by striving toward therapy but by providing active techniques that enable an individual to draw upon his inherent resources for becoming a whole person. It systematically evokes and strengthens the inner capacities of persons by working from a non-medical vantage point and proceeding without analytic or diagnostic categories. It establishes a person's sense of his own being by

draw each person's life toward wholeness

enriching his inner life with new experiences of a creative and spiritual quality. Since these experiences happen to him and are recorded by him in his *Intensive Journal* while they are actually taking place, each person accumulates a tangible and factual validation of his personal growth as it is in process.

Many persons have already had experiences in which they have sensed the presence of an underlying reality in life, a reality which they have recognized as a personal source of meaning and strength. It may have come to them in a brief, spontaneous moment of spiritual exaltation, or it may have come as a flash of awareness in the midst of darkness and pain. They came very close then to the deep, unifying contact, but it slipped away from them because they had no means of holding it and sustaining the relationship. Some could not break through because of their inherited overlay of religious doctrines or other intellectual concepts. Others missed their opportunity because they had so low an opinion of themselves that it did not occur to them that there could be depth and meaning in the experiences of their lives.

The *Intensive Journal* is specifically designed to provide an instrument and techniques by which persons can discover within themselves the resources they did not know they possessed. It is to enable them to draw the power of deep contact out of the actual experiences of their lives so that they can recognize their own identity and harmonize it with the larger identity of the universe as they experience it. Where they had negated themselves, they can by means of their *Intensive Journal* work, give their lives full value.

The specific means of achieving this contact with the inner resources of one's life is by the regular and disciplined use of the *Intensive Journal* with its progressive exercises. The effective principle operating in this is that, when a person is shown how to reconnect himself with the contents and the continuity of his life, the inner thread of movement by which his life has been unfolding reveals itself to him by itself. Given the opportunity, a life crystallizes out of its own nature, revealing its meaning and its goal. This is the self-integrating principle of life which the Journal procedures make available to us as persons.

As an individual works in the Journal Feedback process, the past experiences of his life gradually fit into place, times of exaltation and

10

times of despair, moments of hope and anger, crises and crossroads, partial failures and successes. As we use them over a period of time, the procedures of the *Intensive Journal* make it possible for all the events and relationships of our life to show us what they were *for,* what their purpose was in our lives, and what they wish to tell us for our future. Thus we gradually discover that our life has been going somewhere, however blind we have been to its direction and however unhelpful to it we ourselves may have been. We find that a connective thread has been forming beneath the surface of our lives, carrying the meaning that has been trying to establish itself in our existence. It is the inner continuity of our lives. As we recognize and identify ourselves with it, we see the inner myth that has been guiding our lives unknown to ourselves.

In the course of the gradual and cumulative work by which an individual recognizes the nonconscious guidance that has been directing his personal life involvements, he perceives that the peaks and the valleys are of equal importance. From one point of view, all are necessary, for the high is not possible without the low. In a more fundamental sense, however, he recognizes that the essence lies not in the events of his life in themselves, not in the things that have happened to him, but in his inner relationship to those events. At the moment when they were actually taking place, his relation to those events may have been inadequate because of many small fears and limited understanding. For that, he may feel guilty, angry, and negative toward himself. As the larger perspective opens through the Journal work, however, a new quality of relationship can be established to the events of the past. The continuity of our life renews itself, and we have a fresh opportunity. In the light of our new recognition of the inner movement and meaning of our lives, it actually seems that we can now begin our life anew. That is what the ageless symbolism of rebirth has been trying to say to people since the beginning of religion.

One of the most significant realizations that has come to me personally in the course of this work has been the observation of the *extra increment* of meaning that is added to an individual's awareness as the *Intensive Journal* procedures reopen the possibilities of his life. As the events of a life set themselves in order, giving perspective for the past and guidance for the future, *something additional* happens. It is as though

11

previously untapped knowledge is activated so that a person is brought face to face with the ultimates, and the meaning of his personal existence. It is there before him, collected in his own handwriting in his *Intensive Journal.* We often find that the experience of this deep opening in a person's life spontaneously expresses itself in the language of the spirit, regardless of the individual's religious background. Many of the entries written in the Journal at such moments of realization have the style of natural poetry or personal prophesy, the language of the Self discovering itself.

Experiences of this kind take place in the midst of the *Intensive Journal* work regardless of the social or economic level on which a person is living. To reintegrate and renew one's life perspective has a transforming and spiritually renewing effect on every person in whom it takes place, whether young or old, wealthy or impoverished, intellectual or unlettered. Observing this has served to strengthen the social use of the *Intensive Journal.* It has fortified the central concept of renewing society by renewing individuals, specifically by giving all individuals, wherever they are in the culture, an opportunity to contact their deep sources by reconstructing the inner continuity of their lives.

The process of using the *Intensive Journal* can fairly be described as a method for all seasons in a person's life. We may use it actively and intensely during times of conflict and difficulty; we may use it softly and slowly when our life is more relaxed, letting that be the time for philosophic deepening. At certain points in the cycle of our experience, we may let it fall into temporary disuse. Sometimes we shall use it at a Journal Workshop in the company of others; sometimes we shall use it by ourselves in our privacy; and sometimes we shall use it in the one-to-one relationship with a qualified Journal Consultant. The essence of the work, however, and its capacity to bring about personal growth, lies in the continuity of the process as the Journal is used in a diversity of modes.

Experience with the *Intensive Journal* over the past several years has demonstrated that the most effective way to begin its use is by attending a Journal Workshop. After that, the Journal Feedback procedures can be used in privacy and may have various kinds of emphasis. But the Journal Workshop is the basic first experience. This is the experience for which we are now preparing ourselves, and in which we shall participate with the exercises and experiences described in this book.

There are two main achievements to which you can look forward when you attend your first Journal Workshop. One is the experience of drawing the present situation of your life into focus in a broad perspective that includes both past experiences and future potentials while it opens deeper contact with spiritual and creative sources. The second is to learn, while you are thus engaged in *positioning* yourself in the movement of your life, the numerous techniques of the Journal Feedback method so that you will know how to use the *Intensive Journal* continuously as an effective personal instrument after the workshop is over.

The first purpose in attending a basic Journal Workshop is indeed important. It is to enable us to experience in a full and open-ended perspective the movement of our lives as a whole. Through the Journal Feedback process, we establish a large overview in which we can recognize the cycles of change, of development and diminution, that comprise our life history. This gives us the *context of continuity* in which we can perceive our individual existence, and within this context we *position* ourselves between our past and our future. The composite of entries and exercises which we record in the course of a Journal Workshop places us in a position to answer the question: Where am I in the movement of my life?   *NB*

We place ourselves between the experiences of our past and the possibilities of the future, and we do this in an active way. We do not construct a merely intellectual perspective of our life. We do not analyze our life as though we were an outsider to it. But we enter the inner movement of our whole life history and connect ourselves to it from within. In that way we extend our life in harmony with the inner principle that is trying to unfold through it. We are dancers joining the dance of our life as it is going on, and continuing it toward its fulfillment. We experience an inner perspective of our life as we work with the self-enlarging exercises of the Journal Feedback method.

The active inner perspective of our life which we build in the course of our first Journal Workshop enables us to position ourselves so that we know where we are at those times when we are at a crossroad or at a point of transition in our lives. The perspective of being positioned in this way is especially helpful in enabling us to make a well-considered decision. As we use it to place ourselves, the workshop becomes for us a mid-point in the movement of our lives, a moment in time that is midway between our past and our future. Insofar as the past is over and the future has not yet transpired, this midpoint is an open moment of possibility. Properly used, it becomes like the eye of a hurricane, a quiet place at the center of life, a free, unconditioned moment of opportunity.

For many persons the experience at a Journal Workshop is like entering a sanctuary, for it provides a protected situation safe from the outer pressures of the world in which an individual can quietly reappraise his relation to his life. The procedures that are followed through the workshop give him a methodology to use, and the compactness of the workshop program will enable him to cover the salient areas of his life experience within a limited time. The presence of other persons in the workshop, each exploring the individuality of his own life history, builds an atmosphere that supports and strengthens his inward work at the same time that the *Intensive Journal* insures his privacy. Being with many others while each is delving into the uniqueness of his own life, has the effect of reinforcing our intuitive sense of the integrity and validity of each individual existence. A Journal Workshop thus serves as a retreat in the traditional spiritual sense of the term. It provides a protected pause in our life activities during which we can deepen and expand the perspectives of our existence.

The first purpose in attending a basic Life-Focus Workshop is to establish an overarching perspective of our whole life history, and to begin the process of drawing ourselves into harmony with the inner movement of our lives. Toward this end, our second and very important goal at such a basic Journal Workshop is to become familiar enough with the sections of the *Intensive Journal* and the procedures for using them so that we can work with the Journal by ourselves after the workshop is over. The Journal Feedback method gives us access to an open-ended instrument for balancing and directing our growth throughout the continuity of our lives. If, therefore, once we have had our basic introductory experience in the use of it, we feel that its style of approach is personally congenial to us, our first Journal Workshop will become the launching point for a continuous program of inner discipline. We shall have taken the first step in the ongoing use of a self-adjusting technique that will be available afterwards for us to use according to our own rhythm and sense of need.

One context in which we can understand the relevance of the *Intensive Journal* is the conception of *self-reliance* of which Ralph Waldo Emerson spoke and which he described as the basis for human growth and dignity. Emerson saw self-reliance as a general principle of truth. The *Intensive Journal* program takes that principle as its starting point, and then provides a practical method by which each individual, at whatever his present level and condition, can experience the active power of self-reliance as a capacity available in the actuality of his life.

Emerson pointed out the easy temptation and the entrapment into which we fall when we place our reliance upon external things, on property, the chance of good fortune, and especially on our expectations of what other persons will do for us. He showed us that the fallacy lies in our placing our center of balance outside of our own inherent abilities. When our reliance is upon things or people outside of ourselves, we are not drawing upon the strengths that are inherent within us, and what is more important, we are not developing them further. The progressive strengthening of our inherent capacities gives us a resource that draws upon itself, and that is, therefore, self-sustaining and self-amplifying. Its energies and abilities arise increasingly from within itself. It is, in Emerson's phrase, "that which relies because it works and is." It is self-reliant because its capacities lie within itself and are progressively being enlarged as they are used.

The *Intensive Journal* and its procedures for personal work provide an instrument and a method by which we can each develop interior capacities strong enough to be relied upon in meeting the trials of our life. It gives us a means of private and personal discipline with which to develop our inner muscles. When we rely upon these, we are indeed self-reliant because these inner capacities *are* ourselves. Emerson says in his essay on *Self-Reliance*, "Nothing can bring you peace but yourself." The *Intensive Journal* is offered as an instrument with a day-by-day method to make this realistically possible and progressively true for each of us.

Chapter 2

The Beginnings of
the Intensive Journal

SEEKING THE TAO OF GROWTH

Since the *Intensive Journal* evolved out of a slow distillation of depth procedures and experimental studies, it will be helpful for our understanding of how to use it if we begin by retracing the thought processes that led to it.

The particular dynamic effect that is achieved by using the *Intensive Journal* is not brought about by the mere act of writing in a journal. It is the result, rather, of the special structure of the *Intensive Journal*. The essence of this lies in the cumulative effect brought about by utilizing the combinations of Journal sections with their accompanying procedures to build an inner momentum in a person's experience. Achieving this momentum is based on a fundamental principle that is elemental in its simplicity, but is very difficult to grasp securely enough to be able to work with in a consecutive way. In developing the *Intensive Journal*, the most important steps consisted first in identifying this principle, and then in devising a means of coming into contact with it so that it could be channeled and worked with in each person's life.

This problem was especially delicate because the factors involved in the growth of persons are exceedingly elusive. They are comprised primarily of subjective feelings, states of mind, and states of emotion. One moment we see them clearly, and the next moment they have disappeared from view. And yet they are present constantly and working within us, for they are the contents of the inner process of human development. No wonder that Lao Tse said that the growth principle in life, which he called the *Tao,* is too elusive to be named or to be grasped at all.

When I had reached the point in my work where it became clear to me that the next necessary step was the development of a method for the growth of persons, the elusiveness of the growth principle became a major concern. In practice it becomes clear that the inner growth of a person is irregular, for it often disappears from view for long periods. The psychological cycles of growth move so slowly and circuitously that even when something very important is germinating underneath, people are often misled into believing that no growth is taking place at all.

It is quite different in the case of plants or other nonhuman species in the world of nature. There it is easy to recognize and relate to the process of growth as it proceeds. We see a chick grow larger, we see a plant sprout buds. Even in the human child, which is so close to the elemental processes of nature, we can observe and respond to its growth. We see the child grow another inch, begin to speak in sentences, learn to use numbers, and think conceptually. We can observe this because the qualities of growth still have an outer and objective quality in a child. This is the case in all species below that of the maturely developing human person. Once the process of growth reaches the level of mature human individuality, it acquires the elusive inner quality that is difficult to grasp and define but which eventually becomes the essence of human development.

In the human being, objective physical growth is only the foundation and starting point for the important phases of the growth process. The visible growth which we see in a child and which continues through adolescence provides the necessary base for the less tangible growth by which a Self and a creative being come to maturity. It is this intangible growth that becomes the carrier of the meaning of human existence. At its ultimate point, where this intangible essence is experienced at its highest refinement, it is the content of aesthetic art and the life of the spirit.

The growth of a human being consists of so many subjective experiences, hidden and private to the person, that the markings of change are difficult to discern. *Especially misleading is the fact that the active germination of a growth process often takes place at the low, seemingly negative, phase of a psychological cycle.* Thus, at the very time when the most constructive developments are taking place within a person, his outer appearance may be depressed, confused, and even disturbed. Physical growth is easy to recognize, but personal growth is inward and elusive. In the metaphor of Lao Tse, it is evanescent, like smoke going out the chimney. We know it exists, but its shape keeps changing. It has no shape that we can fix in our mind; we cannot contain it in any mold. We know it is real, but soon it has disappeared and is beyond us.

Lao Tse's image of smoke is a very apt representation of the inner process of growth. The movement of smoke is real and visible, and yet we cannot grasp hold of it. The question then is how one can establish a personal relation to so elusive a phenomenon. How can I make contact with the moving image of smoke, envisioning the smoke as moving out of a chimney and proceeding shapelessly to dissipate itself in the sky?

This image became a riddle that stayed with me, even to the point where it obsessed my conscious thoughts. It became for me very much like a Zen Koan, an imponderable, symbolic conundrum full of paradox and eluding rational solution. At this point I applied a procedure already familiar to me from other work: the procedure of taking a problem we are dealing with on the rational level and converting it to the language of imagery. This is *Twilight Imagery,* an approach that is developed further in the *Intensive Journal* and which we shall use actively in the course of our workshop.*

Working with the problem in the form of an image made it possible to move beyond the level of rational solution. I let myself see inwardly the formless changing movement of the smoke, perceiving it on the

---

* See especially Ch. 6. For background, see Progoff, *Depth Psychology and Modern Man,* Chapters 8, 9, 10. See also, *The Symbolic and the Real,* Chapters 3, 4, and 6.

imagery level as smoke, and on the symbolic level as representing the inner process of growth that takes place within an individual. The smoke became the ever-changing movement of feelings, thoughts, fantasies, wishes, emotions, fears, and every kind of subjective content that is in our conscious and unconscious mind. I perceived this smoke as moving within a person, moving through him, out of him, and finally beyond him. I saw the smoke as being separate from the person, and yet influencing him intimately.

This led me to recall the phrase of William James when he describes the inner movement of our minds by saying that it is not a case of "I think it," but rather that "it thinks me." *The inner process works within the mind at the same time that it functions as a separate process and reaches beyond the mind into our actions.*

I concluded that the best way to locate this smoky process of the mind was to look for it *behind the mind.* At the point where this formulation came to me, placing the inner process "behind" the mind, the riddle changed its form somewhat. Now it became a question of learning to perceive and relate to a process whose movement is hidden from the very capacity that is seeking to understand it.

Considering this, the first step toward a solution seemed to me to bring about some type of mirroring effect. To perceive a process that is taking place behind the mind presents a problem that is very similar to what we encounter when we try to see our own face. We cannot see it directly, but we have to manage to have it reflected back to us. A person can see his own face only by the indirect process of mirroring. The realization of this carried my riddle one step further, indicating that the next task was to devise a mirroring procedure. But it could not be a mirror that would reflect a static picture. It would have to reflect the *movement* of the human psyche to itself.

This formulation helped, but I was left with the problem that the psyche does not have as definite a form as a face. It is not physically visible, and its essence is subtle movement and change. The inner process of the psyche cannot be specifically mirrored as a face can. At this point I began to experience the consequences of the fact that the metaphor of the psyche as smoke is all too correct. To reflect the psyche posed a problem no simpler than catching something as evanescent as smoke in the sky. But the contents of the human psyche are more subjective than smoke, more subtle, and therefore even more elusive.

As the image proceeded out of its own nature over a period of time, it took many shapes and representations. As it varied itself, it continued to move back and forth between the opposites of the formlessness of smoke and the definiteness of each particular human life. As I watched the movement of the smoke with my inner eye, I saw it move into definite patterns and shapes. It would hold its shape for a brief moment, become formless again until a new pattern formed, and then quickly change again. Through this, it was made clear to me that even smoke takes definite, though fleeting shapes in the course of its movement. It led me to recognize also that it is very possible for the moving patterns of these shapes to be described, and that something of their elusive quality can thereby be captured.

In the course of my exercises in imaging the movement of the smoke, I had the experience of describing in writing the variations of the smoky shapes as they passed before my eyes. When the smoke was gone, my description of the succession of its changing shapes remained. It seemed correct to say that the written description made while the smoke was in motion had captured at least a reflection of the elusive movement. Recording it while it was happening had the effect of mirroring the movement of the image. More than that, it reflected the *sequence of the changing shapes.* Thus, in addition to the record of the individual forms and the totality of the pattern, the written description preserved the feeling tone of the movement of the smoke. Reading it afterwards, I found that the inner continuity of the imagery experience was still present, and that, in fact, I was able by reading it to reenter the image and to follow the further movement of the smoke on this symbolic level.

At that point, parallels between smoke and the inner movement of a human life began to suggest themselves, indicating ways of solving my riddle. If the contents of a person's life were condensed at least to the point where they would be as definite as the fleeting shapes of smoke, they could be concretely described as they are experienced. A life may have its source in the shapeless, evanescent inner process of the psyche, but it does take definite expression in the events and actions of the life. Recognizing this, it becomes clear that the record of these events, the actions and the inner experiences that accompany them in a person's life, can be brought into a form definite enough so that they can be reflected and perceived. If all these events, outer and inner, can be drawn together in one place they will comprise one definite picture. They will constitute a collage of a life in motion, and represent the ongoing continuity of each person's existence. If this drawing together of events is achieved, it converts the elusive process that moves behind the mind into a *form* tangible enough to be reflected back to us.

The key lay in finding an instrument that was capable of drawing together the multiplicity of contents of a human life, compressing them into a manageable space while not losing the quality of movement and change that is their essence. Seeking such an instrument, there were two main sources in my previous experience upon which I could draw. One was my decade of work as Director of the Institute for Research in Depth Psychology at the Graduate School of Drew University where we systematically collected the life histories of persons. The other was my experience and experimentation with the use of psychological journals, both personally and in my therapeutic practice.

At the Institute my research lay in collecting intimate documentation on the full life development of people from many walks of life and types of personality. Among them were persons whose attainments in life led to their being classified as "creative," and others whose difficulties could lead to their being labelled "neurotic." Among them there were public figures both of historical and modern times, contemporary celebrities, and persons living a quiet, private life.

Out of the data that was brought together there, various sets of hypotheses were formulated in an attempt to find a single, succinct, unitary means of reconstructing the range and movement of a human being's life. Over the years many alternate constructions were experimented with, tested against the varieties of lives, and reformulated. The goal was to develop a formulation that would be both encompassing as a general concept and open-ended in its categories. Of especial importance was my concern that no analytical theory be inadvertently built in as a hidden interpretation in reconstructing any individual's life.

Eventually, out of these numerous attempts, a set of hypotheses was crystallized that made it possible to mark off the successive time-units of experience through which an individual passes during his lifetime. By means of this, it became possible to study the continuity of a person's life both chronologically and qualitatively: chronologically in terms of the age spans of life in passage, and qualitatively in terms of the contents of the life experiences. Most important, it made it possible to study a broad range of lives from the point of view of the seed of the person in the midst of the difficulties of his life. Further, it was now possible to do this without resorting to analytical categories or psychiatric diagnoses. This last aspect was of the greatest value.

From the point of view of my personal quest, and the special goal which I had set for developing an instrument and method for individual growth, this period of work was primarily a time of data gathering. It provided a base from which to proceed in constructing a workable method for human development, a method for evoking the potentials of a person through all the phases and time-units of his life.

It turned out that the information which became accessible through being able to set large numbers of lives side by side was a major resource for devising an instrument that would reflect the inner movement of a human life. By this means, it became possible to see the underlying patterns and rhythms that are established in the midst of the most diverse lives, by people who are following very different life styles and are striving toward very different goals. It was especially valuable in providing a perspective in which to see the relation between the encompassing life-cycle of a full human existence and the many small cycles that come and go within the passage of a life.

By means of this comparative study of lives it became possible to recognize the overlapping transitions that occur within a full life cycle. The successive cycles of self could then be identified, marking off the phases by which maturation takes place and by which varying degrees of meaning emerge in a human existence. With this, the inner continuity of the *transitions* of individual lives could be seen and the common qualities underlying their differences could be described.

These descriptions became an indispensable resource at a later point in the development of the *Intensive Journal* because they provided the guidelines by which the major divisions and the individual sections within the Journal could be marked off. Without these data the development of the *Intensive Journal* in its present format as an active life-reconstructing instrument might not have been possible at all.

On the one hand, it was essential to give the Journal a structure definite enough to carry the continuity of a method with specific procedures. On the other hand, it was equally important to make sure that this structure would be harmonious with the natural flow of human life, so that it would never be necessary for an experience to be contrived or artificially forced to fit the format of the Journal. The data drawn from the comparative study of human lifetimes provided the basis for the flexibly open-ended structure of the *Intensive Journal* which was eventually devised.

THE VALUE AND LIMITATIONS OF DIARIES AND JOURNALS

The work in the comparative study of lives brought another type of evidence in favor of using a personal journal as the basic instrument for personal growth. It was impressive to observe the number of persons in other cultures and other periods of history who have spontaneously kept a journal of some sort to meet various needs in their lives. These journals are primarily a chronological record of events. They are diaries elaborated to a greater or less degree depending on the temperament of the person and his life situation. Sometimes they are focused on a particular area of experience or a particular task, as is often the case for artists and novelists. In those cases a journal serves as the spontaneous psychological tool that makes it possible for the inner creative side of a work in progress to be carried through.

The keeping of private journals has played a particularly important role in the history of religion, wherever the reality of inner experience has been valued in the religious life. From St. Augustine to Pascal to the Society of Friends, some form of personal journal has been called upon. Sometimes these journals deal with the full range of personal experience including all the intimacies of life from marital quarrels and sexuality to the visionary moments when a person feels himself to be hovering precariously between prophecy and insanity. Those, of course, are the dramatic journals. But more often the journals deal with an area of religious behavior that is specifically defined by the particular religious group to which the individual belongs. In those cases, the goals set by the sect's beliefs are the basis of keeping the journals. The individual uses the journal as a means of measuring his progress along the particular religious path that he has chosen.

That use of a private journal is exceedingly common, not only in the religious life but wherever a person has a fixed goal toward which he is trying to direct himself. Journals are used especially in those situations where a person is having difficulty in attaining his goal. A private journal is then drawn upon first as an instrument for recording and then for evaluating how far he has attained his goals and to what degree he has failed. Such a use of a journal becomes a self-testing device. It is helpful up to a point in providing a means of reflection for the contents of the life. Being judgmental, however, it has a tendency to increase whatever feelings of guilt the person had before he began to keep the journal.

As I was drawn further toward the conclusion that a private journal is the essential instrument for personal growth, it was very instructive to recognize that there are ways and situations in which the keeping of a journal works against itself and has a negative effect. Since that time, as our experience has expanded in the Dialogue House program, we have been able to gather considerable data regarding the difficulties and inadequacies involved in certain ways of using journals. Especially we have been able to see what is involved in the misuse of journal-keeping when it is done without the guidance of dynamic principles and without a protective discipline; or when, under the guise of communication, the keeping of a journal is used as a stratagem or as a weapon in order to impress our point of view on someone else.

As is often the case in scientific work, a close study of the failures and the negative instances provides the clue to finding solutions that reach beyond the difficulties. This has certainly been true of the process by which the *Intensive Journal* was developed. Both the Drew Institute studies and the practice of therapy disclosed many instances in which the spontaneous keeping of journals in historical as well as contemporary times had a self-curtailing effect. These studies provided criteria that were of the greatest value in devising an approach to the use of journals that would be large enough in concept and would possess inherent protections.

One of the significant observations that emerged from the comparative study of lives was the narrowing effect of using journals in a self-contained way. It is often the case that when people use private journals as a means of helping themselves reach a particular goal, as the writing of a novel, or establishing a specific love relationship, or achieving a closer relationship with God in some special theological framework, the definitiveness of the goal restricts the space in which the inner process can move. It has the effect, therefore, of limiting the person, especially since it limits the range of the goal for which he is striving. In situations of this type, it is also usually true that once the specific goal has been attained, or when the interest in it and the motivation for achieving it has diminished, the practice of journal keeping also tends to drop away. Since journal keeping of that kind is not related to the larger development of the life as a whole, it lacks a sustaining principle. Thus the journal easily falls into disuse when it has been misused in that way; and its disuse leaves a vacuum in the person's experience.

Of particular significance was the number of times when journals were used to help a person achieve a goal he had set in advance rather than to reach forward to new goals and to discover new meanings in his life. At such times when the framework of the journal was enclosed by a set of fixed attitudes, it became a static tool. Then it was used not as an instrument for growth, but for self-justification. In such contexts individuals have often employed a journal to insulate themselves against questions they did not wish to face. This use of the journal has the effect of narrowing the scope of a person's life, and of limiting rather than enlarging the possibilities of his personality. A notable contemporary exception to this is found in the *Diaries* of Anais Nin, where a person of great literary creativity used a journal also as a vehicle for her total life development. The tendency of journals to turn in upon their own subjectivity, however, and move in circular patterns is a common pitfall that must be borne in mind.

When I first became aware of the fact that there are limitations in the use of journals, I thought that the reason for this was to be found in the way that the journal was used by people in their personal circumstances and in the situations of history. I thought that the problem lay in the *how* of journal usage. It did not occur to me at that time that there might be alternate kinds of journals which might be used.

All the journals previously used were essentially of one type. They all were personal chronological records of the movement of events in a person's life. They might be reportings of the outer events of life, or they might be introspective and record the inner events. In the latter case, they would have a tendency to extend themselves with observations and reflections, and sometimes with imaginings.

In sum, the basic type of personal journal used throughout history wherever persons have felt the urge to use a journal at all has been an unstructured chronological journal kept either systematically by dates, or written in spontaneously from time to time as suited the temperament of the individual. Accordingly, I made the assumption that this was the only form of journal that was possible. I assumed further that, if some additional steps were to be taken and improvements made, it would have to be in the *way* the journal was used. I therefore turned my attention toward devising new techniques, and especially toward establishing situations in which it would be possible to work with a personal journal more fruitfully.

In this context I began in 1957 to use a journal as an adjunct to psychotherapy in my private practice. I merely asked people to keep a notebook in which they recorded the events of their inner life. Only a notebook was necessary because the journal at that stage involved nothing more than a loose, unstructured recording of their experiences as they were perceived from a particular point of view. That point of view was provided by the questions I asked them, and by the specific points in the course of their work with me where I placed the emphasis by directing their attention and by asking them to make further elaborations.

This procedure seemed to have a very favorable effect therapeutically, so I extended it. The kinds of questions that were raised became more definite, more refined, and more pointed. As I worked in this way, it became increasingly clear to me that there is a specific process working at the depth of a person, and that this process can be evoked more actively by the use of a journal procedure. Increasingly, then, I directed my work toward drawing the inner process forward in persons. I did this by raising the specific questions that seemed most relevant in the context of the principles of depth psychology which I was using at the time, enlarging the issues both by discussion and imagination. I then asked the individual to collect in his journal all the material and experiences that came to him by these procedures. The cumulative effect of doing this was very helpful to the clients, and thus I extended the procedures. I was still, however, using only a blank unstructured notebook as the journal. At that time I called it a "psychological workbook," and it was under that name that I described its use in *The Symbolic and the Real.*

After that book was published in 1963, I had much larger opportunities to experiment with the use of the "psychological workbook" and to observe its effects. I found that I could use it fruitfully in an increasingly wide range of therapeutic situations, and I discovered also that it could be used as an adjunct to the group workshops which I was conducting at the time. At first I was surprised by the results of using journals in groups. I did not quite understand why it should work so well, but I also recognized that something more was necessary.

A great deal that was therapeutic was achieved by working with this psychological journal. Much of it also went beyond therapy and opened the way to personal experiences that gave people a dimension of wisdom that was new to them. I observed, however, that the affirmative effects of using this unstructured psychological workbook were too closely connected with the questions I raised or the way in which I raised them. The results for the individual were at that point very closely linked to my personal style in conducting the therapeutic consultations, and the way I led the group sessions.

The inference from this was that since there was no structure built into the psychological journal, its effectiveness as a tool was dependent on the person in authority who was using it. To the degree that this was true, however, it failed to fulfill a main reason for using a journal procedure, namely, to meet the need for having an instrument capable of mirroring the inner process of the psyche of each individual without falsification of any kind and without the intrusion of special doctrines or authorities. A primary purpose in using journals is to establish and strengthen the integrity of the individual person. Toward this goal it was essential that the journal become an instrument that would be capable of functioning well by means of the individual's own use of it and that it not be dependent upon another person, least of all upon an authority figure.

In addition I observed that there were many people who could work well with the psychological workbook when they were with me personally, but that when they were by themselves they could not carry it further in more than a perfunctory way.

I observed also, at the other extreme, that persons who had a natural fluidity in their writing had a tendency, when they wrote in their workbook, to go around and around verbally until they were eloquently moving in circles. Whatever pattern of analytical thought they were accustomed to following, they tended to repeat in interpreting themselves in their journals until the grooves they were in became ruts. They ended, then, by being more deeply entrenched in these ruts than they had been before.

All of this pointed to the need to take the psychological workbook a step further in its development so that it could reach beyond these limitations. Of special importance was the possibility of developing it in such a way that it could sustain itself if an individual worked with it alone, or at least that it be capable of sustaining the person in the interim times between his contacts with his therapist, or with his group, or with whatever type of dialogue guide he was working.

From the theoretical point of view, what needed to be done was to replace the authority side of psychotherapy with a method of working within oneself, a method that would be self-contained and autonomous, and would therefore sustain the integrity of the individual.

I recognized also that if both the factors of personal authority and of special interpretive concepts were to be neutralized, the first effect would be to leave a vacuum. It was essential therefore to have a definite instrument that would be capable of filling the void. This meant that the journal needed to be developed into a format that would enable it to contain and carry all the potent psychic material, all the energies and ideas and feelings, that would be set loose when a person was freed from the directiveness of a therapist's authority. It would focus all of these back into the context of each individual's own life. If this were done, the journal could serve as the required instrument.

The task then was to draw the psychological workbook into the form of a structured journal capable of rechanneling a person's energies in terms of new patterns of behavior which would regroup themselves in the context of each individual's development. The directive and reintegrative factor had to come from within, and not be imposed by a concept from the outside. It would be possible to achieve this if a person's life experiences could be fed back and forth within the journal. What would be necessary, however, was the correct sectional divisions and a means of active movement within the journal that would have an integrative effect. When this was developed, we had the operating structure of the *Intensive Journal* with its method of Journal Feedback.

Chapter 3

Operating Principles

THE DYNAMICS OF JOURNAL FEEDBACK

The shape of the *Intensive Journal* became clear only gradually out of a series of provisional attempts. The criteria by which the sections of the Journal were marked off were provided largely by the data that had been gathered in the comparative study of creative lives. Beyond the categories, however, was the essential step of establishing an interior structure for the psychological workbook that would enable it to reflect and carry forward the process of growth as it was taking place uniquely in each individual. It required a dynamic of feedback in terms of the person's life experiences out of which new patterns of conduct would be formed.

A period of experimentation, of trying and testing and changing, was necessary in order to bring it about. When that was done, however, the psychological workbook emerged altogether transformed and given a wholly new shape. It was now the *Structured Journal*. A little later, when the next step was taken in devising the exercises and methods of using it, it was renamed the *Intensive Journal*. This name was chosen when we discovered how the journal in this format lends itself to being used intensively, within a short space of time, especially at a group workshop. Its use as an intensive instrument enables a person to crystallize the present situation of his life in a telescoped perspective of the whole of his past and thus to place himself in a better position to move into his future.

When the structure of the *Intensive Journal* was being established, it was clear that it should include much more than the act of keeping a diary. It needed to be an instrument that could reflect the inner movement of each life within its own terms. It should have ample room therefore for all the various aspects, fluctuations, and transformations contained in a human existence. It should provide the context and the mechanisms that would enable a person by working in it to identify, in the midst of the cycles and transitions of his life, his underlying direction and potentiality.

To achieve this, the journal needed to be divided into sections, but the sections could not be merely compartments for a filing system in the psyche. The divisions within the journal had to be of such a nature that they could be integrally connected with exercises and practices and disciplines of various kinds, so that the very process of working in the journal would have the effect of stimulating the development of the person. To fulfill this role, the *Intensive Journal* had to be much more than a passive instrument for reporting. It had to provide a method for actively extending life experience.

As it happened, the structure of the *Intensive Journal* moved directly into the development of an active method. This took place naturally, almost inadvertently, because the structure of the Journal was specifically modelled after the process of inner continuity and growth which I had identified in the comparative study of lives, especially in the lives of creative persons. In retrospect, the most important factor in making possible an active method was that it was not the contents of persons' lives that were taken as the model but the *essential process,* the fluidity of the inner movement.

The distinction involved in this is especially important because it is the Journal's capacity to carry the dynamic of the inner process that gives it its constructive results. It does this by compressing that process to its essence so that the active force in the person's life can be carried forward without being weighted down by the details of events and emotions. This was achieved by embodying the elements of the inner

31

process in the structure of the Journal, but in such a way as to produce a mirroring and feedback effect.

At the beginning, the way I approached this was to set up the format of the Journal so that it would draw attention not to the contents of a person's life, but to his *interior relationship* to those contents. This would emphasize the active, nonanalytical quality of the Journal work. It was clear that the effectiveness of this approach would depend to a large extent upon the kinds of exercises that could be used with the individual Journal sections, and this in turn would depend upon the way in which the sections themselves could be defined. What would they include, and from what point of view could we determine whether to deal with them in one division of the Journal rather than another?

During the early years of using the *Intensive Journal*, a great deal of experimentation was carried out in this regard. At the workshops I tried various conceptions of how the individual sections should be defined and what they should contain. Always the answer to these questions depended upon the kinds of exercises and journal usage that became possible when the sections were defined from a particular point of view. It depended further on the results that could be obtained from the exercises that accompanied particular conceptions of the Journal sections.

The trial-and-error testing of definitions and procedures was extensive and continuous over a period of several years. The essential methodology of Journal Feedback, however, is the result. One of the major problems came from the fact that many of the exercises that seemed to be the most "successful" in that they evoked the enthusiasm or enjoyment of the participants, were not actually productive for the long range task of reconstructing and redirecting a life. They were dramatic or titillating and therefore "popular," or they satisfied people by enabling them to work with the old analytical concepts with which they were familiar. But they did not meet the requirements of the larger *life-integrative* goal. They therefore had to be set aside.

In determining which procedures should be accepted into the permanent core of the method of Journal Feedback, one important criterion was the progressive building of the inner movement of energy drawing the life toward wholeness. Another criterion was that each technique should have more than one, and if possible several, constructive side-results or applications. Especially because the *Intensive Journal* undertakes to have room for everything in an individual's life and to exclude nothing, it was essential to have an economy of techniques, enough to do the work but not so many as to be cumbersome. The protracted experimentation with the Journal in practice produced the refined core of Journal Feedback techniques that is currently in use, but it also led to some theoretical realizations that may have far reaching significance.

In this regard, one important observation that came from working with the *Intensive Journal* during the transitional years of its development was that the Journal Feedback effect is cumulative. The reports of persons using the method indicated that, as it generated energy and built a momentum, it accelerated the process of growth and deepened the life-awareness of persons. At first I did not understand why this should be so. The results were easily observed, but the reasons were difficult to identify. It seemed clear, however, that something of great importance for the larger process was involved in what was taking place.

Using a method that is now part of our regular Journal Feedback practice, I approached the problem by first reconstructing the sequence of previous events. The origin of the *Intensive Journal* lay in my discerning the main aspects of growth in the lives of creative persons, and embodying these in the form of journal sections. That was the first steppingstone in the development of the Journal. The next step was to devise working exercises that would make it possible to explore the contents of our lives by using the various sections of the Journal. As this was done, it became apparent that one entry led to another. What was written in one section of the Journal evoked old memories and new awarenesses and stimulated further entries in other sections. By the second year of working with the *Intensive Journal*, it became apparent that the effect of using it consistently was to generate additional energy and movement in a person's life. At first I thought that the reason for this was simply that the original exercises were based upon a depth psychology that was active and evocative rather than analytical and diagnostic. But after a few years it became clear that the reason for the increased energy and growth in people did not lie in the depth psychological concepts with which I had begun. It was something other, something even more fundamental and of larger significance.

The creative effect of the use of the *Intensive Journal* seemed to derive from the fact that its structure was drawn from the study of the lives of creative persons. One of my original hypotheses, in fact, was the thought that, if the structure of the Journal could embody a composite and quintessence of creative development, it would be able to assist the growth of persons whatever the context of the individual life might be. In marking off and defining the particular sections of the Journal, I had consciously sought to reflect the main aspects of the lives of creative persons. Now I realized that there were larger implications than I had originally understood. Reflecting the fact that the lives of creative persons are strongly in motion and are full of change and energy, the sections of the Journal did not focus on the specific contents of their lives, but on the particular processes of their lives. Had the emphasis been on content, it would have led eventually to analysis, and the result would have been essentially static. The format that was chosen, however, had the effect of making each section a place where a mini-process in the unfoldment of a total life was being expressed and was carried forward.

The fact is that I did not recognize this to be the case at the beginning, but only some years after the *Intensive Journal* was in use. The experiences and regenerative changes which were demonstrated in the lives of persons who worked with the *Intensive Journal* indicated that inner energies were progressively activated by the use of the method. The reason for this lay primarily in the fact that the Journal sections were not categories for analytical classification, but mini-processes reflecting the individual aspects of a life in motion. Being processes of active experience, the effect of working with them in the format of the Journal was to generate energy and carry the life to further levels of expression. Realizing this opened further theoretical implications and led to additional developments in the method.

As the public use of the *Intensive Journal* proceeded, the nature of these mini-processes and their relation to one another became increasingly visible. Through the Journal experience they defined themselves more specifically, especially as they demonstrated their active qualities, their capacity to unfold from within themselves, and to interrelate in an interior way, feeding back and forth to one another by means of the Journal exercises.

It became apparent that here was the source of the momentum of energy that was cumulatively generated by continuous work in the Journal. I began then to look more closely at these *mini-processes* as they were embodied in the individual sections. Reflecting as they did the unfoldment of life in creative persons, it was clear that they were very close to the fundamental growth principle in human existence. In fact, they indicated one of the primary characteristics of creative persons, namely, that creative persons experience their lives not in terms of static contents but in terms of the active unfoldment of multiple mini-processes within them. The contents of their lives are perceived by creative persons as being not the major realities but merely the raw materials of the process by which their artworks and other achievements are brought to fruition. *Outward activity propelled from within* is the essence of the creative existence. Thus one of the main indications of the strength of creativity in individuals is the degree to which they have brought themselves into connection with the multiple and interrelated movement of the mini-processes in their lives.

In this perspective and considering the events that were taking place at our Journal Workshops, the next major task was clearly indicated. It was to develop a framework and techniques that would coordinate the various mini-processes so that they could feed into one another systematically and progressively. There would thus be a multiplication of energies activating one another, all feeding into a single integrative process of growth. It would be like many streams feeding into one river which draws their energies into itself and flows strongly out to sea as a unitary force. Something like this had been taking place in the first years of the Journal Workshops, but now it could be restructured on the basis of our experiences and observations so that the mini-processes would be able to feed smoothly in and out of one another.

Taking the lives of creative persons as the model for the *Intensive Journal* led to a much larger principle and process. The dynamic factors were always implicit there, but it only became possible to see what they are and how they function when the *Intensive Journal* gave them a place in which they could become tangible. Here they could disclose their form, and by means of the early procedures of the *Intensive Journal*, they could indicate the styles of movement and the rhythms that are natural to them. At this point it thus became possible to take a further step and to refine the method into a concise operational form. This next step was the development of the fundamental concepts and the specific techniques of *Journal Feedback*.

The feedback effects that occur in the use of the *Intensive Journal* take place on several levels. One form of Journal Feedback is elementary and essentially mechanical, but it is important nonetheless. This is the feedback effect that is achieved simply by writing down non-judgmental entries that record the inner and outer events of our lives. Following this, there is the feedback effect of reading these entries back to ourselves in our silence. Further there is the feedback effect of reading aloud the entries that we have written. We may read them aloud in our own privacy or in the presence of a group. Additionally, we may read our entries into a cassette recorder and then play them back to ourselves. Each of these provides an additional aspect of feedback and serves to carry the inner process a step further.

With the passage of time and the sustained use of the *Intensive Journal*, a significant additional experience of feedback becomes possible. After we have accumulated enough of them, we can read back to ourselves the entries we have made in the various sections over a period of time. This experience of *continuity feedback* is a valuable means of maintaining a perspective of our lives in the midst of movement and change, and of readjusting our perspective to meet current situations.

All of these aspects of Journal Feedback are related directly to the elemental fact of writing and reading back to ourselves the entries we have made in our Journal. In this sense they are derived from the basic mechanics of journal keeping, and are classified under the heading of *operational feedback*.

There is, however, another, more subtle phase of Journal Feedback that is specifically connected to the movement of the mini-processes. This is the feedback that becomes possible because the sections within the Journal provide a means by which our subjective experiences can become tangible to us and can express their energy in contact with other subjective aspects of our lives. Experiences that would otherwise be too intangible and therefore too elusive to grasp thus become accessible to us so that we can work with them. Indefinite bits of thought and emotion which would ordinarily be lost to us like water down the drain are transformed into specific Journal entries which feed back into other mini-processes and activate the energies of other subjective experiences. We thus progressively build a cumulative movement that is fed into by the mini-processes of our inner life as they interact with each other and with other aspects of our interior life generating new energy as they go. The combination of these interactions via the interplay of Journal exercises brings about new constellations of subjective experience which have not only a greater energy but also a more clearly discernible content and meaning. They therefore often provide the base from which new directions and goals of life are formed, since what was intangible and inaccessible before now becomes a specific and active component of our inner life.

The composite of entries, exercises and procedures by which this transformation of the elusive into the tangible is brought about is *experiential feedback*. It is that part of Journal Feedback by which the mini-processes of subjective experience are enabled to interrelate with and cross-fertilize one another within the context of each individual's life history.

The conception and formulation of experiential feedback on the basis of the first years of experience in using the *Intensive Journal* was a major step toward drawing the Journal techniques into concise, effective form. It is, in fact, the principles underlying experiential feedback that have made it possible to expand and refine the program of Journal Feedback into a full method of individual development capable of being used in exceedingly diverse social situations. In the succeeding volume of this *Intensive Journal* series dealing with the fundamental principles of *life integration* by means of journal work, the various phases of the process of Journal Feedback are discussed in greater detail. Here, however, there are two additional points about Journal Feedback that are essential to be described as preparation for our Journal Workshop.

37

These concern, firstly, the difference between the *Log* sections and the *Feedback* sections; and secondly, the general characteristics of the three dimensions of *experiential feedback.*

In the structure of the *Intensive Journal,* one basic distinction is that between the Log sections and the Feedback sections. The Log sections are those parts of the *Intensive Journal* in which we gather the factual data of our lives. As the Journal Feedback procedures have evolved there are now five such sections: The *Period Log;* the *Daily Log;* the *Dream Log;* the *Twilight Imagery Log;* and the *Life History Log.* In each of these we record the facts of our inner experience from a particular vantage point, always without judging, censoring, embellishing, criticizing, justifying, or interpreting the facts.

Each event is a fact of experience and we describe it as it took place. In the Log sections we make our entries as objective as we can, recording what occurred briefly and directly. Although a great deal of emotion may be involved in them, our entries in the Log sections are simply the *neutral observation* and recording of the inner and outer events of our lives. We may, for example, be filled with intense anxiety or great joy, or we may have a dream of terror or of exaltation. We simply describe these subjective states in as neutral and as objective a way as we can, without comment and without elaboration. That is the basic factual role of the Log sections. They are the collectors of the raw empirical data of our lives.

The Feedback sections, on the other hand, are the place where we carry out the active exercises that generate the energy and bring about the transformations of awareness in the Journal work. It is in the Feedback sections that the mini-processes are expressed and have their opportunity to unfold by means of the active feedback exercises.

The raw material for these active exercises is supplied by the Log sections. The neutral reporting of our experiences in our Log entries supplies the data that is fed into the Feedback sections. In the course of this Journal process of feeding in and feeding back, a very significant transformation takes place in the nature of the material. When the entries are made in the Log sections, they are simply raw, empirical data. In that sense, they are information regarding the contents of our lives. When they are fed into the Feedback sections, however, they are immediately absorbed into the movement of the mini-processes that are embodied there. They are thus transformed. They are no longer static informational data regarding the contents of a life; but they become active elements in the mini-processes by which the potentials of life are seeking to unfold.

This transformation has a major theoretical significance, but it also has tremendous practical effects. In it we can see the reason and the consequences of the fact that the Journal sections are not focused on the contents of lives but on the *inner movements of experience*. The Feedback sections carry the mini-processes of lives-in-motion. As a result, the Journal Feedback process does not get bogged down in intellectual or analytical interpreting. It is constantly in motion, absorbing the factual content of experience into the mini-processes within the life. This feeds into the larger process by which the contents of experience are consumed as logs in the fire of our individual existence, generating light and heat, awareness and emotion as they provide the energy that carries the life toward its meaningful unfoldment.

REACHING THE ELAN VITAL: THE MINI-PROCESSES AND THE DIMENSIONS OF EXISTENCE

In structuring the Journal so that the individual sections could serve as channels for the mini-processes, *three natural divisions* established themselves. The reason for this is that the Drew Institute studies of creative persons indicated three main types of inner movement taking place simultaneously. Each involves a particular aspect of life content, and unfolds within its own contexts, with its distinctive rhythms, tempo, and style of movement. Within them there are various mini-processes, and each of these is embodied in a particular Journal section. These clusters of mini-processes comprise the three *dimensions* of inner experience and provide the base for the experiential feedback procedures. Each of the dimensions is a major division of the Journal with its own set of individual sections.

At the time of designing the *Intensive Journal* there were several indications, mainly operational, that it would be helpful to emphasize the distinctions among the three dimensions by using different colors for each. Thus the sections of the *Life/Time Dimension* are red; those of the *Depth Dimension* are blue; and those of the *Dialogue Dimension* are orange. There is no symbolic or esoteric significance to the particular colors used in this way. They are simply there as indicators of the different dimensions of experience and the style of mini-process carried by the individual sections. In practice, as our Journal Feedback exercises have stimulated movement back and forth within the Journal, the space within the Journal representing the inner space of our lives, these color distinctions have turned out to be very useful in expediting the active inner work.

The term *dimension of experience* has a very specific meaning as it is used within the context of the *Intensive Journal*. By dimension is meant a composite of aspects of inner experience that not only comprise their own context in which a person's life-reality is perceived, but also carry their own modes of movement on the subjective level. The dimensions are self-contained realms of experience each with its characteristic contents and style of unfoldment.

The *Life/Time Dimension*, for example, contains the mini-processes that reflect the inner continuity of a person's life history. It deals with the basic and obvious fact that our lives take place in objective or chronological time on the outer level of experience; and it deals also with the fact, which is central to our Journal work, that on the inner level our experiences take place in terms of subjective or *qualitative time*. The interior perception and experience of the movement of time is what we mean by Life/Time. The Life/Time Dimension includes all those phenomena or mini-processes that carry the progression of our experiences and cumulatively form our personal life history.

We perceive the events of the Life/Time Dimension in terms of the inner movement of time. Life/Time is time perceived and experienced qualitatively from within each individual's subjective perspective. Like a ray of light through a crystal, the movement of Life/Time breaks into many rays, or mini-processes, in each existence. The various mini-processes are reflected in the individual sections of the *Life/Time Dimension*. These are: *Life History Log; Steppingstones; Intersections: Roads Taken and Not Taken;* and *Now: The Open Moment.*

The Depth Dimension is the realm of human reality in which the mini-processes move in terms of symbolic forms. It contains those aspects of experience that are primarily nonconscious in the moment when they transpire within us, but which are guided in their unfoldment by a profound quality of consciousness that underlies their movement. This consciousness is more a *directive principle* than a literal piece of knowledge. It is a consciousness that discloses itself actively, but mainly in indirect forms as it guides the life process. In the beginning this consciousness is only implicit, invisible, and hidden in the depth, as a scientist is hidden in a child, as a tree is hidden in a seed, or as an inspiration is hidden in a person who has not yet had even the dream by which the new idea will be awakened.

To be transferred from the depths, where it is still unconscious and not yet visible, to the surface where it is expressed in life activities, consciousness requires a means of movement. The mini-processes of the Depth Dimension provide this interior locomotion as they are embodied in the individual Journal sections. There are five sections in this division of the *Intensive Journal: Dream Log; Dream Enlargements;* The *Twilight Imagery Log; Imagery Extensions;* and *Inner Wisdom Dialogue.*

The Depth Dimension deals with the nonconscious levels of the psyche from which consciousness comes. Its contents are sleep dreams, waking dreams, and the varieties of intuition by which we make our direct connections with the implicit wisdom of life. Of particular importance is the active style of intermediate depth experience, Twilight Imagery. This has a particularly important role in the Journal Feedback process because it gives us a nonanalytic way of evoking those potentials of our life that are veiled by the language of symbolism. Although the Depth Dimension is a realm of experience with many obscure symbolic contents, it is also the source of much of our creative and spiritual life. Its characteristic style of movement is allusive and metaphoric rather than direct and literal, and the mini-processes by which it unfolds therefore tend to be elusive. The exercises in the Journal sections of this dimension seem, however, to have a special capacity to activate sources of energy that have powerful effects in our life.*

---

* Of the three dimensions of experience with which we work in the *Intensive Journal*, the Depth Dimension is the one that is dealt with in the work of C. G. Jung. For the conceptual link between Jung's theories and this aspect of the *Intensive Journal*, see Progoff, *The Symbolic and the Real*, Chapter 3.

The Dialogue Dimension deals with the connective relationships within our personal life. It is the *realm of interior communication*, and it contains the mini-processes that have the effect either of drawing us together with harmonious relationships within ourselves, or of keeping us split and inwardly distracted. The Journal sections in which we work with the mini-processes of the Dialogue Dimension have the special function of opening the channels for interior communication, and of providing the techniques by which a vital inner contact can be maintained among the various parts of our lives.

Basic to the Dialogue Dimension is the realization that the main aspects of our existence unfold as persons in the universe. We shall see and experience the numerous implications of this as we proceed with the various procedures for using the *Intensive Journal*. They all reflect the underlying process by which a unique person emerges in the course of each individual existence. A human being begins his life as a seed of possibility, and these possibilities are unfolded, frustrated, transformed in the midst of the varied circumstances of his life. Out of the composite of our experiences and relationships in contact with our environment, we each build our unique life history. And at the center of this life history is the emergent person who is our self. It is this person within our life history who meets with the person in the life history of others and thus forms the *dialogue relationships* that are the basic units of experience of the Dialogue Dimension.

As we move more deeply into our lives, it becomes apparent that not only human beings but artworks that we do, institutions in which we believe, situations in which we become involved also have life histories. To that degree, human or not, they also are persons, and they can be related to as persons. It thus becomes possible to enter into dialogue relationships in all the meaningful aspects of our lives. This is the main content of the mini-processes of the Dialogue Dimensions. The individual sections in this division of the Journal provide the place where we work actively on several levels with exercises that extend the range and possibility of our interior dialogue relationships.

These sections are: *Dialogue with Persons, Dialogue with Works; Dialogue with Society; Dialogue with the Body;* and *Dialogue with Events, Situations and Circumstances.*

It is significant to note that these sections are not entitled simply, Persons, Works, Society, Body, Events, but in each case it is "Dialogue with." The reason is that these sections are not simply categories by which we mark off and catalogue the various aspects of our lives. They are not for the purpose of analyzing ourselves, but to enable us to establish ongoing relationships with the various mini-processes of our experience. Because of the way that we carry out the exercises in the Dialogue sections, we are able to establish a contact and communication with each of the mini-processes as though it were a person. It is by means of this that extraordinary and enlightening experiences become available to us, opening deep inner relationships with the contents of our lives.

All the dimensions of experience with which we work in the *Intensive Journal* express the forms of energy movement taking place on the subjective level of our lives. In the individual sections of the three dimensions we work with the specific mini-processes that carry this movement. Primarily we use procedures in each of the dimensions that are in accord with its characteristic style of movement. For example, when we are working in the dream sections, we use procedures that follow the symbolic style of the Depth Dimension; when we are building the context of our individual life history, we use procedures that fit the characteristic style of the Life/Time dimension. Eventually, when we have progressed to an advanced level in the use of the Journal Feedback techniques, we learn how to combine the styles of movement of the various dimensions; thus we are able to evoke a broader range of inner experience. This is the later work of *Journal Interplay*.

All the dimensions of experience that underlie the Journal sections possess an inherent and evolving activity. We do not analyze or diagnose the mini-processes that carry this activity, but we record them and we evoke them. We draw them forward so that they can express the purpose and goal that lies behind them. By means of them we build the inner momentum of our lives and reach new levels of capacity and awareness. This is the core of the difference between working in the *Intensive Journal* and merely keeping a diary.

At its essence, the method of Journal Feedback is a means of drawing upon the structure of the *Intensive Journal* in order to generate energy, and to draw the movement of the life forward. The feedback procedures become possible because of the active quality of the dimensions that are contained in the major divisions of the Journal, and because of the variety of life-materials that are brought to the fore by the mini-processes of individual existence as we work with them in the special sections. With the full range of life-contents as its raw material, the Journal Feedback method draws upon numerous sequences of exercises to reach into the life of the individual. The combination and interrelation of these procedures have the effect of drawing the energies and the unused potentials forward and fusing them into new integrative units.

The Journal Feedback method achieves its results by bringing about a multiplying effect within the psyche. Its impact is cumulative, and this generates a progressively stronger momentum. In time, as the force of this momentum increases, it attains an autonomous power, as though at that point it had become self-generating and self-directing. It then seems to be able by its independent capacity to carry the person forward to the next step of growth in his life. Often it is able to provide this accretion of energy despite the enervating effects of a person's anxieties and negative self-image. It is able to carry him forward despite himself, once the critical, turning point in the work has been reached. This turning point can often be clearly discerned and marked off, for it is the moment when the balance shifts, as on a scale or a seesaw, and one side becomes definitely the heavier and the dominant one. In the context of our work with the *Intensive Journal*, it is the point at which the cumulative build-up of energy by the process of Journal Feedback has become greater than the energy available to habitual consciousness and old styles of behavior.

This self-multiplying, cumulative effect of Journal Feedback gives it a great force. It generates a power which accumulates in the unconscious depths behind the mind in the very midst of conscious thinking and writing. And then it thrusts forward in the form of new experiences, new recognitions, new ideas and emotions. Thus the force of Journal Feedback breaks apart and breaks through the shells of our habits and those other psychological impediments which are the heavy baggage most of us carry from the past. It does this by building its energy invisibly, and then thrusting forward from behind the mind, drawing its new solutions out of the context of each person's unique existence and phrasing them in the terms of each person's life.

The movement of Journal Feedback is impressive when it begins to show results, but it follows irregular rhythms and these can be misleading. Often it remains behind the mind for what seems a very long time before it begins its swing upward. It is not uncommon that in the early stages of the process nothing at all seems to be happening; and then, all at once, the cumulative effects show themselves one after another.

The effect of Journal Feedback upon the cycles of the psyche results in an elusive pattern of movement. It is a style of movement that is very difficult to evaluate from any point of view that is external to it. That is another way of saying that while we are in the midst of our cycles of inner experience and something is being worked out within us, our intellectual and analytical minds cannot be of much help to us. They are external to the inner process that is working in the depth of us behind our minds.

Since we cannot understand our inner process from the outside via our intellectual minds, we must learn to reach it from within. Underlying the irregularity of its rhythms, there is a consistent principle, and this we can learn to identify. As we perceive its movement, we are able to cultivate it from within and align our lives with it. To do this requires a capacity that is much like the *creative intuition* of which the philosopher Henri Bergson spoke. By means of it we can contact the *elan vital*, the vital force, in our lives.

From one point of view it can be said that the method of Journal Feedback provides a practical means of achieving that quality of being which Bergson envisioned and described. To achieve this requires a combination of intellectual understanding, intuition, and direct experience so that we can comprehend the operative principle that underlies Journal Feedback and document it with our own life. As we fill our *Intensive Journal* with our life, the cycles of unfoldment that are reflected there generate a further movement. This is the elan vital of our inner self. It is being reawakened and reenergized, and given a personal frame of reference that will enable it to do its work and find its unique meaning for each of us in the context of our life history as we live it in the midst of the world.

Chapter 4

Privacy in the Group:
The Atmosphere and Rules
of a Journal Workshop

There is a basic metaphor that sets the tone and atmosphere of the Journal Workshops. It is the image of the well connecting to the underground stream.

When we come together at a workshop with our *Intensive Journal*, it is as though each of us is a well. We are each engaged in entering that well, which is the well of our life, and in reaching as deeply into its sources as we can. As we carry out the various procedures of our Journal work, we are taken progressively to ever more fundamental levels. This is our guiding principle of progressive deepening by which we use the *Intensive Journal* as our instrument for making contact with and drawing upon the ultimate sources of life.

We each go down individually into the well of our life. The well of each personal existence is separate and distinct from every other. Each individual must therefore go down his own well, and not the well of someone else's life. We find, however, that when, as individuals, we have gone very far down into the well of our life, we come to an underground stream that is the source of all the wells. While the wells of our personal existence are each separate from every other, there are no separations here. There are no walls or dividers in the underground stream. We are all connected here in the unitary continuum of being.

Our lives are separate as individuals, and each human being must live his own life history. Just as we cannot live someone else's life, so we cannot go through someone else's well to reach the underground stream. We each must go through our own personal existence, but when we have gone deeply enough we find that we have gone *through our personal life beyond our personal life*. This is the transpersonal connection which we experience in the underground stream. We each work toward it individually within the context of our own life history. When we reach it, however, we do not remain in the depths. Those waters have the effect of renewing our energies and giving us access to abundant resources for our life. We draw upon these sources and carry them back with us to the surface of the well where we incorporate them in living out the next time-unit of our lives.

The symbol of the well and the underground stream thus carries us through a continuing cycle of experiences. While the outer events of our lives take place at the surface of the well, we go inward to the underground stream to reach our deep sources, and to have the revitalizing experience of reconnecting ourselves with the larger unity of life. Having broken through the walls of individuality to enter the deep source, we then return to live our personal existence in the world of external reality.

This cycle of experience, symbolically understood, provides the prototype of the way we proceed in working at a Journal Workshop. Each individual is engaged in entering the well of his existence as deeply as he can so that he can draw new resources for his life from the underground stream. Another way to say this is that each existence is engaged in finding the way of life and of being that will be true to its own nature. It is seeking its own integrity, and in the course of this quest the inner person emerges and grows. It is this *inner person* that is the essence and the meaning of the life.

The essence of the *Intensive Journal* concept is that it provides the fullness of psychic space and a method of moving about within that space so that each inner person will be able to emerge in his own way and in his own timing. In order for this to take place, the privacy of the inner process must be protected as a sacred trust. For this reason, the work that we do in the *Intensive Journal* is a sanctuary of privacy for the individual not only when we are alone but also at a workshop. It is an *active privacy*, however.

Using the *Intensive Journal* at a workshop, we direct our attention inward so as to nurture the inner person who is seeking to grow strong in us. We are seeking the seed of our Self, for in that is contained the person who is concealed by the social styles and social roles that we enact in our outer lives. Living in the world, we are all subjected to external pressures and conditionings. We respond to those pressures by allowing habit patterns to form, and these eventually direct our actions for us as though they were independent of us. The result is that we live our lives as though they were being conducted from an outer rim of ourselves. By letting this happen to us, we are able to survive the depersonalizing pressures of society, but we survive at the cost of the private person within us. Our psychological shells and our behavior habits protect us, but increasingly they usurp the function of the unfolding seed of the self.

The seed of the inner person is the essence of a human being. It carries the potentiality of life, and it is unique in each individual. The urge to live is an affirmation of this seed, but its growth especially in its early stages, is soft and delicate. Like the young shoot of a plant, its life is precarious. It is especially vulnerable to the pressures and whims of the social environment. If it is to survive, it must build its own inner strength. It must be able to affirm the private person within itself.

At a Journal Workshop we come together to work actively each in our own privacy using the *Intensive Journal* as our instrument. We systematically draw back to the hidden part of the self where the seed is. This means feeling the inner movement of our life, being in touch with it, being deeply connected to it at its roots, and working to nurture its growth. In the nature of things, this kind of inner work cannot be done while we are engaged in external activities, nor while our energies are moving outward. We must draw ourselves inward and give ourselves sufficient time to turn our attention into ourselves so that we can work with commitment in our own privacy.

In this context, *active privacy* is the basic means of inner contact available to an individual. It does not mean working alone, nor does it mean holding ourselves aloof from others, for privacy does not involve a physical place or a physical condition. Privacy is primarily an inner place and a quality of being. Especially it is the condition of being that is established in a person when his attention is focused toward nurturing the seed and deepening the roots of his life. *Active privacy* is the relation of a person to himself as he works with the inner processes of his life.

Often it is necessary for a person to be alone without the physical presence of others when he is engaged in this inward work. That is why those religious traditions that have emphasized the contemplative life have generally recommended a retreat from the world, or at least a period of withdrawal, for the time during which the inward work is being done. The effects of such disciplines vary, however. Their success is generally dependent upon belief in the particular doctrines which the religion espouses; and such beliefs usually present considerable difficulty in the circumstances of modern life. Without such a belief, or without the traditions to provide a cultural background for at least the equivalent of a religious faith, those disciplines that require spiritual withdrawal tend to have only a transitory effect. They need to be bolstered by something with stronger roots in the life of the society.

It has become clear that modern man requires an approach that is different from traditional spirituality in order to meet the special psychological needs of our time in history. If attention to the inner life of the private Self can only be practiced by individuals who are withdrawn and in isolation, a condition of imbalance is bound to arise that weakens the entire experience. The one-sidedness of isolated aloneness creates a precarious emotional situation which the modern mind can seldom sustain. On the other hand, if balance and support are provided to strengthen the individual who is in quest of the private person within himself, he will have a means of safely traversing what has been called "the razor's edge" of inner experience.

To provide this outer support for the private inner work is one of the main reasons that a basic part of the private work of the *Intensive Journal* is carried out in a group environment. *Journal Workshops* provide a place where an individual can combine two essential experiences that are often thought of as opposites. He can work in the depths of his own privacy while being supported by the sustaining atmosphere of a group. The principles by which a Journal Workshop is conducted make it possible to draw strength from the *presence* of others without infringing on the privacy of the individual. This is because the Journal Workshops concentrate their attention upon actually doing the Journal work.

At *Journal Workshops* people come together in a group, but not in order to communicate with one another, and not to relate to one another. Judged by the usual conception of "group" experience, this is a strange, even paradoxical, situation. People meet in a group, the size of which may vary from a dozen to more than a hundred, but they do not necessarily speak to one another, nor respond to one another on any external level. That is because they come together in a group with the explicit purpose of each working individually in his own life.

From time to time in the course of the workshops, individuals do read aloud from their Journals. This is part of the Journal Feedback experience. When they read, however, they do not expect that anyone in the group will necessarily be listening to them. Some may listen; and some may half-listen, hearing not so much the words as the overtones and the psychic vibrations of what is being said. They will be only half-listening because they themselves will be engaged in writing in their own Journals. Each participant is engaged primarily in moving deeper into his own life. Even those persons who will be listening to what is being read will make no judgment, and no interpretation of what they hear. If anything at all is said about it, it will be little more than a neutral comment, just enough of a response to indicate that someone else is there and has heard what was read. That is why it is usually the leader of the group who makes the response. The others are involved in working in their own lives.

This style of procedure is an essential element of the *Intensive Journal* methodology. Persons who have become accustomed to the more extroverted types of group interaction occasionally find it difficult to adjust to this quiet way of proceeding, at least at their first contact. The training of our culture has accustomed us to look outward for our meaningful experiences. We are gradually learning, however, that the depth resources for our lives lie within us. It is a basic truth of human existence. To recognize it intellectually, however, is not sufficient. It is necessary that each of us *experience* for ourselves the reality of our inward resources and learn to reach them. This comes gradually as a progressive awareness and capacity. The Journal Workshop method provides a continuous means of working by which each person can establish this depth contact within the context of his own life and steadily expand it.

In order for the dynamic factor within Journal Feedback to become effective within the group situation, it is necessary for the participants to overcome their desire to respond to one another emotionally or inter-personally at the workshops. They must also forgo their urge to an-alyze and interpret one another's readings. If we turned our attention outward toward others while we are engaged in the Journal work, the effect would be to split the movement of the process. The energies available to us would then be divided, thus cutting the inward momentum that is essential in order for Journal Feedback to be effective.

To build and maintain this momentum, it is necessary that we bypass the surface interplay of feelings among the members of the group so that we direct our attention intensively to the underlying seed level of the person. The guiding principle of a Journal Workshop is to follow procedures that will deepen, extend, and accelerate the feedback process within each of the individual participants. Everything that is read in the course of a workshop contributes to this process. The specific entries that are read may not necessarily be "deep" in the sense of being philosophically profound; but they are always *deepening* because each one expresses an additional act of reaching further into the unfolding process of a life. One small, outwardly unimpressive entry at a time, we move ever deeper and more strongly into our lives as individuals. No single entry or exercise achieves this by itself. But the cumulative movement of the Journal exercises at a workshop stimulates the feedback process and brings it about, at a different tempo and in a different form for each person.

We may still wonder, since the emphasis is so strongly on the experience of the individual in the depth of his privacy, why, then, do we meet in a group? What is to be gained by bringing many people together in order to have each of them remain essentially private?

The heart of the matter was very succinctly stated by a participant in a Journal Workshop. As the weekend session was coming to a close, we were engaged in writing a meditative reflection in the closing section of the *Intensive Journal*, the section that is called, "Now, The Open Moment." That particular exercise is one that leads to many diverse forms of expression, but for one woman in the group the meditation became a short poem dealing with her group experience. In it were the lines:

This solitary work
We cannot do alone.

She was expressing her realization that the work she had done in her Journal was at its essence a private work. In the course of the workshop she had dealt with the most intimate parts of her life, in most cases for the first time. She had opened those questions and had let herself explore them. They were exceedingly private; yet she had been able to write about them in the group with a depth and fullness that had not been possible when she was alone. She had written many intimate things and had even voluntarily read some of them to the group. But nothing of her privacy had been violated in the reading.

The task of coming into contact with the depth and fullness of our lives is a "solitary work," for the essence of it is privacy. The paradox is that it is not a task that can be carried through successfully when an individual works at it altogether alone. He requires the assistance of others, and especially he requires the presence of others. He requires a situation and a method that will enable him to work *side by side* with others while doing the solitary work that reaches deeply into the private person within himself.

The presence of others, each engaged in reaching into the past and the potentials of his own life, seems to have the effect of assisting the "solitary work" of everyone. One of the goals of a Journal Workshop is to provide such a situation, a place where people can come together to meet at a deep level, with full freedom of expression and with their privacy protected. Here we are shielded from the outer pressures of our life. In a sense we are withdrawing from those pressures, but in order to escape from them. We are withdrawing into the protected depth of the group in order to be better able to work more actively at resolving the truly fundamental questions and issues of our lives.

In the meeting place of the Journal Workshop we are free from judgment by others and any artificial restraints upon either our conscious or our unconscious thoughts. It is not a negative freedom as in drawing away from something we do not like. It is a freedom with the purpose of enabling us to work with a specific method that will build a dynamic movement at the depth of ourselves. And especially it is a freedom that enables us to use that method with the benefit of the psychic support and validation of others, while we ourselves are giving the support of our sincere presence to the other participants in the group.

This active quality of many working together each in his own depths, each giving his silent and psychic support to those around him, is a great source of psychic energy. In an intangible way it generates a power very much as prayer does. Working in one's *Intensive Journal* in a group is not just an introspective and psychological work. It is a systematic attempt to build a reintegrative effect in our lives by working deeply in our inner process using the *Intensive Journal* as our instrument. We do this as a private work carried out by each within the context of his own life. We do it alone, and we do it together.

For these reasons, the Journal Workshops are not group workshops in the ordinary sense of the term. We do not come together for the purpose primarily of being in a group situation. We come together rather for the specific purpose of being able to work more deeply and freely in our *Intensive Journals*, making fuller use of the Journal Feedback method, drawing upon the psychic assistance that comes from doing an intense and dedicated work in the company of others who are similarly engaged. Once again, a group participant spontaneously offered an apt description of what the Journal Workshops are about. "These are not group workshops," she said, "These are working-in-the-Journal shops." And that is indeed their essence. We come together in order to work in the *Intensive Journal* with a depth and extent that would not otherwise be possible.

Once we have defined them as "working-in-the-Journal shops," we have a clear criterion to guide us in the methodology to be followed at a Journal Workshop. There are two main factors. The first is that we require specific techniques that will enable individuals to build a momentum that carries them to a greater depth as they work within their privacy in the midst of the group. The second is that we require an *atmosphere* in the group that progressively forms from the moment the group convenes. At public workshops it is usually the case that most of the participants have never met before, but that does not impede the formation of a deep atmosphere. Just as in a cathedral the atmosphere does not depend on the prior acquaintance of those present, so it does not in a workshop. Since we come together to work in the cathedral of our lives, it does not matter whether we have met before. We have each come to the Journal Workshop to perform the equivalent act of private dedication. To the degree that we each focus on that act in our individuality, a deep atmosphere forms around us in the Workshop. We find then that the specific techniques that we use at a Journal Workshop contribute to the forming of the atmosphere; equally, the atmosphere deepens as the exercises proceed enabling us to carry out our private work at ever deeper levels. Thus the two aspects of workshop methodology, the exercises and the atmosphere, mutually support one another. The interplay between them sets the pace and rhythm at which the Journal work can proceed. The guidance of this interplay is a primary factor in conducting a Journal Workshop.

The atmosphere of the group makes it possible for each individual to work at a deep level; but the work that is done is different for each person since each is at a different point in the process of his life. For each one, the purpose of Journal work is to pick up the process of growth wherever it is in the individual and to draw it forward to its next stage of unfoldment in keeping with its own inner timing. Since we are working in a group situation, we must allow that as a person moves through the cycles of his life, there is a change from moment to moment in the inner conditions that will best nurture his growth. Multiplying this by each of the individuals participating in the workshop gives us a seemingly impossible number of special needs to harmonize in the group. But we find that we are able to harmonize the multiplicity of special personal requirements simply and naturally by enabling each person to go down to the *underflow* level of human experience in his own terms. Each goes through the well of his own life to the depth level that is beyond the well and beyond the person.

In this way the opposites of multiplicity and privacy are naturally reconciled. They complement one another, and they blend into one another to form a larger whole. The working etiquette of the group is essentially designed to establish a situation that will reinforce a mutuality of respect for the delicate process by which the inner growth of a person takes place. We seek to protect the psychic space around the individual so that the seed of potentiality may grow in him, and so that the growth that begins in a workshop can continue to be cultivated afterwards in Journal self/work until it bears its fruit. In order to do this, we maintain our privacy and separateness at the same time that we are working together. We each work in our own well; by maintaining that integrity of focus, we assist the process in everyone.

In the course of a workshop, it sometimes happens that the Journal entry which a person reads expresses a difficulty or a painful problem in his life. He may become upset, distraught, or tearful while he is reading it. How shall we respond to him?

We may feel love and sympathy for his situation, but we do not rush in to help him. We may feel that being neutral outsiders to his life, we see the solution to his problems and we wish to help him by telling him what to do. But if we do really wish to help him, we will maintain our good wishes in silence. We will preserve for him the space and freedom that will enable him to find his own answers to his problems in the rhythm that his life requires. If he is allowed to have the leeway in which to experience both his pain and his searching, he will eventually not only be able to solve his problem, but something much more meaningful will take place for him. He will be able to hear the larger message for his life and consciousness that the problem is trying to disclose to him. In the course of discovering this, he will also be strengthening the inner muscles of his psyche. This is of the greatest importance, since it is this that enlarges a person's capacity for further growth.

Because we follow the principle of honoring the integrity of each person's inner process, we restrain ourselves from graciously giving our advice and guidance in a workshop. We keep our own counsel, and thus we give one another a far greater gift, the gift of freedom and time. We also give one another the silent support that comes from trusting the self-healing wisdom of life. There is a great power in this that cannot be put into words. By our silent restraint, we express not only our love for the other person, but also our respect for the integrity of the life process at work in each of us. This is a most basic rule to follow in participating in a Journal Workshop.

In a similar way, it sometimes happens that a person who is working in his Journal at a workshop is moved to tears, even to heavy sobbing. Then also we may feel an urge to rush over with our loving hugs and caresses, to tell that person that we care and that everything will be all right. But should we do that with our intentions so pure and full of love, we may actually be preventing the person we wish to help from fulfilling the needs that his sobs are expressing. We must hold firm to our fundamental awareness that the psyche knows what needs to be done, that it will eventually do it in its own authentic timing, and that we have the responsibility to protect its freedom to move through its necessary cycles.

A person who cries at a workshop may have been waiting for many years to gain the courage and strength that would enable him to release the long-stored pains of sadness in his life. If we rush in with our embraces and assurances, we will close off the space in which he can express those old emotions. Our good intentions may then stifle the open expression that was just beginning to be strong enough to let itself be heard.

Often the tears and sobs are the mourning that was not allowed to take place when we suffered a death in the course of our life. It may have been the death of another beloved person, a person who was important or dear to us. Of even greater significance, and an even greater reason for mourning, it may have been the death of a part of our lives that was cut short before it could grow. Holding the perspective of the principle of inner continuity in the life of persons, we recognize that such spontaneous mourning is the internal ritual that is necessary before a person can be freed to take the next step in his life.

We wish to be especially careful not to close in on another person and limit the space and time in which he can live through the necessary mourning for the past sadnesses of his life. Especially in those persons who have repressed their sadnesses for many years, when they finally find a situation, as many do in the Journal Workshops, in which the open atmosphere gives them the inner freedom to let the crying happen, it is important that no one intrude. If we did intrude with our well-intentioned comforting, we would get into the other person's well. We would close it off at the point where it was freeing itself from the excess material so that it could regulate itself from within. We must give it more time so that it can eventually restore its own inner balance and reestablish contact with its deep sources.

Sometimes, when a person is experiencing this spontaneous psychic ritual of mourning, the external manifestations may seem to be very extreme. Sobs may rack a person's body, and the wails of sadness may have an eerie sound. Many of us, then, having been conditioned by the prevailing belief in a psychology of pathology, will feel that we recognize a syndrome and feel that there is a diagnosis to be made. We will then rush to the quick judgment that the person is caught in a serious psychotic disturbance, and that something immediate and drastic has to be done.

In all our experience in the workshops, we have found that only one thing needs to be done, and to do it properly always balances the situation. What is necessary is that each of the persons in the workshop remain quietly in his own well, reaching within himself toward the underground stream that sustains us all. Feeling that quietness and stability in the group around him, the mourning person finds that the waves of pain go past their crest within him. Passing their crest, they gradually subside. Soon he begins to feel quiet again with a sense of having been carried by something greater than himself.

He is indeed being carried by something from beneath himself, for the waters of the underground stream are buoyant. They sustain him through the cycle of his tears. When he emerges on the other side of the crying, he has added to his life the experience of having passed through a full cycle in the process of the psyche. He now possesses a direct knowledge of what is involved in passing through "the valley of the shadow," reemerging, coming up the mountainside again. Having been left free to express his inner pain, the person has begun to learn of a process and a power in the depth of his own life. Having endured a full cycle successfully, he now knows it directly. In the future, therefore, he may be able to rely upon it, and even trust in it. Having experienced it once, he will now be able to draw upon it again and again in the future to help him pass through the cycles of the crises of life that inevitably lie ahead.

Just as a person is free in a workshop to express whatever is at the fore at that moment in the process of his life, so he is also free not to express it. In the course of the workshop we have an opportunity to write in the various sections of the Journal, and we are then invited to read. But no one is required to read. No one is required to speak. It is against the principles of the workshop to prod a shy person into speaking or reading from his Journal. We never go around the room so that we can all take turns at participating. We maintain the privacy and integrity of everyone so that the workshop situation can be a place where each person is free to honor and express the inner principle of his own being.

Just as we make no judgment about the content of what a person reads, so we make no judgment about the person who holds his silence in the workshop. We do not say to him: "What are you hiding? What are you afraid of?" We respect his silence with our own.

We let each person follow the integrity of his own inner promptings. We leave it to him to decide whether or not he shall read from his Journal—now or later—and whether or not he shall speak in the workshop at all. We know that there may be experiences in a person's life that carry with them a great need to be spoken in the group, but that are not yet able to push their way through to the surface. The person does not yet feel strong enough to say them in public. The time when they can be spoken by him has not yet come, and we must therefore respect his reticence. There may be something maturing in the depth of him that we do not yet know of, since it has not been able to reveal itself. We therefore allow it the time that it requires.

There also are some things that cannot be spoken in a group because, in doing so we would intrude on the writer's or someone else's privacy. There are some experiences that are so delicate that they would break if they were spoken aloud. And there are some experiences that cannot be told without violating the integrity of a larger principle in one's life. For all of these reasons, we respect the validity of silence. They need not be spoken in the workshop, but these experiences can be written in the Journal and developed in the various exercises in the course of the workshop.

It has often happened in our experience that a person participates actively in a full weekend workshop without saying a word in public. He may converse at mealtimes and talk freely with the other group members during coffee breaks, but not speak at all during the group meetings. Then at the close of the workshop he comes to the group leader and indicates how important, even transforming an experience it has been. As partial verification, he points to the Journal and to the large amount of writing he has done in the workshop. He may also point to himself.

I recall a man in California during the early years of the Dialogue House program whose experience provides a good illustration of silent participation in Journal Workshops. Travelling to different locales, he attended three consecutive workshops within a period of two weeks, but he did not speak a word in public during any of them. As he phrased it to me afterwards, however, he "wrote reams."

His reason for attending such a concentrated program was that he had reached a major crossroad in his life. He felt that if he could gain a perspective of where he was in the Now-moment of his life, he would be able to make a valid decision for his future.

Hearing me speak at a public lecture, he had grasped the conception of *repositioning* one's life through gaining a new time perspective by means of the *Intensive Journal*. He felt that the concept spoke to his present condition, and he resolved to put the Journal method to a full test. He had, in addition, a particular problem which arose from the fact that his career had involved him with public figures in the entertainment industry, and he did not feel ethically free to reveal the nature of his relationship to them. Therefore, he could not speak openly in the group. But he had a great and immediate need to put his life in order and to be able to see his inner processes from a new vantage point.

When he had first come to the workshops, he thought that he, as an intellectual person, would receive from the *Intensive Journal* with its structure and classifications an objective understanding of his subjective life. What did take place for him, however, was something of a different and more far-reaching nature than he had anticipated. It was not so much that he gained an intellectual perspective, as that his life was actively repositioned in the course of the workshop. He was placed in a new relationship to the inner movement of his experience. From being at a dead stop, his experience of working in the Journal at the workshop set him into motion upon a new path without his consciously or deliberately choosing it. He achieved this in silence, by working intently in all the exercises of the Journal during the workshops which he attended. Especially he achieved it by working in his Journal in his privacy during the days that intervened between his workshop experiences.

When the series of workshops was over, he said that even though he had not spoken in the group, the fact of his being part of a group situation at this critical time of transition made it possible for him to work intensively in his Journal. The presence of the other members of the group gave him strength, and the atmosphere of the group quieted his nerves. The fact, also, that other people were seriously involved in the same process, and that each in his own way was directing his attention inward to achieve a deeper relation to his own life, helped him stay on an even keel. Thus, he said, he was able to write in his Journal with a consistency and fluidity that would not have been possible had he been working with it at home alone. At least at that early point in his work with the Journal, he said that he could not have sustained his work in privacy without the supporting presence of the group.

When the three workshops were over and he had had time to survey the results, his judgment was that the intensity of his use of the Journal in the workshops had had the effect of crystallizing the multitude of his jumbled thoughts and feelings into a single perception of his life. What had seemed to be very complicated decisions had thus fallen naturally and simply into place. In the course of the sustained Journal exercises in the workshops, decisions he could not make by conscious thought had seemed to form by themselves. They were shaped beyond analytical consciousness through the working of the inner process. He added to me that he thought that an analytical therapy would not have made such a consolidated experience possible. It would have taken a great deal longer, if, indeed, it would have happened at all. The fact was, he told me, that the reason he had come to the workshop in the first place was that analytical therapy had held him at his impasse.

Reflecting further on what had taken place in him, he felt that even with the use of the *Intensive Journal* he could not have worked through to the change by himself. His jangled nerves and anxieties would not have permitted him to concentrate and devote himself to the work for a sufficient length of time. But the atmosphere of the group enabled him to do this because it calmed him. The presence of the others in the group, each working in his own way, strengthened his resolve and enabled him to return to his central task whenever his attention wandered.

The group had a steadying and sustaining effect upon him. It was as though, he said, he were held up and carried by the group whenever he faltered. And he felt this as a great suffusion of love in the room. But there was no specific or overt relationship of love taking place between him and anyone else in the room. He was aware of that because no personal communication was occurring in the form of speech. But he felt that a tone of love in the room rose up around the persons present while they concentrated on their individual work and reached into the depth of themselves. This love he felt as a mode of communication that did not require him to speak. It left him free to explore the wide range of past and potential in his life. It gave him an energy and a capacity he would not otherwise have had; this enabled him to stimulate new inner experiences and awarenesses and to record his most private feelings.

That atmosphere in the group strengthened him in another way. It sustained him when the workshops were over, so that when he was by himself he was still able to continue his communication with himself in his Journal. At those times, he needed only to recall the situation of the group and place himself back in its atmosphere. Because of this, the days that intervened between the workshops which he attended were especially fruitful for him. He was able to enlarge explorations that had begun in the group. When the series of workshops was over, the momentum that had been generated enabled him to reenter his Journal and extend the process he had started there. By now the Journal had established itself in his consciousness as an instrument that was securely his to use. It carried with it the quality of feeling that had been present in the workshops, so that this atmosphere was now as much a part of the

Journal as its pages and its sections. Thus, he felt free and able to use it in the future on all occasions, whether he attended further workshops or not.

The feeling of being free to use the Journal after the workshop is over is a very important part of the whole program. It is this that gives continuity and ongoingness to the discipline of personal growth. The Journal Workshop begins the work, but the work itself continues for the whole of the road of one's life. With this in mind, a primary goal in attending a workshop is that as you become familiar with the use of the Journal through carrying out the exercises, you will become increasingly comfortable in using its procedures. You will then be able to take the *Intensive Journal* with you out into the midst of your life and continue using it in all circumstances. At that point it will become much more than a book in which you write. It will become a companion, a portable alter ego, and an intimate friend who will respond and discuss with you in dialogue. A person's relation to his *Intensive Journal* becomes, with time, very similar to a musician's relationship with his instrument. It is a special kind of friend, a friend whose nature it is to be used. And in this type of relationship, the more one friend is used by the other, the greater are the possibilities of what the two can achieve in living relationship together.

Let us now come together for our fundamental experience in the use of the *Intensive Journal*. Our purpose is to reach into the context and the continuity of our life as a whole so as to draw it all into focus with respect to our present circumstances. Once we have had this basic integrative experience, we will be able to continue by ourselves in our own timing working in the specific facets of our lives by means of the Journal Feedback procedures. The first step toward this ongoing experience is to participate in a Journal Workshop, to lay the groundwork and learn the basic procedures.

When we attend our first Journal Workshop we each receive our registered copy of the *Intensive Journal*.* In order to preserve our privacy, we do not write our name in the Journal. But each Journal is numbered, and the number is registered with Dialogue House in New York City. If

* See Appendix.

it is lost, it can be returned to us anonymously through that channel without our names being divulged. Thus our privacy remains intact.

At the beginning of a workshop when we first receive it, our *Intensive Journal* is indistinguishable from anyone else's. It is a black notebook, empty except for the twenty printed dividers that separate the sections in which we shall do our work. The dividers are in several colors to distinguish the various dimensions of our life experience and to facilitate the active movement of interplay among them. Those who work actively and continuously with the *Intensive Journal* have found that the use of different colors to distinguish the major divisions of the Journal helps them move more fluidly through the many interrelated aspects of their lives and expedites the self-integrating process within them.

We come together now as though in a group ready to begin a work and an experience that will be profoundly private for each of us. As we wait for the workshop to start, we sit in stillness. We let our breathing become slow and deep. The workshop is a pause in the active, outer movement of our lives. It is a time of sabbath, a quietness in which a new kind of inner movement can begin. We sit in silence, our thoughts at rest, waiting to begin to work in the depth and magnitude of our lives.

Chapter 5

Beginning the Journal Work:
The Period Log

Now that we are at a Journal Workshop, where shall we begin the work of drawing our life into focus? We begin with *Now*. But *Now* is not limited to the immediate instant. It is not just "here and now," not just the spot on which we stand, nor this moment when we speak. Our *Now* moment is elastic. Therefore, as we begin our work of life-focus, we stretch the present moment back as far as it needs to go in order to include as much of the past as is still an active part of the present.

The *Now* of our life thus becomes more than a moment. It is a unit of time that is as long or as short as each situation requires, and it includes the most recent part of the past that is a meaningful factor in the present. This forms the period that is the Now of our lives, our most recent relevant past as it moves into our present. This is the *period* to which we turn our attention in the *Period Log* section of the Journal at the start of a workshop, as we do now.

For each person, this elastic Now has a different content and a different duration. We may now be in the midst of a great love, or between loves, or deprived of a feeling of love. We may now be in the midst of a meaningful work, or between meaningful works, or feeling ourselves to be without meaning in our work and seeking it. We may be in a time of exhilaration, or in a time of depression, a time of gathering fruits, or a time of planning, and planting, and preparation. Whatever it is, it is the Now for us, our own Now. It is the particular present moment in which we find ourselves.

This present moment of our lives may cover a short period or a longer period. Whatever its duration, whatever its content, whether pleasant or painful, this is the unit of time, the period with which we begin our work in the *Intensive Journal*. It is a unique period for each of us. The *Period Log* is the section of the Journal in which we make the entries, succinct and objective as can be, to record this period as a whole. We describe the main outer and inner events that come to the fore of our minds when we reflect on the period and recall its primary aspects. Thus we begin our work together, but each with a different base, and in the context of a life-situation that is distinctive to ourselves.

The length of the period that we choose as our starting point varies with each person and with each life situation. For one person this present period in his life may reach back three years since he had a car accident and was hospitalized. Because of the changes it brought about, the period of time since that event is the Now in which he is living. For another person this present period may be merely a few weeks since he met a new friend, moved to a different city, began a new job, or underwent some other significant change in his circumstances. Since that time his life has borne the imprint of that event, and it, therefore, is the definitive factor in his present period.

The period that is Now varies with each individual. It is our basic point of departure whenever we prepare to do any significant work in the *Intensive Journal*. This is true whether we are coming together for a full workshop, or to work in privacy or in Journal Dyad. Our focus and starting point is always the present moment in time, for it is by means of that that we can position ourselves in the time movement of our lives. We begin by placing ourselves between the past and the future with reference to the particular situations that are at issue in our lives.

We do this by working in the Period Log. Let us begin by closing our eyes, relaxing, and quietly, inwardly, feeling the movement of our lives. We let ourselves feel the implications of the question, "Where am I now in my life?" We let the answer to this shape itself only in general terms behind our conscious minds. We do not direct ourselves into thinking about it deliberately, but we let ourselves *inwardly feel* the movement of our life as it has been taking shape in this present period.

As we do this, the boundaries and characteristics of this present period in our life take shape for us. We find that we are now able to give spontaneous answers to the question of what is this present period in my life? What events mark it off? How far back does it reach?

What have been the main characteristics of this recent period?

Perhaps this recent period began when you had an idea for a new project. Or perhaps it began when you married, or had a child, or had a rift in your marriage relationship. Perhaps it has been a time of hard work, or a time of confusion, or a time of waiting.

Perhaps this recent period began a few months ago, or perhaps it began long ago and has lasted for several years. Perhaps it is marked off by a specific event like a marriage or a birth, or an illness, or a new job; or it may be a period that is characterized by a general quality of feeling, like a cloud of depression that sometimes covers a person's life for many years. Even if it has lasted for a long time, we would still have to say that it is the recent period in your life. It would be recent in the sense that it is the situation that sets the context for the present moment in your life.

Very often we find that when a person is beginning to use the *Intensive Journal*, the period with which he works first is a period that covers many months or years. That is because he has not been paying serious attention to his life, and there are long spans of time to which he must relate himself. He must begin with them. After a while, however, when a person has been working closely with his experiences, the relevant periods tend to become shorter and shorter, moving closer to the immediate present. It is then as though the person has caught up with the movement of time in his life and is on a current basis with himself.

This will continue until he comes to another point of major change in his life. At that time, as he prepares for that new transition, he will perceive his present moment in the perspective of the large sweep of time in his life. At such a point in his experience, the period with which he works will cover a long stretch of time. When the situation has passed, his Period Logs will tend to revert to time units of shorter duration.

Now let us prepare to use the Period Log in its basic beginning exercise so that we can each place ourselves in the changing contexts of our lives. We are positioning ourselves in the movement of inner time.

We begin by becoming quiet. Let us sit in silence for a moment and once again feel the movement of our lives. We are quietly bringing ourselves into harmony with the continuity of our life experiences.

We do not at this point "think" of our life, but we "feel" it. We feel its movement in a general and flexible way. We specifically do not think about it, for if we did, we would only have the same thoughts on the subject that we have always had. We know from our experience that the self-analytic, self-judgmental thinking process tends to move in circular grooves, turning in upon itself and repeating itself.

We wish instead to open the way for something new to enter our experience. We therefore do not do what we have been accustomed to doing. We do not think about our lives, but we sit in silence and we *feel* the inner movement of our recent experiences without judgment. We do not direct our thinking, but we let awarenesses present themselves to us regarding this present period of our lives.

At first this may seem to be a vague and general procedure. And that is part of the reason for it, especially at this early point in our work. We hold ourselves in a condition of openness in which no particular thoughts are dominating our mind. We are silent. Thoughts may come, but they are not any particular thoughts. They are not directed thoughts. They are not thoughts that we consciously seek. They are thoughts that simply come to us. We let them come, and we let them go. They will soon return to us, but in the form of images.

We sit in stillness paying no attention to any special thoughts, not thinking, but feeling the movement of our life. We sit in this quietness for some moments. We find that there comes to us a generalized awareness of what this recent period in our lives has been. An inward sensing of the tone of our life in this recent period. Now we let the quality of our experiences during this time of our life express themselves to us. Perhaps they will take the form of an image, a metaphor, a simile, or some spontaneous adjective that describes it in a word. If so, we will take notice of this inward awareness in whatever form it appears to us.

We are in silence, our eyes closed, feeling this recent period in the movement of our lives. While our eyes are closed, as we sit with no thoughts, in the quietness, images may take shape in our minds. We see them inwardly, and they carry a feeling of the movement of our lives. They reflect the quality of this recent period in our experience.

Sitting this way, many different images and feelings can come to you, reflecting the quality of movement in your life. Whatever form it takes, let yourself perceive it. Do not reject or censor it. Neither should you affirm it; certainly you should not interpret it. Simply observe it and take note of the fact that this is what came to you when you closed your eyes and let yourself feel from within yourself the inner continuity and movement of your life. Then record it briefly in the Period Log of your *Intensive Journal.*

In doing this, many different kinds of experiences can come to people, different kinds of perceptions and images reflecting the present situation in their lives.

One person sees an image of dark smoke stuck in a chimney. "It can't get out," she says.

Another person, a student, sees a seed under the ground. It is softening and breaking apart. It is beginning to grow.

Another person sees an airplane flying a bumpy course through heavy clouds. Presently it comes into clear skies where the sun is shining.

Still another person sees nothing, but hears strains of music. This is not a visual image, but an auditory image. The tone and tempo of the music expresses his feeling of the movement of his life.

Another person neither sees nor hears an image, but feels a movement of emotions within herself. She experiences a welling up of joy, a suffusion of love. This is a "feeling" image. One person experiences the love in relation to a particular individual in her life. Another experiences it as a promise of deeper connection to life, as a love of God.

Still another person feels the movement of the recent period of his life and perceives a visual image of darkness, followed by a feeling image of heavy sadness, followed still further by a body image that becomes a knot forming in the pit of the stomach. All are expressions of the present situation of his life.

Whatever comes to us in this way, we record in our Journals; and we make no judgment about it. We do not say, "Oh good, I have an optimistic or encouraging image of this time in my life." And we do not reject the image because it was dark or doleful, or because it indicated that further difficulties may lie ahead.

We bear in mind, rather, that the significance of such images is that they express the quality of feeling that corresponds to this present moment in our life situation. Whatever it is at the moment, we accept as a fact that this is what it is, and that these are the images by which the inner situation of our lives is being reflected to us. We also know that whatever the images and our life situation are, they will inevitably change as they continue in their movement. If we perceive a plane flying in clouds, the cycle of the image will carry it through to clear light and sunshine. If it is an image of a seed in the ground, the organic movement of the image will carry it through to growth. If it is a flower blooming, it will wither; eventually it will become a seed again. Therefore we make no judgment in the midst of the movement of our imagery experience. We simply observe the movement of our images, write them down, and continue with our experiences.

As we are feeling into this recent period of our life, a simile or metaphor may come to us. "It has been like walking along a desert road and not seeing any trees." "It has been like eating at a banquet where each dish is more surprising than the last." This period in my life has been like a . . .

As we write down the comparison, some additional adjectives may come to us, describing this time in our life. Not words that we deliberately think about, just words that come spontaneously to us. When we allow words to come to us without thought in this way, they often say a great deal to us about our lives. And they say it in a very cogent form. They are verbal images.

Now, after preparing ourselves by working at the nonconscious level, we are ready to focus more specifically into the contents of this recent period of our life. We are ready now to write in our *Intensive Journal*. When did this period start? Was there a particular event with which it began? Or, more likely, is there a particular event that stands out in our minds as we think back over it, an event that we identify with the beginning of this period?

Sometimes the period is marked off by very obvious and dramatic events, the death of a friend or a relative, finding a new job, or being fired, moving to a new city. Frequently we find that a lengthy and significant period in a person's life begins without anything specific happening. Basic situations often establish themselves in ways that are hardly observable while they are taking place. Gradually, without announcing themselves, they become a fact of our lives; and they may be there for a long time before we recognize what the situation has actually become. In such circumstances, there is often some particular memory with which the period is identified. It may not be a memory of the event that started the period, but the memory expresses the essence of the situation. Often this is embodied in the moment of realization, the time when we recognize the nature of the situation as it has developed. If there is such a memory, write it down, then add to it any other facts that define the period and mark off its boundaries.

When we began to work in the Period Log, first closing our eyes in order to look inward for images, and then letting the essence of the period express itself in a metaphor, we were not proceeding by conscious thought. We were simply relaxing our conscious controls and letting images and feelings come to us. Now we are ready to work consciously again. As our next step, we reconstruct the outlines of the period. We begin by recalling the salient and specific details of this now period in our life.

We let our minds go back over this time. What memories come to us? Were there special events that took place? Were arguments, angers, physical fights of any kind important in the period? Were there events of friendship, of loving, spiritual or physical loving that played a significant role? Were there family relationships, or work involvements, or social activities that we now recall? Were inner experiences important? Did you have any particularly striking experiences of a spiritual or artistic or extra-sensory type? If so, indicate them briefly here. At a later point in your Journal work you will be able to deal with them in the detail they require.

Do you recall any dreams from the period? There may be dreams that stand out in your mind because they were especially striking or dramatic. Or there may be dreams that continued to recur although they had first appeared in an earlier period of your life. Dreams that continue to return should be considered carefully, for they are like persistent callers who have a message that needs to be heard.

Do you recall any strange or uncanny events, coincidences or psychic events that seem to have a meaning for you? Were there strong religious experiences during this time? Were there inspirations, great new ideas? Were there times of great good luck or of misfortune? Were there physical illnesses?

All that comes to us as memory relating to this period is to be written in our Journal in the Period Log section. As we do this, we should bear in mind that the concept underlying the keeping of a "log" section is that its entries are to be brief. Working in our Period Log, we jot down as many of the relevant facts and memories as we can, simply getting them down on paper, not elaborating them at first. With brief entries, we can in a short while recapitulate the period as a whole and bring ourselves up to the present moment.

There will be some entries in the Period Log which will lead us to feel, even as we are writing them, that they need immediately to be described in full detail. Others can first be recorded briefly and then elaborated at length later on. Many of the entries that we make in the *Period Log* suggest to us as we are recording them that they merit a great deal more of our attention. Such events and memories often have a great deal to say to us about our past and future. They are especially important in providing the starting point for the feedback exercises that we do in other sections of the Journal. In general, however, it is best to limit our Period Log entries to the essential factual description of our experiences. At a later point in the workshop or when we are using the active Journal Feedback exercises in our post-workshop private work, we can explore them more extensively and enable them to reveal their further message for our lives.

Working in the Period Log serves several very important functions in the use of the *Intensive Journal*. Primarily it provides the point of focus at which we begin the process of positioning ourselves in the movement of our lives. For this reason, the Period Log is the first section of the Journal to be used at each Journal Workshop. We begin with it in order to give ourselves a reference point in the present time unit of our lives.

It is important to bear this in mind if you are undertaking to have your first experience in using the *Intensive Journal* by using this book as your guideline without actually being in the atmosphere of a Journal Workshop. In that case, you will find it best to begin with the Period Log as we are doing, and to carry through the exercises as described until you have brought yourself up to date with respect to the current situation of your life.

Take care, however, not to write too much at this point. It is not beneficial for you to be exhaustive in the descriptions and statements that you write in your Period Log. Remember that it is a *Log* section, and that a primary quality of Log entries is that they be written briefly. Our experience has shown that brevity in the Log sections is especially helpful in the early stages of the work. This is true for several reasons, some of which may not be apparent at this early point in your Journal work. One reason is that it enables us to develop a large perspective for our life in a relatively short period of time. A second reason is that the brief entries in the Period Log enable us to gather a large number of small pieces of information which increase in relevance when they are brought together. Taken in composite, these brief entries establish the context of our life experience as a whole and provide an immediate framework against which the larger scope of our work can be carried out. Furthermore, as our Journal work proceeds, these varied and brief entries in our Period Log serve a very productive function in providing the points of departure for the active feedback exercises that will follow. We must ever bear in mind as we carry out our Journal work that the basic entries which we make in our Log sections are a *feeding-in* of our life material which the Journal Feedback process will progressively integrate in a dynamic way by means of its exercises and the varied procedures of Journal Interplay.

To make it possible for this reintegrative, life-focusing effect to occur at a later point in our work, it is essential that we overcome at the beginning the temptation to overwrite in the Period Log. Sometimes the excitement of a new discovery as the movement of our thoughts and memories accelerates makes us want to continue writing on and on. It is important to remember, however, that excessive writing at the beginning may weaken the larger dynamic of the Journal Feedback process as a whole. It will draw us off into the type of experience that characterizes ordinary journal or diary writing; then we will lose our access to the special re-integrative powers which the Journal Feedback process provides.

We are especially vulnerable to the temptation of excessive writing in the Log sections when we are beginning our Journal work in our own privacy without the disciplines and atmosphere of a Journal Workshop. Working by ourselves, we are not restricted by the limitations of time. One memory will then beget another, and our writing may then become exceedingly fluid and extensive. It is important to bear in mind then the reason for which at a Journal Workshop we deliberately set a time limit upon writing in the Period Log. We do this in order to establish a nonconscious process of selectivity that will draw into the foreground of a person's attention those factors that are truly of primary significance in the situation of his life. We wish to achieve this in the shortest possible time, and with as little interference as possible from our self-conscious thought processes. We want to leave as little time and temptation as possible for a person to rationalize his life to himself, thereby obscuring and possibly falsifying the facts of his experience. To encourage spontaneity, therefore, it is best for the entries in the Period Log to be brief and direct without amplification and without premeditation.

Each person must be aware of his own tendencies, and they are different in this respect for each individual. We have found it often to be the case that when a person writes on and on in the Period Log, his extended verbalization tends to lead him away from the basic factuality of his life. Educated people may especially be seduced into quasi-literary writing instead of basic, unvarnished statements of their inner experience. The factual and objective description of the inner subjective states is an essential step in the Journal Feedback process. Any degree of literary amplification at the level of the log entries opens the back door for self-consciousness in the Journal work, and this draws us back into our old patterns of analysis and intellectual interpretation. To the degree that we allow this to take place, our Journal will become a retrospective and introspective diary of a more traditional type. If that tendency is not corrected, the Journal work loses its force, and the results which the feedback procedures of the *Intensive Journal* can otherwise achieve are diluted by that much.

There are two general approaches for us to follow in gathering data for our Period Log. The first is to recapitulate the occurrences of the period spontaneously as we have done, drawing upon the memories that come directly to mind when we turn our attention to this recent time in our lives. The second way is to review the events of the period briefly but systematically. The structure of the *Intensive Journal* gives us a convenient means of doing this. We refresh our memory by using certain of the feedback sections as checkpoints recalling to our attention the relevant contents of this period in our life.

The basis of this checklist is its reference to the individual feedback sections. The nature of their contents and the way that we use them will be better understood later on when we have carried out their specific Journal Feedback exercises. In the meanwhile, however, we can begin to refer to these checkpoints in a general way in order to assist our work in the Period Log.

Going back in your mind once again over the period that you have marked off, let yourself now recall the relationships with individuals that have been important during this time. They need not have been pleasant or satisfying relationships. Whether they were fulfilling or frustrating is beside the point. It is important that they were meaningful to you. Jot down in your Period Log now the names of the persons with whom significant experiences took place during this period of your life. Do not describe the occurrences in detail, but merely add some comments and brief descriptions after the name of the person. A few phrases followed by two or three explanatory sentences should be sufficient to express your memories and record your feelings and observations. Do this for each of the individuals who are significant for you during the period. These brief entries will then give you a starting point for additional exercises that you may carry out in the feedback sections later on.

Now we move to a further checkpoint. What work projects or outer activities were important to you during this period? It may be that you did not have a definite work involvement and that you were seeking one. Or it may be that there were frustrations and tensions in your life during this time because of the lack of a meaningful work. If so, that is an important fact to be entered in your Period Log.

If you were engaged in a project or work activity, it will be valuable for you to record briefly the various phases and changes through which it passed. What were the hopes and plans and difficulties that you encountered? What is the situation at the present moment with respect to your work? The cursory entries that you make in this regard now in your Period Log will also be the base for further experiences in the feedback exercises.

Let us now continue moving through the Journal checklist for additional brief entries to be made in the Period Log.

What events were important with respect to the physical aspect of your life during this time? Was health or illness a significant factor? Do any particular events now come to mind with respect to diet or athletics or love-making or drugs or the enjoyment of nature? If so, record them and add only whatever brief comment or explanation is necessary.

Have there been events during this period that involved you with social or political issues? Was it a time when your beliefs or group identifications were called into question? Was this a time when you had a particularly strong experience with respect to music or drama or any of the other artforms? Record these briefly now, making a mental note of the fact that you will elaborate them further at a later point in your Journal work.

Consider now whether any events have taken place during this period that were particularly striking or dramatic or meaningful in your life. Was there any single event that drastically changed the course of your life experience? Perhaps there was an accident of some kind or an event of unexpected good fortune. Perhaps there was a striking coincidence, an experience of extra-sensory perception that was particularly meaningful to you, or perhaps you had a strong experience of a religious quality, whether in a church or in direct closeness with nature. If such an event occurred during the period and now comes to your mind, record it briefly. Its significance will be expanded for you in your further experiences in the Journal.

When you have made the brief entries to record the contents and occurrences of this recent period that are recalled to your mind by using this checklist, your basic entry in the Period Log will be complete. Bear in mind that you are interested in recording memories and facts of experience without judgment and without censorship. Your Period Log is the place where you draw together an outline picture of this recent time in your life. It contains the specific contents of our experience, but not the details. It is our first step toward positioning ourselves in the larger movement of our lives and drawing our life experience into focus.

Chapter 6

Twilight Imagery
and Its Life Correlation:
The Period Image

Having completed our basic entry in the Period Log, we sit in stillness again. We shall now reapproach this present time in our life from another vantage point.

While we were reviewing our recent experiences and describing them in our Period Log, our attention was directed toward the memory level of our minds. This was necessarily so because we were engaged in recalling specific events and situations. In order to do so, our attention was focused toward the surface of the psyche where conscious thoughts and rememberings take place. To that degree, it was turned away from the depth levels where our deeper-than-conscious intuitions occur. As we work in our lives in the *Intensive Journal*, we wish to have access to the knowledge that comes not only from the conscious and rational side of the psyche, but also the direct awarenesses, hunches, and inspirations that come from our nonrational depths. For this reason, having made our first entries from the vantage point of conscious memory, we now *shift our psychic position* and reapproach the present period of our life from a depth point of view. We do this by means of *Twilight Imaging*.

The key to *Twilight Imaging* lies in the fact that it takes place in the twilight state between waking and sleeping. We find that by working actively in that intermediate state of consciousness, we are able to reach depths of ourselves with which it is very difficult to make contact by any other means. Once we have learned the Twilight Imaging procedures, however, we find that these experiences are relatively easy to achieve. As long as its essential guidelines are observed, many authentically creative contacts and spiritual awarenesses can be gained. To achieve this, however, it is necessary to follow the basic principles of Twilight Imaging which require that it be carried through in a nonguided, nonconscious way, with the flow of imagery being neither manipulated nor directed.

We can understand what is involved in Twilight Imaging by referring back to our metaphor of progressively entering the well of inward experience until we are able to reach the underground stream. When we follow the symbolic discipline of moving into the well of our Self, we find that we develop an increased capacity of inward perception. This capacity seems to be inherent in human beings and is a natural mode of awareness. Since it is inward, however, it tends to be little used in cultural situations where the individual's attention is constantly being preempted by the pressures of the outer environment. When, on the other hand, we establish an atmosphere that makes it possible for the attention to be turned inward in a quiet way, this capacity shows itself to be very actively and strongly present in persons who would have thought they did not possess it at all. At such times it often expresses itself in a way that catches the person unawares, but that possesses an enlightening and even an inspirational power.

The term *imagery* has the overtones of a visual experience. It implies specifically that the experience involves images that will be seen inwardly. This is misleading, and is not actually the case. The primary quality of Twilight Imagery lies not in its visualness, but in its *twilightness*, the fact that it takes place, as though by itself, on the intermediary, or twilight, level of consciousness. The term *imagery* refers to the fact that its main expressions are not literal in the sense of being thoughts or ideas, but that they are rather representational or symbolic. They may indeed be visual, as they often are; but in many cases they are not visual at all. They may take the form of perceptions that come through any of the other, non-visual senses. But they are *inward* perceptions, and thus, if they carry an aroma or come as sounds or body feelings, they are to be understood as being not actual and literal as physical perceptions are, but as being symbolic and inward.

Of primary significance is the fact that we do not consciously or deliberately put these perceptions there. We ourselves do not determine what they shall be. Rather, being in a quiet and passive position, we behold them. We turn our attention inward and we wait in stillness, and let ourselves observe the various forms of imagery that present themselves. We let them come of themselves. We do not put the imagery there, just as we do not put our dreams there. They just appear unbidden. We do not guide them, nor make suggestions to them; but as they take shape out of themselves, we perceive them. As they appear in whatever form and in whatever sensory aspect they choose, we take notice of them. With our attention turned inward, we observe them as though they were dreams. We follow the direction of their movement without directing or altering their contents. Then, at various convenient points in the process, we gather our observations and our beholdings together, and we record them in our *Twilight Imagery Log*.

We describe the contents of our Twilight Imagery experiences in the same neutral, non-interpretive, non-judgmental way that we record our dreams. We describe them as we perceive them, with just enough elaboration so that a reader, primarily ourselves reading our Journal at a later time, will be able to recognize what took place in the experience. As we proceed in the movement of our lives working in the *Intensive Journal*, we keep a record of these experiences consecutively in the section of the Journal called the Twilight Imagery Log. This log section becomes an empirical sourcebook for us of the facts of our inner experiences as we perceive them on the twilight level.

As part of our general, ongoing Journal work, we gather our Twilight Imagery experiences together over a period of time, so that at the right moment we can turn to this log section and draw upon them for a variety of Journal Feedback exercises. The exercises that begin with the data drawn from our Twilight Imagery Log often have a special power and productiveness. They draw upon the personal depths that are unique to each individual, but they reach into the transpersonal depths as well.

Now, however, we wish to work in the Twilight Imagery Log from a special point of view and with a particular purpose. We have made our basic entry in the Period Log describing our memories and adding brief observations and comments. We let that entry rest there without further elaboration in the Period Log section while we turn to the Twilight Imagery Log. Here, at the head of a sheet, we write the phrase, *Period Image*, and the date. It is well to note at this point, and to emphasize and remind ourselves that we must remember to mark down the date at which we are writing each entry. At a later time, when we draw together our cumulative entries and reenter them by the procedures of Journal Feedback, the dates at which they were written will be important facts contributing to our further experience.

The significance of the phrase, *Period Image*, is that it opens a sub-section within the Twilight Imagery Log that enables us to reapproach this recent period of our lives from a symbolic point of view. Having described from the side of rational consciousness the unit of Life/Time that comprises our Now-moment, our experience of the Period Image will give us the perspective of the depth dimension. It opens to us the dual perspectives of both conscious and nonconscious awareness.

It is good to have our *Intensive Journal* open to the Period Image subsection, keeping it open with our pen handy while we sit in stillness. We breathe slowly, softly, letting thoughts drop away without our thinking them. We remain in quiet calmness.

Sitting in quietness, our eyes close. We let this take place gradually. It is as though the stillness and the softness of our breathing draw our eyelids together so that they seem to close of themselves. We realize that when our eyes close gradually and softly in this undeliberate way the darkness we enter is not unpleasant. It is, in fact, rather comfortable. It carries an atmosphere of calmness with it as we let ourselves quietly drift into the twilight level. Our attention has naturally readjusted itself and has turned by its own tempo to the inward dimension. Here we may perceive the realities of life, and especially the realities of our personal life, in the varied aspect of their symbolic forms. This *inward beholding* gives us the added vantage point of a depth perspective.

As we are doing this, we let ourselves *feel* the tone and quality of the period we have described. We do not think about it, we do not evaluate nor make judgments about it. Having described in the Period Log the main factors that came to our mind, we now do nothing further on the conscious level. We merely sit in quietness, our eyes closed, our attention turned to the twilight level of experience. Here we let images come to us again, images of every kind. We do not specify what kind of images they shall be, whether we will see them, smell them, hear them, intuit them, feel them in our body. Whatever their form, they will be twilight images, coming to us out of the middle level of consciousness between waking and sleeping, and just presenting themselves to us so that we can observe them in a natural way and record them.

We also do nothing to specify or determine the content of the Twilight Imagery that comes to us. We merely let ourselves feel the content of the period that we have described, and with that as the background, we let the imagery form itself out of its own nature. We specifically wish to keep our conscious mind out of the way, so that our imagery will reflect the flow of our life, and will not be slanted to reflect our subjective desires.

This experience of twilighting which follows the writing of the Period Log can be considerably fuller, freer in its flow, and longer in duration than the imagery experience which preceded the writing. The purpose of the first Twilight Imaging experience was primarily to deepen the atmosphere and to provide an opportunity for the mind to quiet itself. The imagery at that point, therefore, was not extended. It was sustained only long enough to take us to a deeper than cerebral level and to let our individual image or metaphor set the tone for the conscious remembering and recording that followed. Now that we have completed the conscious part of our exercise with the goal of positioning ourselves in the present of our lives via the Period Log, we are free to let our Twilight Imagery extend itself as fully as it wishes. We can let it range as far as it requires in order to reflect to us the other-than-conscious side of this present period in our lives.

Now our eyes are closed and we are sitting in stillness. Our attention is turned to this recent period in our lives which we have described and explored in the Period Log. We are not thinking of it but letting it present itself to us in the form of images, impressions, emotions, and especially through symbolic awarenesses that come to us in many sensory forms. We may see them, hear them, smell them, intuit them, but always by *inward perception* at the twilight level. It may come at first as stirrings in our body, as joyous surges or as stomach knots. By whatever form of perception they come to us, we observe them neutrally, without judgment, and we record them under the subsection which we have marked off in the Twilight Imagery Log with the heading of Period Image.

In the silence now we open ourselves to these Twilight Imagery awarenesses, and we record them as they come to us.

When this has been completed, we have one further question to pose to ourselves with respect to the entries we made in the Period Log and the experiences we have recorded in the Twilight Imagery Log as our Period Image. As we consider these two side by side—the actual outer events of our lives and the spontaneous imagery that comes from our inner depth—do we observe any perceivable relationship between them? Do they seem to be the same? Or opposites? Or parallel to one another? Or at a tangent to one another?

Do they seem both to be saying the same thing, but in a different style of language? Or does the meaning of our imagery seem to be different from the message that comes to us when we recapitulate our life experiences with our memory? To say it another way, does the information that comes to us from our nonconscious depth confirm the opinions we have in our consciousness? Do they contradict one another? Do they balance and complement one another?

There is a great deal that we can learn about the inner movement of our lives when we set our conscious and our nonconscious perceptions side by side. It is essential, however, that we let ourselves truly feel and give full value to the perspective that is given to us from each side. We must not prejudge either one, but consider each one fully within its own terms, and then balance both together.

Considering and balancing these two types of experience which we have just had is not a thought process. It is not helpful to approach the question by thinking about it, nor by intellectually analyzing and interpreting the contents of our life and our images. What we wish to do, rather, is to establish an *inner correlation* between our life events and the imagery that reflects the movement of our experience and comments upon it in symbolic form. The best way to do this is simply to let the two fit themselves together out of their own natures, and to present their comment upon each other in their own terms.

To do this, it is best to sit in silence while setting side by side within ourselves the conscious experiences of our life and our twilight imagery. We let ourselves *feel* the quality and the tone of each of them. We do not analyze them; we merely feel them, we enter into them, and we let ourselves respond to them in an inward, undirected way. Thus they can balance themselves within us in relation to one another. Together they form a *whole message* which can speak to us without words from within ourselves.

To be able to hear the larger message which the two can give together, it is important that we refrain from making a judgment regarding any single experience taken by itself. This is particularly so when our imagery experiences seem to be saying the opposite of our recent life experiences. It may be, for example, that while we have been living through a period when our projects and relationships have been going well, we have a visual image in which we see a glass fall off a table and break. Or we may see an automobile driving along a thruway at high speed and suddenly come to a place where the traffic is at a standstill, or where there is an accident.

By the same token, although the period we have described may have an optimistic tone, when we come to the quiet of our Twilight Imagery a nonvisual image may come to us that is nothing more definite than a vague feeling of uneasiness of difficulties or dangers lying ahead. At such times, it is best to avoid drawing any rash conclusions, but it is advisable also for us to consider seriously the opposites that have been presented to us in the totality of our Journal Feedback experience, and to set them side by side within ourselves.

A similar experience may come to us from the opposite direction. The recent period of our lives may have been filled with pain and disappointments, but the image that comes to us may have an optimistic or encouraging tone. It may be of the sun rising out of darkness, or of a child being born, or a seed germinating beneath the earth. If it comes in a nonvisual form, it may be a choir of voices, or a symphony of joyous music; or, less definitely, it may be a feeling of strength or renewed energy welling up inside us.

In whichever direction the correlation experience moves, we should not rush to any premature conclusions. We should not jump too quickly to joyous celebration, nor should we let ourselves fall into a negativistic fatalism. What is important is that we learn to observe objectively the nature of our subjective perceptions. We *perceive inwardly* the wholeness of the situation of our lives as it is presented to us in the many aspects of its organic movement. By means of the interior perception of Twilight Imagery we see that each moment contains its opposites inherently within itself. Growth and decay, conflict and harmony, all the opposites, are part of the movement of time. One overarching truth that presents itself repeatedly to us as we observe the organic continuity of life is that whether they are pleasant or painful, all circumstances will eventually be transformed in their time and in accordance with their inner nature. The indications of that change in their next immediate stage within the context of our lives are often shown to us ahead of time on the symbolic level by means of Twilight Imagery.

When we set the two together, the outer and inner perceptions combine to enable us to perceive the organic wholeness of time as it is moving in our lives. If we become alarmed when our imagery tells us that there is an element of difficulty around the corner of our present optimism, or if we begin to celebrate when an encouraging image indicates that a period of pain is coming to a close, we are cutting short the whole movement of time in our experience. There is an *organic inner continuity* in the movement of our lives, and it is expressed both inwardly and outwardly.

Perhaps, for example, it has been a time of rapid change in our life, one new situation coming in after another. In the turmoil we feel a mixture of emotions, confidence and fear, and the tension which the two produce. These are our conscious attitudes. In our Twilight Imagery we see a forest in full bloom, then in fall colors; we hear the chirping of birds, then silence; we see the trees barren in winter, then in spring growth again. Through it all we feel the process of change continuing in its permutations.

It is apparent that the many contents in this imagery reflect the active movement in the person's life. The two run parallel to one another, each reflecting the other. The inner experience of this Twilight Imagery, however, adds an additional dimension when it is set side by side with the outer movement of the life. It gives us an additional awareness, an *interior perspective* by which we can recognize the integrative principle that is present beneath the surface of our lives and is the connective thread of our existence.

To experience the inner continuity in the movement of our lives through the opposites of change is the purpose of our exercises in inner correlation. From time to time as we work in the Journal Feedback process we shall come to phases of our life experience that are difficult and ambiguous, and at those times we shall find that the quiet work of inner correlation is an especially valuable source of quiet guidance from within. At this point in our work we let ourselves perceive the inner relationship between the movement of the outer events of this recent period and the imagery that has come to us on the twilight level. We record whatever recognitions or impressions or intuitions come to us in the Twilight Imagery Log in addition to the entries we made describing our Period Images. When we have written all the awarenesses that have come to us in this regard, we return to quietness in preparation for the next phase of our Journal work.

feeling of strength or renewed energy

vague uneasy feeling

visual image

Chapter 7

Keeping the Daily Log

By working in the Period Log, we begin the process of positioning ourselves in the movement of our lives. It places us between the past and the future in such a way that, both intellectually and symbolically, we are able to have a larger perception of the path our life is trying to take.

The work in the Period Log places us in contact with the continuity of our life experiences so that we form an inner perspective for our relationship to their movement. Its exercises enable us to recapitulate our recent past in a compressed format so as to bring us up to date with the movement of our lives. Once that has been done, we require a means of maintaining the relationship that has been established. This next step is a primary function of the *Daily Log*.

In the *Daily Log* we make the entries that enable us to continue on a current basis with the movement of our lives. We work day by day as much as possible to keep ourselves in an ongoing relationship with whatever is taking place inside ourselves.

Because of its regular use, the *Daily Log* is the section of the *Intensive Journal* that most closely resembles a diary. Anything that we would otherwise record in a diary may also be written in the *Daily Log*, but the *Daily Log* itself has a special purpose. It has the function of gathering into one accessible place a running record of the subjective experiences of all kinds that move through a person's mind and emotions in the course of a day and a night. The *Daily Log* is the primary section of the Journal in which we gather the source material for the active experiences of Journal Feedback.

It is similar to a diary mainly in the respect that entries are recorded in it regularly and that it is maintained on a continuing basis. Entries are made in the Daily Log however from the special point of view of their reflecting the inner process of the individual's life. As we become accustomed to working in the Daily Log, we find that we use it increasingly to record our current life data in a form that moves most directly to the Journal Feedback exercises.

The primary purpose of the Daily Log is to provide a continuing source of Journal Feedback material for the other sections of the Journal. This goal sets the focus and style of the entries we make in it and defines also the differences between the Daily Log and the ordinary keeping of a diary. Diary writing usually involves the unstructured, chronological recording of the events of a person's life as he perceives them. We have to recognize, however, that the mere fact of continuously writing entries, as is done in the keeping of a diary, is not sufficient in itself to bring about deep changes in a person's life. To achieve a significant transformation in a personality, strong forces of energy must be generated. This is done by the feedback procedures as they draw upon the Log entries and build a momentum through the interplay of the various sections of the Journal.

To enable the Daily Log to play this active role in the Journal Feedback process provides the main criteria for the entries we make in it. The entries should include only an essential minimum of descriptive material dealing with the external events of life. Whatever is necessary to record in this respect may be included, but it should be brief, so that we will be free to focus primarily on the interior aspects of our experience.

In writing in the Daily Log, we especially wish to record the unpremeditated flow of the events of our inner experience. Often a very few words are sufficient to indicate the quality of the experience that is taking place. The important thing is that we record it as close to the time of the actual occurrence as possible, and that we write enough to enable us to hold it for our memory and for our future use. Afterwards, when we have written sufficiently in the Journal so that we can draw together several entries and read them in continuity, we find that each entry fills in and recalls the context and details of the others. Thus, with relatively little being written at any one time, it becomes possible, even in the midst of a very busy life, to accumulate the data that will enable us to gain the long range benefits of working in the Daily Log.

One first guideline for writing in the Daily Log is that the individual entries be succinct reflections of the mental, emotional, and imagery occurrences taking place within us. As much as possible, our writing should focus on the essence of the experience. Entries should be brief, but brevity is by no means a fixed rule. It is merely that brief entries enable us to record the largest range of material, so that we can then have a greater flexibility in choosing the subjects and the directions in which we shall proceed in the active feedback exercises.

Sometimes, when we begin by making a brief entry in the Daily Log, we find that, without realizing it, we have launched ourselves upon a strong-flowing stream of inner experience. As the movement of it builds, the experience enlarges itself. At such times, a creative process is spontaneously taking place in us in the midst of our writing in the Daily Log. We certainly do not wish to bring such entries to a short and arbitrary stop by our rule of brevity. On the contrary, we want to encourage them and evoke them further so that we can draw to full expression the possibilities and the implicit awarenesses which they contain. We have to take advantage of the strength and momentum of our writing while it is in motion. Later on, after these entries have extended themselves as far as they could, we can transfer them to another section of the Journal. We often find that there is an especial value in these extended segments which we write spontaneously in the Daily Log under the stimulus of a strong impulse or inspiration. They are not always relevant for the immediate situation with which we are dealing in our Journal work, but it is good to encourage them and let them continue nonetheless. Though they are written originally in the Daily Log, they may be exceedingly relevant in the context of the section of the Journal to which we transfer them, especially when we return to them in another perspective at a further point in the Journal Feedback process.

Sometimes, because of the overlap of the pages on which we have written, it is not feasible to transfer our entries physically from one section of the Journal to another. In that case, it works perfectly well merely to make an additional brief entry in the feedback section where it would belong, describing the gist of the original entry, its date and general content, and telling where it is to be found in the Journal. It is often helpful, also, to include some indication of the aspect of the Journal work to which you feel it may apply. Thus, when you are working in Journal Feedback later on, you will have something specific to spur your memory and reconnect you with the context and the process that was in motion at the time of your spontaneous writing.

Transfers and cross-referencing of this kind play an important role in building the momentum of Journal Feedback. We try to make our entries in such a way that our material will be available to us in the various other feedback sections to which they may pertain for possible future experiences. At a later time, then, as the circumstances of our lives unfold, we will immediately have access to our earlier thoughts and feelings and be able to feed this material into our new exercises and explorations.

As a general principle when we are working with the *Intensive Journal,* it does not matter much in which section we are doing our actual writing. It does matter a great deal, however, where we keep the material for future reference. If we can have access to our accumulated entries by means of transferring them or cross-referencing them, we are able to incorporate them in our further experiences and use them as starting points for additional feedback exercises. In this way we build the momentum of our inner process.

There are two main ways of working in the Daily Log. One is by recapitulation. The other is by current recording.

In the first, we recall and recreate the events of a day treating the day as a unit. We do this at the end of a day, or as soon afterwards as we can. Sometimes, in the nature of our lives, several days must pass before we have the opportunity to make our entries. Then the memory may begin to blur, and too many events may accumulate in our minds for any to be clear. Nonetheless, even though we may lose many of the details, there is a great value in trying to recapture for the record of the Daily Log as much of the general movement of the days as we can.

To recapitulate day by day is of course preferable. Some people prefer to make use of their work with their Journals at a quiet time at the end of each day, even if they have time then only for a brief entry. Others leave a free period at a point early in the day, some time during the morning, when they recapitulate the previous twenty-four hours.

Inevitably there are times when several days pass with no entry being made. Since those tend to be the busy times, it often seems that so much accumulates during those times that we hardly know where to begin when the time comes for us to catch up with our Daily Log.

There are several ways to overcome this difficulty. Many people have found in practice that it helps them to begin by writing a general description summarizing the several days that have passed. They find that, after writing the summary entry, they are able easily to write retroactively, beginning by describing the events of the most recent day, and then moving backward as far as their memory will allow. The act of describing the most recent events often has the effect of stimulating flashbacks of earlier experiences, and thus it becomes progressively easier to recall events which we thought we had forgotten. After a while, with practice in these procedures and drawing upon the experience of others, we find that there are numerous combinations of methods that we can adapt to our personal situation in order to enable us better to recapitulate our experiences in the Daily Log.

The second way of working in the Daily Log, the way of *current recording,* has certain obvious advantages, but it is not always convenient or feasible. To the degree that it is possible, however, it enables us to gather the raw data of experience before it can be forgotten, and before our memories can falsify it.

In actual usage, much more of the Daily Log entries are made by current recording, writing in the very midst of the experience, than we might expect. The reason for this is that, when a person makes it a practice to write a recapitulation of his day as often as he can, the act of doing this connects him more and more closely to the inner movement of his life. The tendency is then that, as he writes his recapitulations of events that have happened, new inner events are stimulated. His is thus led, while in the very act of recapitulating his day, to fresh experiences that come into existence in the immediacy of his Journal work.

Entries like these are a natural result of Journal Feedback when it is practiced systematically. Working with regularity has the effect of building a momentum that is generated by the movement of the material itself. The continuous use of the Daily Log therefore has a self-propelling effect, as the act of making regular entries leads beyond itself. It stimulates new experiences and new awarenesses, and these are recorded in the act of their happening in our Journal Feedback work.

We find, then, that in the practice of Journal Feedback, the two ways of working in the Daily Log combine in different phases of the work. To get started, we recapitulate a day, or that part of a day that is most meaningful to us. While that is taking place, additional experiences are being stimulated within us, inner experiences of all kinds, pleasant and unpleasant. And we record these currently in the immediacy of their occurrence with our active entries in the Daily Log.

Let us now work together in a basic recapitulation exercise of the Daily Log. We choose a recent period of twenty-four hours as the focus of our exercise. But first, before we begin the exercise, let us become quiet.

We sit in stillness. We breathe slowly, regularly, steadily slower. We close our eyes, breathing slowly in the silence, and reaching into ourselves. We let ourselves feel the inner movement of the events of our lives.

In the silence, now, with our eyes closed, we let ourselves go back in memory for a day, covering at least a period of twenty-four hours. It is often best if we take ourselves to the time when we awakened on that day. We let ourselves recall as fully as we can how it felt lying there in bed, drowsing, just awakening.

We prod ourselves to remember as many specific details as we can. Where were we sleeping? With whom? How well had we slept? Was it a quiet sleep? Or was it restless? Were there dreams in our sleep? It may be relevant at this point in our recording to bring back the situation of the night before as the background of the dreams or of the half-waking thoughts of the night.

What special events took place before we went to sleep? What feelings were moving about within us toward the end of the day? We write them down as fully as we remember them, and as far as we feel their relevance for our dreams and our thoughts of the night. We recall to ourselves and record, as much as we can, the feelings and thoughts and emotions that have passed through our mind both on conscious and nonconscious levels. We take note of all the small details as they return to our memory, and we record each briefly in the Daily Log.

When you awakened in the morning, how did you feel physically? Did you awaken slowly, as though you were emerging from a dream? Or did you awaken quickly, full of energy and alertness? Are you aware of having had a dream during the night? Did you write it down during the night, or did you assume that you would remember it in the morning? Do you remember it now? All of it? Or some small part of it?

Now is the time to record as much of your dream as you can recall. Even if you remember only a very small fragment of it, that small part is worth describing. While you are writing it, additional segments of the dream may be recalled to your mind. To remember a small piece of a dream is like catching a fish by the tail. If we hold onto it, we can draw the whole fish in.

The Daily Log, however, is not the section of the Journal where we describe the fullness of the dream. The Dream Log is the section where we do that.* In the Daily Log it is sufficient if we make a brief entry recording the fact that we did have a dream, and indicating briefly something of its general nature. In the Dream Log, which is in the division of the Journal dealing with the Depth Dimension, we describe the dream as fully as we can, not analyzing or interpreting it, but simply recording the events and impressions of the dream in a neutral, non-judgmental, reportorial style. We wish to have it on record so that, at a later time, we will be able to accelerate the process of Journal Feedback by working with the continuity of our dreams.

In the Daily Log we record merely the fact that we remembered having a dream, and we say only enough about the dream to enable us to identify it. We may give the dream a name there, indicating also the

* See Chapter 16. "Working With Our Dreams."

primary image in it. As we do this, the identifying image becomes the title of the dream and gives us an easy means of referring to it if we have occasion to work with material from that dream in other sections of the Journal. The dream entry that we make in the Daily Log, for example, may simply be, "I had a dream of riding horses in the desert"; or, "I had a fragment of a dream about eating ice cream cones that all tasted like sand." We mention just enough in the Daily Log to identify the dream and enough also, when we are pressed for time, to fasten it in our minds until we are able to describe it more fully. We indicate also the cross reference to other sections of the Journal where we have worked with that dream, and especially to show that we have described it more fully in the Dream Log.

Now, holding our minds back at the time of the beginning of the day for the recapitulation of the Daily Log, let us begin to reconstruct the events and feelings that drew the day into motion.

We begin once again by being quiet. As our writing proceeds, we find that we are able to recall more and more of the thoughts and emotions that were present in that transitional time when we moved from sleep to waking consciousness. Often the memory of these thoughts and emotions are wispy and difficult to hold. But whatever small "tails" of these we are able to grasp are helpful in enabling us to draw it all back so that we can reconstruct what has been taking place within our minds at the dim edges of consciousness. Even small pieces of memory are valuable for recapitulating the movement of the day.

What were the emotions and desires, the anxieties, the hopes, and the plans as you began your day?

Was there a basic tone of emotional feeling, or of body feeling? Was it enthusiastic, or was it anxious? Was it light or heavy, as you were emerging into the waking state?

While you were not quite asleep and not quite awake, did visual images, or intuitions, or strong, clear feelings come to you? That time between sleep and waking is a twilight state in which important awarenesses often come to us, if we are able to perceive them. Did fantasies come to you at that time? Imaginings? Or sexual feelings? Without censoring and without judging, record whatever you can recall of that early part of the day in your Daily Log.

Now let us proceed to the further movement of the day. Let us bring back to our minds the sequences of events and emotions as the active part of the day began.

How did you begin doing the tasks of the day? What were the thoughts that came unbidden to your mind? While you were doing the things that were necessary, were you aware of feelings and fantasies moving through your mind without your wanting them to be there? Did you find yourself worrying about things that you did not want to be thinking of? Did you find hopes or wishes entering your mind without your consciously putting them there, or wanting them to be there?

What kind of relationships came about in the course of the day? Were there experiences of love and affection? Did you experience frustration and anger? Now let yourself feel again the emotions that arose in you and that were brought forth in others. Record them briefly and describe as well as you can the movement and the interrelationships of your emotional responses and those of the other persons involved with you during the day.

Do not judge the emotions, but simply report what took place. As you describe the movement of your emotions, you will find that the external movement of events will fit around them, and the pattern of the day will take shape for you. To follow the movement of our emotions enables us to retrace the formation of our lives from the inside. Thus you will begin to recognize how your day unfolded from within yourself.

Now, as you are retracing the inner movement of your day's experience, let yourself feel again the atmosphere of the various moods through which you passed. In particular, let yourself recall the variation in your feelings, as your mood of the morning continued or changed as you came to lunchtime, and then midday, and as different people entered the scene of your experience. Consider how it varied in the latter part of the afternoon, and in the evening. What was your mood and the tempo of your thoughts and feelings as you continued into the night, and as you prepared for bed? Are you aware of how your body and your emotions began to be fatigued, and how they prepared for sleep?

Now, as you view the day in retrospect, consider the rhythms of the day. More important than the rhythm of outer events is the rhythm of your inner experiences. We find these rhythms not on the surface of our actions but in the changes of feeling tone and attitude that take place at levels deep below our consciousness. To reach these rhythms and to identify them, we let our minds go back over the movement of our inner experience as it took place in the course of a day. As much as possible, we reexperience the fluctuations that took place in our feelings so that, as though we were marking off an interior graph of our lives, we record the shifting phases of our moods. We do this not in order to analyze our inner "patterns," but in order to bring ourselves into accord with the movement of our inner process. Whatever recordings we can make of the factors and sequences involved in the variations of our moods will be of great value for our later work in the Journal Feedback exercises.

The questions we have raised and the areas of experience that have been indicated are to serve as starting points and guidelines for the entries we make in the Daily Log. Even when our lives seem to be uneventful on the outside, the range of content and movement within us is very great. That is why we realize, when we have worked regularly in the *Intensive Journal* for some time, that it is truly worth our while to record in our Daily Log without censorship and without judgment everything that we can perceive as it is taking place in the inner movement of our lives. Later, when we reapproach this material from the point of view of Journal Feedback, we are able to see how large and varied a resource we have been carrying in the depths of ourselves.

As you write these entries in the Daily Log, take care that you do not inadvertently censor or edit the material you are recording. It is all too easy to slant your reporting without even realizing that you are doing so. Do not exclude some things because you are ashamed of them. Do not emphasize other things because you are proud of them. It is important for us to maintain a strongly neutral position in the recording that we do in our Journals. This will not be difficult, however, if we bear in mind that what we are recording in our Daily Log is only for ourselves and for our own later use in the Journal Feedback procedures. We are engaged in gathering honest, empirical data for use in deepening our own inner process. There is no point, therefore, in our writing entries with a view to our being praised or clearing ourselves of blame. We need the empirical facts for our later use, and these entries in the Daily Log are the means by which we draw them together.

We find, also, that this goal of neutral fact gathering is best achieved if we write in the Daily Log primarily in the form of brief entries. It is also best if we write in the Daily Log as much as possible without premeditation, recording our entries spontaneously in the order in which they come to us. We should not be concerned at all if, upon rereading our entries, they seem to be haphazard and disorganized. We should remember, then, that when we write in our Journal, we are not composing an essay but we are only recording the unedited expressions of our inner experience. Therefore we should pay no attention at all to the style of our writing. The Daily Log is not an exercise in literature; it is an exercise in our lives. There is no need for us to be concerned about our grammar, nor our literary style, nor the use of polite language. It is important, rather, that we feel free to write in our everyday language, letting the flow of our words reach the paper with neither editing nor censorship.

It may be good at this point for us to pause in our reading in order that we can carry out the writing exercises describing the past twenty-four hours in the Daily Log. When you have finished writing the recapitulation of this period, or when you have written as much as feels sufficient and right for you at this time, let yourself become quiet again. Sit in stillness, breathing slowly, not thinking, but letting your whole being absorb the feelings that you have been describing.

What feelings do you find within yourself now that you have recorded these varied facts of your experience?

How did you feel while you were writing them?

As you consider this, record whatever additional feelings and thoughts and memories and observations come to you.

Once again, after making this additional entry in your Daily Log, return to quietness. Let your breath become slow and regular, and for at least a few minutes, let no further thoughts enter your mind. The exercise we have done of reentering the movement of our life is bound to stir up a variety of emotions and energies. We therefore wish to make sure that we give ourselves sufficient time to settle ourselves and become inwardly quiet. We do not rush ourselves when we work in the inner experiences of our lives. Certain exercises are carried out with intensity and in a brief time so as to assure spontaneity, but for the most part we allow ample space to surround each of the exercises that we do.

Now, having written a basic entry in the Daily Log, we sit in quietness. We do not analyze nor interpret, but we let ourselves absorb the movement of the day as an integral piece of our life. It is an atom of time in our existence. In this stillness we prepare ourselves also to work in the larger cycles of time that comprise the movement of our lives.

Chapter **8**

Working in
the Life/Time Dimension

LOOSENING THE SOIL OF OUR LIVES

We are ready now to begin one of the major aspects of our Journal experience, working in our life history.

Although they are largely concerned with the contents of our past, we find that the techniques of *Time-Stretching* which we carry out in the Life/Time sections of the Journal tend to extend themselves throughout our Journal work.* They involve a variety of entries and exercises that enable us to reach both back and forward in the movement of time in our lives. We use them first for the basic task, which we begin now, of gathering together the material of our life history, and later we use them in the feedback sections in order to apply the Life/Time dimension to special aspects of our life. Working in our life history is progressive. Its cumulative effect is to draw our life into focus so that we have a basis for making the decisions that are pressing at the moment, and also to give us a perspective of the pattern and context of our life as a whole. We work in our life history not because it contains our past experiences, but because our life history is our unique life story, and it is continuing to unfold in our present experiences. Working in it by means of our

* The basic procedures of *Time-Stretching* are contained in Chapters 8–11.

Journal experiences enables us to have an inner perspective of the movement of our life, and thus we can eventually have a dialogue relationship with our future.

The sequence of exercises that we follow at a Journal Workshop is designed to build this inner perspective of our life. It involves a progressive enlargement of our sensitivity to the movement of Life/Time within us. Through our life history, we reconnect ourselves to the elan vital, the life force within us, but in the meaningful context of our whole unfolding existence. Thus we are able to reposition ourselves at critical points in the process of our lives with ever more sophisticated perspective and awareness.

We can already see how the sequence of exercises at a Journal Workshop has begun to move in this direction. We began with the Period Log in order to place ourselves in the present moment of our lives. In doing that, we were positioning ourselves between our past and our future, deliberately interpreting the present moment as a period of time large enough to give us a flexible perspective. To make our contact with time specific, and to maintain a current relationship with our life movement, we then worked in the Daily Log. Our work in these two Log sections sets the basis for our relationship to the inner movement of time in our lives. With them as our foundation, we can proceed to expand our framework of time, and we can place ourselves in a more intimate and understanding relationship with the cycles and variations that have occurred in our lives. As we do this, our specific goal is to build a large enough working context so that we can develop a sense of inner timing with which to guide ourselves as we move into our future.

At this point in our work in the *Intensive Journal,* having carried out the exercises in the Period Log and the Daily Log, we may notice something beginning to happen inside ourselves. As we perceive it, it may feel like a loosening or a breaking open. This is a sign that we are beginning to be able to move around inside ourselves. We have opened channels in the inner space of our lives.

At first the experience of this may seem strange to us, for the necessities of life have accustomed us to live much less flexibly. Under the pressure of events, our lives become hard packed like soil that has not been tilled for many years. One experience is added to another so rapidly that we have neither time nor opportunity to consider their implications, nor the possibilities they open. We do not have time to savor their pleasantness, to feel their pain deeply, nor to establish an inner relationship to them. They pile up and are pressed tightly together inside of us, leaving no room in between for the fresh air of consciousness to enter, nor for something new to grow.

As we work in our Journal, however, we gradually break into this hardness. The soil of our lives is loosened and softened. The solid clumps of past experience are broken up so that air and sunlight can enter. New awarenesses come in and have a fertilizing effect. Soon the soil becomes soft enough for new shoots to grow in. That softness inside of us is a new feeling, and it opens new possibilities. It can be the beginning of a new period of Life/Time, the birth of a new self, and a new unit of existence.

A major goal of our work in the *Intensive Journal* is to bring about this softening within us and thus to make ourselves more sensitive to the contents and the continuity of our inner lives. As we do this, it gradually becomes possible for us to move about more freely within ourselves, opening up experiences, exploring them, letting our feelings move fluidly through memories and hopes, and giving ourselves access to corners of our life to which we previously had no avenues of contact. We wish to reach the point where we can feel comfortable in moving with full freedom into every crevice of our lives, not having to leave any stone unturned, nor any memory or emotion untouched, having at least neutralized our fears if we have not totally overcome them.

Ultimately all the contents of our lives then become accessible to us. Our whole existence becomes like good soft soil through which we can run our fingers, enjoying the touch of it. We find that we are free to explore our inner world without judgment, beyond personal praise or blame, and without fear. Without making mental or emotional reservations, we are able to move throughout the depth and breadth of our life experience, remembering, describing, writing, exploring everything that has been, everything that is, or is emerging as part of our unfolding experience.

We find then that no matter how difficult the circumstances that our personal destiny has brought to us, we have become strong enough and capable of handling them without being thrown off our course and without losing our momentum. This quality of sensitivity and openness to the inner unfoldment of our lives becomes a major source of life-confidence enabling us to overcome the anxieties and trials of our existence.

An essential factor in developing this capacity is the work that we do in the Life/Time dimension of the *Intensive Journal*, especially the exercises of *Time-Stretching*. These exercises have varied and wide-ranging applications in the practice of Journal Feedback because of their value in helping people navigate their lives through periods of transition. They play a central role, also, in carrying through the basic life focus experience.

The concept and practice of *Time-Stretching* enables us to move back and forth through all the segments of time in our existence. It is based upon the fundamental distinction between *chronological time* and *qualitative time*. Chronological time refers to the objective sequence of events as they are perceived by an observer who is outside of them and who therefore sees them externally with no emotional involvement in their content. Qualitative time, on the other hand, refers to the subjective perception of objective events in terms of the meaning and value they have to the person who is experiencing them. Qualitative time is the movement of Life/Time perceived from within the process of a life.

In the Time-Stretching exercises, we use the Life/Time sections as the outer embodiment of the inner process of our lives, and we move flexibly in and out of these sections in a manner that corresponds to the inner movement of qualitative time. The nature of the entries that we make and the procedures for using them enable us to move in and out of the present and the past and the future, going back and forth among them, drawing forth their variations, their interrelationships, and especially, their implications and possibilities. Because of the nature of the inner movement of time that is involved in these exercises, we do not carry them out by working in one section of the Journal alone. Rather, in order to enlarge the range of the interplay in the movement of Life/Time, we work simultaneously in the three main sections of the Life/Time dimension. We begin with a series of deepening exercises in the Steppingstones section to give ourselves a sense of the fluid and changing contexts of our life. We then reach into the various corners of our life by moving back and forth between the Life History Log and Intersections: Roads Taken and Not Taken, opening out the contents of our lives with an open curiosity that is non-judgmental. We are stretching our relationship to Life/Time so that our perception of it can include whatever is relevant or necessary for us in order to reposition ourselves in our lives. We use the Time-Stretching exercises to achieve this, and the Steppingstones sections is the hub of them. It is here that we begin.

LISTING THE STEPPINGSTONES

When we speak of the *Steppingstones* of our life, we are referring to those events that come to our minds when we spontaneously reflect on the course that our life has taken from its beginning to the present moment. The *Steppingstones* are the significant points of movement along the road of an individual's life. They stand forth as indicators of the inner connectedness of each person's existence, a continuity of development that maintains itself despite the vicissitudes and the apparent shifting of directions that occur in the course of a life. The Steppingstones are indicators that enable a person to recognize the deeper-than-conscious goals toward which the movement of his life is trying to take him.

Essentially what we mean by Steppingstones is what Dag Hammarskjold was referring to in the title of his autobiographical book, *Markings*. Hammarskjold's "markings" were drawn from an unstructured journal which he kept, and they record the main points in the movement of his life. The "markings" or Steppingstones which Hammarskjold recorded here were by no means always affirmative or productive events. Some of them were very painful experiences, and involved the failure of highly valued projects in which a great deal of hope and energy had been invested. Nonetheless they were important markings in the continuity of Hammarskjold's life. They were his Steppingstones.

The metaphor that Hammarskjold uses is one that is natural to him as a lifelong mountain climber. The climber leaves markings behind as he proceeds up the mountain. But Hammarskjold points out that he does not leave markings only when he has gone upward. Sometimes the course takes him downward into a valley or ravine, and then it is equally important to leave a marker so that there is a record of the path that has been followed. In Hammarskjold's book he records all the variations of his climb up and down the mountain of his life; the same principle holds for our working with the exercises in the Steppingstones section. The Steppingstones are neutral with respect to pleasure or pain, progress or failure. They are simply the markings that are significant to us as we reconstruct the movement of our life.

The special value of working with the exercises of the Steppingstones section is that they serve as vehicles by which this reconstruction can take place concisely and effectively. They enable us to draw out of the jumbled mass of our life experiences the thin and elusive connective threads that carry our potentialities through their phases of development toward a fuller unfoldment. The exercises enable us to mark these off and strengthen them, especially during those stages when we are weak and still unsure of ourselves. At certain points in our lives there may be more than one connective thread of growth moving as a line of continuity through our experiences. Sometimes the lines overlap, or they may disappear for long periods as though they have entered a dark underground cycle from which they eventually reappear. By working with the Steppingstones, we make contact with these elusive lines of continuity that are seeking to establish themselves as patterns of meaning in our lives. By discovering them and identifying them, we are able to affirm possibilities in ourselves that might otherwise be lost. We shall see the details of this a little later in our Time-Stretching exercises.

Working with our Steppingstones, we go back into the past of our lives, but not because of fascination with the past. We do not wish to lose ourselves in the field of memory. We go back into the past by means of the Steppingstones in order to reconnect ourselves with the movement of our personal Life/Time, and so that we can move more adequately into our future. In this respect, the work we do with Steppingstones is comparable to a running broad jump. We go back into our past in order to be better able to leap forward into our future. This is the essence of our work in the Life/Time dimension.

To enter the atmosphere in which we can best work with our Steppingstones, we close our eyes and sit in silence. In this stillness, we let our breathing become slower, softer, more relaxed. As we are quieted, we let ourselves *feel* the movement of our lives. We do not think about any specific aspect of our life, but we let ourselves feel the movement of our life as a whole. In our silence we let the changing circumstances and situations of our life pass before the mind's eye. Now we may recognize the varied events in their movement, not judging them nor even commenting on them, but merely observing them as they pass before us. We perceive them and feel them in their generalized movement without actually seeing the details of them.

As you do this, it may be that the events of your life will present themselves to you as a flowing and continuous movement, as a river moving through many changes and phases. Or it may be that your life will present itself to you as a kaleidoscope of disconnected events. Whatever the form in which the continuity of your life reflects itself to you now, respond to it, observe it, and let the flow continue. If images present themselves to you on the twilight level, images in any form whether visual or not, take note of them. As soon as you can, record them as part of your Steppingstones entry.

Sitting in quietness, breathing deeply at a slow and measured pace, let the continuity of your life as a whole move before you. Let yourself feel its movement as a total and unfolding process. Passive receptivity is the best attitude to adopt in doing this. As you sit in silence, let the cycles, the rhythms, the tempos of your life present themselves to you. Let them be free and undirected so that they can shape themselves into whatever form truly reflects their basic qualities; let yourself be free in your quietness to perceive them as they come to you without editing or falsifying them.

They may come as memories or visual images or inner sensations of various kinds. Especially they may state themselves in the form of similes or metaphors in addition to expressing the literal facts of past experience. Let your attitude be receptive enough that the continuity of your life as a whole can present itself to you both in symbolic forms and in literal factual statements. Whatever comes to you in this preparatory time of quietness should be entered in the Steppingstones section.

Now you are ready to make your first listing of your Steppingstones. Since they are the most significant points in the movement of your life, the list should be limited in number. Spontaneous selectivity is the essence of our marking off our Steppingstones. No matter how old we are and how long our life, the best practice is to place eight or ten Steppingstones on our list, but in any case not more than a dozen.

It is helpful, also, the first time we are listing our Steppingstones to begin by stating the first basic facts drawn from the vital statistics of our life. The first Steppingstone, for example, may be the event of your birth followed by such objective markers in your life as entering school, graduating, changes in your family and in the location of your residence, the death of close relatives, major financial changes in the family's fortunes. These external events have a certain objective factuality in that they have taken place in the outer chronological time of your life. They express the external movement of events. They thus provide the objective background against which we can perceive and reexperience the subjective realities of our lives.

While the external facts of our lives are recorded objectively in terms of chronological time, the events of our inner world take place in qualitative time. They lead to the inner experience of meaning in our existence, but their base and starting point lies in the external circumstances of our life. For this reason we often find that when we are having our first experience of working in our Steppingstones we obtain a truer reflection of the movement of our life if we begin by listing the basic objective events that have taken place in chronological time. By reflecting the outer movement of our lives, these provide a base from which we can proceed to our more intimate and more subjective experiences of meaning.

As we continue with the listing of our Steppingstones, we find that they tend progressively to take the form of events that express the uniqueness of our individual selves. The tendency is to move from basic chronological events, like place of birth and education, to qualitative events that carry the maturity and the private meaning of our lives. Thus the Steppingstones that describe the early years of life tend to be basic and biographical, while the Steppingstones of later years are more subjective and specialized in tone. Correspondingly, the first two or three lists that a person compiles when he begins to work with the Steppingstones exercise usually reflect the factual outline of his life, while subsequent experiences move ever more deeply into the personal, qualitative experience of Life/Time. It will be good to bear this perspective in mind when, at a later point in your Journal Feedback work, you review and reread the Steppingstone exercises that you have written.

It will become obvious to you as you begin to list your Steppingstones that your life can be reconstructed from several different vantage points. How shall you decide on which approach you are to choose? Bear in mind that it is *not* for you to make any decision at all in this matter. This is the reason that we begin our exercise in quietness and adopt an attitude of passive receptivity. We wish to intrude as little as possible of our conscious choice into the listing of our Steppingstones.

To set the process into motion, begin by indicating some basic facts of early years in the first entry or two. Then return to your quietness letting the movement of your life present itself to you. Perhaps a memory of a particular event will come to you. In itself it may not be the most important event of that period of your life, but it is calling your attention to a particular unit of your Life/Time. Make note of it, for you will probably wish to make use of that memory at a later point in the Time-Stretching exercises. Its immediate value for you, however, is that it directs your thoughts to a period of your life that is one of your Steppingstones.

At this point it is sufficient for you to choose a descriptive phrase. Even a single key word will suffice. In making your basic listing of Steppingstones, it is not necessary to be elaborate. All that is required is a word or a brief phrase that will be indicative of the Steppingstone period. After all, no one but yourself will be reading that list, and the brief reference will be intimately clear to you. There is also, as we shall soon see, a special value in brevity of phrase for the basic listing of your Steppingstones. Afterwards there will be ample opportunity to enlarge upon them in detail and to expand them in various directions.

With your eyes closed, there may be a memory that comes to you, an image that represents a particular time in your life, or an indication in any other form that calls your attention to the period of a Steppingstone in your life. Write it down as it comes to you.

It may be that as you are letting the Steppingstones of your life come to you spontaneously, you realize that they are not appearing in chronological order. Steppingstones from the latter half of your life may be coming to you before the earlier parts. Do not let that deter you. Record them as they come to you. When enough have been listed to cover the main movement of your life so that you feel satisfied that you have reflected your life to yourself in a fair and representative manner, it will simply be a matter of renumbering the Steppingstones you have listed so that they will correctly represent the continuity of your life.

Renumbering the Steppingstones that you have listed spontaneously so that they will be chronologically accurate is a simple matter. When you do that, you are not editing or altering your data. You are simply making it more accurate on a factual level. When you come to the feedback exercise of reading back to yourself the Steppingstones you have listed, it will be important for you to read them in the renumbered chronological order, for that will enable you to feel from within the inner continuity of your life process.

Other than renumbering them, however, you should not alter nor edit the Steppingstones you have listed. The spontaneity with which they have presented themselves to you is an integral part of the experience. Bear in mind that the Steppingstones are the significant points of marking along the continuity of your life. As we draw them together out of the depth of our lives in our quiet atmosphere, those that are called up to our minds are the ones that are meaningful to us in the context of the present moment of our lives. The spontaneity of the experience selects the Steppingstones for us from a place in ourselves that is beyond consciousness, and thus it enables us to see a thread of the inner continuity moving in our lives.

Each list of Steppingstones is such a thread of continuity drawn together from the vantage point of a particular present moment. It is called to the forefront of the mind by the circumstances of our life and our consciousness at that moment, and it has the qualities of that moment. After a while, when our work in the *Intensive Journal* has given us occasions for drawing together several sets of Steppingstones, we are in a position to recognize the integrity of each list. Each represents a special thread of continuity in the movement of our life. When, after the passage of time, we reread a number of Steppingstone lists at a single sitting, they come together as the threads that form the tapestry of our life. And we ourselves have woven it.

In order to attain this effect, however, so that we can perceive the continuity of our life in the wholeness of its varied phases, it is necessary that we retain each list of Steppingstones as it presents itself to us. That is the reason why we do not edit or alter the list of Steppingstones as it comes to us spontaneously in our Steppingstone exercise. It is better to let the list stand and to make another list that will reflect the variations that have suggested themselves. In that way we add another thread to the tapestry, and enable ourselves to see the continuity of our life from more of its varied sides.

While the essential tone with which we carry out the Steppingstone exercise is that of undirected spontaneity, the one conscious guideline that is necessary concerns the number of Steppingstones in each list.

As we recapitulate the meaningful markings of our life, it may seem to us that there are a great many events that deserve to be listed. If we place no limit on the number of Steppingstones that we record, we find that we are merely making a chronological list of the striking occurrences in our lives as they now call themselves to mind.

The special point, however, of the Steppingstones exercise and the main reason why it works dynamically to crystallize new perspectives for our lives, lies in the fact that it reaches beyond chronological time. It gives us an awareness of the qualitative movement of our life events as these may be recognized from *within* our experience of them. To achieve this, we insert an element of deliberate tension into the spontaneity of the exercise. We set a limit to the number of Steppingstones that we place on our list. We do not record all the meaningful events of our past, but only those which we feel have been significant factors, affirmative or negative, by which our life has come to its present situation. In this more limited context, we may list eight or nine or ten, but no more than twelve Steppingstones.

We find that compressing the number of Steppingstones does not inhibit the spontaneity of the exercise. It merely introduces a factor of selectivity to insure the fact that the Steppingstones that will be called to mind will be the most meaningful ones and the most relevant for our present situation. The pressure of condensing our Steppingstones has the effect of bringing about a spontaneous and unselfconscious evaluation and crystallization of the movement of our life. It brings to the fore those major elements that have formed the meaningful continuity of our lives, as this is perceived and brought to mind by our circumstances and quality of consciousness at the moment when we draw our Steppingstones together.

Approaching our lives by this procedure has an interesting equalizing effect upon the various age groups. Whether you have lived for seven decades or only for a decade and a half, you will list the same number of Steppingstones. Obviously the older person will have had time for a larger number of meaningful events to take place in his life. The compressed selectivity, however, that is brought about by limiting the list to a dozen or less forces each person to draw his life together into a context that highlights its significant points. Thus, as both the young and the old draw forth the continuity of events that have been truly important in shaping the direction of their lives, all are equal in the number of Steppingstones that are meaningful to list.

These are the essential guidelines that we need to bear in mind in working with our Steppingstones. We begin by becoming quiet, breathing deeply at a slow and measured pace, closing our eyes, and letting ourselves feel inwardly the rhythms and cycles of the movement of our life. As they present themselves to us, beginning with the first event of our being born, we record the main markings of the movement of our life, eight or ten or twelve in number, drawing them forward to the present situation of our life. We record them briefly. A concise phrase, or often a single word is sufficient to denote the Steppingstone as we place it on our list.

When you have completed your list, pause and let your mind return to a condition of quietness. In the silence you may contemplate the movement of the list that is outlined by your list of Steppingstones. Here are some additional questions to consider.

What feelings were stirring in you as you recorded this list? Write this as an addendum to your Steppingstones.

Now you may read your list of Steppingstones silently to yourself. What emotions or awarenesses arise in you as you do this?

If you are participating in a Dialogue House workshop, the leader will ask those who would like to read their Steppingstones to do so. You may wish to take advantage of that opportunity. Bear in mind that the reason for reading your Steppingstones in the group is not at all so that you can tell your life story to the other participants. Your purpose is not to communicate with the others, but to feed back into yourself the experiences of your own existence. That is part of the progressive deepening in the Journal Feedback process.

If you choose to read your Steppingstones aloud in the workshop, it is best to read only the brief headings you have written for each. The same is true if you read them aloud now in your own privacy with only yourself present to hear them. If you have written any elaborations or explanations, do not read them aloud at this point. Merely read the short phrase or single word that you have used to denote each Step-pingstone. By maintaining this crisp conciseness, you will be able to experience the essential continuity of movement in your life. The starkness of the outline of your life will heighten its impact on you. As you read it, let yourself hear it; also let yourself be free to feel whatever emotions are stirred in you as you recapitulate the course of your life.

After the workshop you may wish also to read your Steppingstones aloud into a cassette recorder. You can do this in your own privacy, and it will be especially valuable for you to do so if you chose not to read your Steppingstones while you were in the presence of the group. Reading your list into the recorder will give you the benefit of the feedback experience of speaking the Steppingstones. You should take note of your feelings as you do this and add them as a further entry in your Steppingstones section. Of even greater feedback value will be your experience in hearing your Steppingstones spoken aloud. This places you in the position of being briefly an observer of yourself.

At a workshop, those who read their Steppingstones aloud do so for the benefit of the feedback experience it will give. There is, however, another most significant side effect that accompanies the reading of the Steppingstones.

The reading of the Steppingstones measurably deepens the atmo-sphere of the group. We very often become aware that a profound presence has become part of the atmosphere of the workshop as people are reading their Steppingstones. As the readings take place, it is as though each individual is offering his most personal possession, his life, but he is presenting it objectively, even transpersonally. He is not exalting it, nor embellishing it, nor defending it. He is only reading the markings of his life history in their honest actuality, without comment and without special requests, seeking neither praise nor sympathy. Each human existence is presented as a factual offering placed on an unseen altar before the group. Perhaps the atmosphere of depth and awe that enters the workshop is the cumulative effect of many human existences being set forth as offerings in this sincere, unprepossessing way, each primarily engaged in clarifying itself to itself. Again and again in the Journal Workshops we are shown evidence that the sincere examination of the individual human life is one of man's fundamental religious acts.

Each set of Steppingstones is unique, for no two human beings have the same combination of life experiences. This individuality shows itself also in the diverse ways that people list their Steppingstones. The details of the material must remain private, in keeping with the underlying ethics of the *Intensive Journal* program, but we can see examples of this diversity of forms in the Steppingstone lists that are read at the workshops.

Even though the specifics are left out in the sets of Steppingstones that are made by listing indicative phrases or just a single word, such lists are extraordinarily effective in reflecting the movement of a person's life. Consider the following stark, and yet poetically expressive list of Steppingstones that was read at a workshop: "I was born. I loved. I danced. I wept. I posed. I suffered. I was entranced. I was humiliated. I got lost. I am trying to find my way."

It is obvious that we, who are outsiders to the life that is described in that listing, cannot know the details of the experiences to which those cryptic sentences refer. Nonetheless we do feel the quality of the person and the tone of the life in which he is engaged. It is not for us but for the person whose life it is that the details of what is involved in those Steppingstones have meaning. He alone needs to know, and each person who makes such an outline of Steppingstones is well able to fill in the private details as he continues with the Time-Stretching exercises. To make such a listing of Steppingstones does, however, help us to identify the thread of continuity that has been moving through our life; most importantly, it enables us to wind that thread fine enough to draw it through the narrow eye of the needle formed by the circumstances or the crisis of the present moment of our life.

There are several ways in which we use the Steppingstones exercises as a means of fine-winding the elusive threads of continuity through the narrow crises of our lives. When a person reaches a time of transition in his life, when he comes to a crossroad of decision, or when one phase of his life has ended and he must find the resources with which to begin a new unit of experience, it is of great value to be able to find and to grasp the inner thread of our lives by working with the Steppingstones.

Consider the situation, for example, of a woman who comes to a Journal Workshop at a point in her life where her child-rearing years are coming to an end. She is a housewife, living what she feels to be a regularized existence in the modern suburban manner, and wondering what her future holds for her. Working with her Steppingstones is the first step in positioning herself in the movement of her life so that she can discover her resources and her possibilities. The first listing of Steppingstones that she makes reflects primarily the external events of her life. "I was born. I went to school. I graduated from college. I held a job. I married. I bore three children. The children are growing up. Everything is fine but I am discontented. I don't know what to look forward to."

As we consider them, we realize that those last Steppingstones with their mixture of fear and a vague yearning for something not yet known are the link to her future. At the moment when she lists these Steppingstones, she has no indication of what they imply or where they may be moving. She only knows that she feels troubled as she writes her Steppingstones. When she is asked about them, she says that she feels her Steppingstones are boring and that they are of no interest to anyone. She also says that she felt very much like crying as she was reading the list in the presence of the group.

Her response and description of her feelings are direct expressions of the Journal Feedback process in motion. They are, in fact, continuing the process. The movement of her life was clearly in a low phase. In another situation when she expressed such unhappiness, there would undoubtedly be some helpful person present to give her sympathy, some sensible advice, and a reasonable interpretation of why she is feeling that way. At a Journal Workshop, however, we refrain from doing that. In order for our operational principles to bring about their changes, it is essential that we do not intervene with helpfulness but that we honor the integrity of the individual. We must leave ample room for the organic process of their life to continue through its valleys until it finds the means of restoring itself out of its own resources.

Since the Steppingstones embody the inner continuity of a life, the act of listing them is in itself a step in carrying the life process forward. Writing them and considering them in a focused exercise has the effect of drawing that process one notch further at the nonconscious level.

That movement is often visible in the very first listing of Steppingstones that a person draws together. We could see that in the set of Steppingstones of the woman whom we quoted. She began by recapitulating her life in terms of her birth and the external facts of her early life. The first Steppingstones were general, being primarily objective in content. As she came closer to the present period, however, subjective feelings came more strongly to the fore. We could see then that in describing a Steppingstone of her life as a period of discontent, she was also moving the inner process onwards. The urge to tears was part of this movement as well. An energy was stirring underneath and was in motion. Of necessity, the first forms of the movement expressed her frustration and boredom, since those were the inner conditions creating the need for change. The question that comes to mind, then, is how the change will be brought about. How will a new more meaningful condition of life be established?

As a person begins to think about this rationally, a new sense of frustration and even of panic may be felt. The reason for this is that deliberate and rational thinking cannot direct us to a satisfying and meaningful experience in our life. That can only be brought about in the same way that inspiration comes to an artist, by *cultivated spontaneity* as he works persistently at the nonconscious levels of his inner experience. Working in the procedures of Journal Feedback is the equivalent of the creative process in the artist, not because it is directed toward a particular artwork, but because it systematically stimulates and draws forward the process at the depth of the person. Working with our

Steppingstones and using them as the base points for our later Journal Feedback exercises fulfills this same function with respect to the organic process that is seeking to unfold in our lives.

In the case of the woman of whom we have been speaking, the movement of this inner process will be reflected in the next set of Steppingstones she lists. Especially if enough time has passed for her to have worked seriously in the *Intensive Journal*, the vantage point from which she views her life will have moved to another position. Her perspective will be different. When she lists her next set of Stepping-stones, it is likely that only the very first one, her birth, will be the same and will be in the same position. Instead of making a routine recording of her education, she will focus on a particular subject that interested her, an event or relationship that took place during her college years, or a decision she made at the time which had unforeseen consequences in later years. Instead of stating the cold statistical fact of how many children she bore, she may now place her attention on some particular experiences in relation to her childbearing and child rearing.

On the other hand, with her emphasis shifted toward the lifestyle that is emerging in her future, she may find that she does not even list her children at all in her next set of Steppingstones. This will not be because she is rejecting them, but because she is now evaluating the past events of her life in terms of their contribution to the next step in her develop-ment. She may recall now as a Steppingstone her emotions when she learned that her brother would go to medical school while her own schooling would be curtailed. Or she may now list as Steppingstones quite different events which she would not have considered to be important before. They may have been sources of frustration, or of stimulated imagination, or unfulfilled hopes, satisfactions and detours. As the context of her life is enlarged by her newly opening perspectives, the contents of many experiences in her past become meaningful to her in new ways. Events that seemed insignificant before now take their place as Steppingstones as she sees a meaning and a potential in them pointing toward the future. In the course of this, what may be called a *transvaluation* of her life experiences will have taken place, and new goals, meanings and hopes will have begun to emerge.

This transvaluation will express itself in changed attitudes and a new

114

life perspective. At successive Journal Workshops or in her private experience after she has worked with the Journal Feedback exercises and Steppingstones, she will find that the events continue to change. As she compares the several lists when she rereads them in sequence after some time, she will recognize that hardly any of the Steppingstones that were on her original list appear on the later lists; those that do reappear will be in a different context, for the old events will now have a new meaning. Hearing herself read in sequence these successive sets of Steppingstones will reinforce for her a fact that she already knows, namely that her life has changed. She is now a new person with a different life history than she had before.

In this modern period of history when the life expectancy is much longer than it was in previous generations and when the resources offered by society are much greater, many people are able to live through two or three distinct cycles of life. In each of these, they are a different person with different values and lifestyles. To be able to look forward to such successive developments opens a large potential not only for the later years of one's life but for the fullness of meaning in a human existence as a whole. The main difficulty lies in the period of transition between two major units in a person's life. When the old period has ended and a new period has not yet been substantially established, the emotional burdens of anxiety and self-doubt may be heavy to bear. That is a time when it is especially important to have a progressive and organic method for enabling the perspectives of one's life to reshape themselves.

The woman of whom we have been speaking entered the *Intensive Journal* process when she felt that she was at a dead end in her life and could see no ray of light indicating that something of value lay ahead. Another type of situation is that of the person who has come to a crossroad of decision in his life where he has to choose between two major pathways both of which are already parts of his experience. It may seem that such a person is suffering only from an excess of riches, but the tension can be very great indeed.

In such circumstances it is often helpful to draw up two or even more sets of Steppingstones within a very brief period, even within a single workshop. In that way, if there is more than one thread of continuity seeking to unfold in a person's life, each will have ample space in which to reveal the strength of its roots and the scope of its possibilities.

Sometimes it is not a question of decision or of conflict, but simply of a change in emphasis taking place in a person's life. Situations of this kind come to the fore especially when the time for retirement is approaching, or when other circumstances are bringing about a change in the main activity that has dominated an individual's attention.

I think in this regard of a man who came to an *Intensive Journal* Workshop at a point in his life when he was preparing to retire as chief executive of a large corporation. He had already determined what was to be the new direction of his life. He wished to develop his spiritual capacities to the point where he could serve society effectively in an altruistic way during his later years. Toward this end, he had come to the workshop in order to set his life in perspective.

When he came to the Steppingstones exercise, however, he found that the Steppingstones of his life were not willing to come together in a single list. Following our procedures, he undertook to write them spontaneously with the assumption that they would place themselves in a single unified format. But his Steppingstones had their own point of view in the matter. Like people who will not speak to one another, they would not come together. It strongly suggested that there was a marked antithesis between the two sides of his life.

In that situation there was nothing to do but to let the Steppingstones have their way and to let them record themselves simultaneously in two separate lists. As he did so, he discovered that each set of Steppingstones contained the chronology of a separate development that had been taking place within him over the years. The first list contained the Steppingstones of his rise to business success. It listed his birth, the poverty of his early years, his personal unsureness during his education, his chance meeting with a public figure who became his sponsor, the redirection of his education into the legal profession, and then the various events that led to his progressive rise up the corporate ladder.

Parallel to this, and altogether separate from it, was the list of Steppingstones that marked the continuity of his spiritual life. Among these were his memory of his grandfather as a figure who personified wisdom; various books on philosophy and religion which had come to his attention, but which he had failed to read; hearing a lecture on mystical subjects, rejecting it, but being haunted nevertheless by the speaker's thoughts; becoming acquainted at a later point with an author on spiritual subjects; then, a personal, inner experience that brought about his decision to bring one of his lives, his business life, to a close and to begin an altogether new style of experience.

Reading those two lists of Steppingstones to the group was a very moving experience for him. It was as if he had read the life histories of two separate individuals. It told him, among other things, that the "new" life he was beginning was not at all new to him. It had its own history, and had had its own continuity and growth, but that growth had taken place beneath the surface of his life. Now the rhythm and timing of that "second person" within him was coming to the fore and was ready to become the dominant person in his existence. The fact that the two persons insisted on chronicling their lives with two separate sets of Steppingstones dramatized for him the distinctness of their existence *at that particular time in his life.*

It was not something to be diagnosed as a psychiatric split, but rather an inherent aspect of the transition through which he was passing. While it was establishing its strength, the new self had to insist on its independence and separateness. It was in a position very similar to that of an adolescent establishing his identity and freedom from his parents and teachers. But such times of transition pass. At a later time, after the business man had moved through his transition and had retired from the life of his old business self and had established a way of life for his new self, it was possible for him to experience all the events of his life as part of one larger unfolding unity. Therefore, on a subsequent occasion he could reconstruct his life in one single integrative set of Stepping-stones, thereby giving full value in perspective to both the business side and his spiritual nature.

These examples may give some perspective of what is involved in listing the Steppingstones. Each time we do this exercise we are recapitulating our life from the special point of view provided by a particular moment in our life-history. But it is not merely a procedure that we carry out with respect to our past. The very act of listing our Steppingstones reshapes the context of our life, and thus draws us a step further into our future.

We see in this an important key to the dynamic effect of working with our Steppingstones. The purpose of the exercise is to move us forward in the Life/Time dimension, constantly recrystallizing our perception of our life, and thereby drawing us onwards. It is not at all intended to give us an intellectual understanding of our past. That is one reason why there is no such thing as listing the "correct" Steppingstones. They are inherently in flux. Therefore the key to working with the Steppingstones is to let the list be created spontaneously out of the fullness of the present circumstances of our life, whatever they may be. We should be open and receptive to these circumstances without being judgmental about them. Then, as we begin each exercise in quietness, listing our Steppingstones in an atmosphere of deep stillness as we are listening to the inner flow of our life, directions of experience of which we were not previously aware may be reflected to us. The Stepping-stones thus provide us with essential, nonconscious life-information to feed into the interplay of exercises in the other sections of the Journal. This, in turn, will build the momentum of Journal Feedback, and will provide the inner guidance we require for the next step in our life.

Chapter 9

Exploring the
Steppingstone Periods

The listing of our Steppingstones is the first step that we take in order to position ourselves in the full continuity of our lives. Each set of Steppingstones that we draw together reflects the interior view of our life as it is perceived from the vantage point of a particular moment. By being expressed spontaneously and concisely without self-conscious analysis, the Steppingstone list gives us a direct, inner perception of the movement of our life.

At the first stage of the *Time-Stretching* exercises, we identify each Steppingstone either by a brief phrase or by a single word. This is sufficient, since the connotations and background are familiar to us. We know the personal details to which we are referring with our briefly stated Steppingstones. This conciseness has the advantage of enabling us to draw our life quickly into focus, at least in a general and preliminary way. When we read our Steppingstones back to ourselves they give us an encompassing perspective, and they evoke in us an inner response which carries our life-movement a step further.

The initial impact of reading the Steppingstone list is an important stimulus to the Journal Feedback process. It gives us a direct experience of the wholeness of our life as it has been in motion over the years. The special value of this is that the broad, moving context enables us to recognize the large implications and possibilities which lie implicit, and often hidden, in individual events. On the basis of our lists of Steppingstones we are able to enter the details of particular experiences, drawing forth their significance and opening the possibilities of their still unexpressed contribution to our lives.

The next step in our work of *Time-Stretching* is to explore our Steppingstones in closer detail. We do this by proceeding in stages. First we draw out the context of circumstances in which our various Steppingstones have occurred. Then, by degrees, we progressively explore and elaborate the seeds of future experience as they are contained in the past periods of our lives.

The Steppingstones which we list are mainly specific events that stand out as signposts along the road of our individual life. When we consider them closely, however, we realize that each Steppingstone represents an entire unit of our Life/Time, including events and experiences of many different kinds.

In itself, a Steppingstone is a specific occurrence or situation which comes to the fore of our minds when we go back over the past and review the movement of our lives. Steppingstones are essentially markings which enable us to retrace the pathways of our experience. The fact that they are markings, however, implies that the area of our experience which they represent includes something more than the markings themselves. Each area includes the composite of events and experiences which took place both before and after the markings themselves occurred, and which comprise a full unit of Life/Time.

This is what we mean by a *Steppingstone Period*. It is a unit of Life/Time, a period in our life in which many varied experiences are contained. The period as a whole is symbolized to us subjectively by the particular Steppingstone event which represents the primary and governing quality of that time in our life. In this sense, each Steppingstone that we place on our list symbolizes for us and evokes to our memory the totality of a Steppingstone Period.

The brief listing of Steppingstones which we have made to reflect the movement of our life turns out, then, to have a further significance, and thereby an additional role in our Journal Feedback work. It is more than a listing of events, but a spontaneous demarcation of the *qualitative units of Life/Time* into which our existence has subjectively divided itself up to now. At a later time, when we are looking back at the movement of our life from another vantage point, the divisions will be different. Just as other Steppingstones will suggest themselves to us in the future as markers for our past, so will other Steppingstone Periods be the qualitative units into which our lives will divide themselves when we consider them in the future from a new, or different, perspective.

In the context of Journal Feedback, a *life period,* as we mark it off in the Period Log or in working with the Steppingstone Periods, is a qualitative unit of Life/Time which an individual perceives as a generalized whole. Each life period is governed by a particular life theme, or by a set of themes. We see this expressed at Journal Workshops in the way that people characterize the present period in their lives when they work in the Period Log. They may say, for example:

"It is a time when I am learning how to live in America after emigrating here."

"It is a time when I am getting used to being retired."

"It is a time when I am taking care of my small children, and wondering what I will do when they are grown."

"It is a time when nothing at all seems to be happening and my life is at a standstill."

"It is a time when I have passed through many discouragements finally ending in a new field of employment."

This type of statement summarizing the recent period in a person's life applies also to the Steppingstone Periods. While each of the periods of the past includes a variety of factors that are operating and unfolding at different levels and degrees, there is a generalized unity to each period. This unity is given by the underlying tone of events, goals and circumstances during that particular period in the individual's life. It is expressed in the tonality of what was happening and what was trying to happen in the person's development. "It was a time when . . ."

That phrase serves as a doorway by which we can enter each of the Steppingstone Periods. We wish to recapture for our private experience

121

the atmosphere of the period, the quality of feeling, the tone of energy and striving at that time, the difficulties, the hopes and the anxieties which comprised our inner world and our outer experience during that period.

We begin with our starting-phrase, "It was a time when . . ." As we move from this, the style of the observations that we record tends to be generalized and impressionistic at first. Especially at the beginning as we are reestablishing our contact with the period as a whole, our first Journal entries tend to deal with the underlying tenor and atmosphere of the time. As we continue, however, the reconnections of our memory become progressively stronger and more definite, and they enable us to enter more deeply into specific events. It is at this point that our work with the Steppingstone Periods feeds into the other Time-Stretching exercises and builds the cumulative effect of Feedback Interplay.

We now take our next step in these Time-Stretching exercises. We begin by returning our attention to the list of Steppingstones which we brought together. Each Steppingstone refers to an actual event in our lives, and it also is part of a larger, encompassing time-unit in which many other events are contained. The individual Steppingstone is an indicative marker of the time-unit as a whole. It expresses the tone of the Steppingstone Period as an encompassing qualitative unit of our Life/Time.

We sit in quietness and reread our list of Steppingstones. Each Steppingstone now represents a unit of Life/Time to us. Eventually our goal is to enter and explore each of the Steppingstone periods. Since that is a large task, we proceed toward it gradually, working in one Stepping-stone Period at a time. As we do this, unravelling the past time-units of our life at whatever pace feels comfortable to us, we are establishing a format and learning a procedure that will enable us to work continuously in each of the Steppingstone Periods on our present list as well as those that will emerge from our future Steppingstone exercises.

We proceed by working in one Steppingstone Period at a time. Our first step, therefore, is to choose the Steppingstone Period with which we shall begin our work. While it might seem logical to start with the earliest period in our lives, we have found in practice that our work with the Steppingstone Periods is more productive when we proceed not chronologically but qualitatively. We begin by focusing our attention on a Steppingstone Period which seems to us from our present vantage point to have played an especially significant role in the movement of our life.

In our quietness now, we reread our list of Steppingstones to see whether there is any single Steppingstone Period that stands out from the others with respect to its meaningfulness for the transitions of our life. In this regard, the question of whether it was a period in which we felt ourselves to be successful, or happy, or fulfilled is not relevant. It is important rather to choose as the Steppingstone Period with which we begin the work one in which the most formative events were taking place.

Choose a time when possibilities were opening for you, when alternatives were present in your experience, and when critical decisions were being made, or were being left unmade. If the consequences or implications of those decisions and the events deriving from them are still being felt in your life, that is a good indication of a Steppingstone Period worth your attention. You will find that it is especially valuable to choose a time-unit about which you have serious questions with respect to your own behavior and its attendant circumstances. It is good also to choose a period that held fertile possibilities which, as seen from your present perspective, were not adequately fulfilled. Bear in mind, however, as you reopen the past periods of your life, that this work is not to be done judgmentally. We are to give ourselves neither praise nor criticism, but we are to make neutral observations of our life, being as objective as we possibly can about the subjective experiences of our life.

It may be that as you are going over your Steppingstone list you will feel that there is more than one Steppingstone Period which would be fruitful for you to explore more fully. While we wish to work intensively with one period at the outset, it is not necessary for us to by-pass these additional periods. We can take note of them and set up a format for working with them at a later time. One good and helpful practice we have found is to set up a fresh page within the Steppingstone section for each of the periods that suggest themselves to us from our Steppingstone list as being meaningful and valuable for our future work. We may then concentrate our attention on the Steppingstone Period which we have chosen as being of primary importance; but it also leaves us free to jot down on those sheets whatever thoughts and memories come to us spontaneously while we are working in the Time-Stretching exercises. Later we can return to those pages and complete our exploration of all the Steppingstone Periods that call for our attention.

As a general principle, the work that we do in the Steppingstone Periods follows procedures that are essentially the same as those with which we worked in the Period Log. The main difference is that we are now working in the past, and are continuously gathering data for each of these periods using additional Time-Stretching exercises. Once we have gotten past the basic work in our primary Steppingstone Period, we shall be working simultaneously in the other periods, filling in their relevant information as the memories and awarenesses spontaneously come to us.

Having decided upon the Steppingstone Period with which we shall begin, our first step is to place ourselves in the atmosphere of that time in our lives. We begin by reexperiencing the events of that time in their general aspect, gradually enabling our perceptions of the past to become more specific and definite.

We sit in stillness and close our eyes. Our breathing becomes slower and softer. We become quiet inside ourselves, letting our minds move back to the time of the Steppingstone Period. We do not deliberately try to recall any specific event, but we let ourselves *feel* into the atmosphere of that time in our lives. Gradually the atmosphere of that past time becomes present to us, and we feel the tone and quality and the circumstances of that period in our experience. Now we can begin to record and describe the general aspects of what was taking place in our life at that time.

"It was a time when . . ." Since that phrase is the doorway through which we re-enter the Steppingstone Period, we place ourselves there, and then begin to write, filling in, bit by bit, the relevant pieces of information. With concise statements, we indicate the type of events that were taking place at that time in our life. In general terms we say what was happening, give the tone and the quality of the circumstances, of our inner life and of our environment. "It was a time when
"

What are some adjectives that come immediately to your mind to describe the period as a whole? What are some brief phrases? Write these down. If the movement of events was reflected in markedly different phases within the period, indicate this with the various adjectives that you use corresponding to each sub-unit of time. The nature of the changes that took place is an important aspect of the period and should be reflected in your entry.

Perhaps a metaphor or a simile comes to your mind to describe the content and the movement of the period. "It was a time that was like . . ." Record whatever you now feel it to have been like. Permit yourself to be free and impressionistic in the metaphors that come to you regarding that time in your life. The freer you are, the more fully they will reflect your nonconscious perceptions of that period.

As your eyes are closed while you are re-entering the period and feeling its atmosphere, you may find yourself moving to the twilight depth of the psyche. At that level, images may present themselves to you, visual or non-visual images in various sensory forms, that will reflect the tone of your experiences during that period. Hold yourself in openness for these twilight imagery perceptions and record them directly as they come to you. Do not edit or interpret them, but simply describe them as you perceive them. When you read them afterwards, you may find them to be especially sensitive and spontaneous reflectors of your inner awareness regarding that time in your life.

What you have written up to this point about the Steppingstone Period is of a generalized nature. Now you can begin to become specific. What do you recall about the feelings you had about yourself at that time? Briefly describe the kind of person you were then. If there were ambiguities, or uncertainties, or variations in the kind of person you were, describe them. If they changed from time to time in varying circumstances, indicate the nature of the changes and how they took place.

What was your attitude toward life at that time? Did you have any particular beliefs about your personal destiny, favorable or unfavorable, fortunate or unfortunate? Did you have any intimations about what life might hold in store for you? Did you have any special hopes or plans for your personal development? Did you have any strong religious beliefs or commitment to any social group or teaching? Did you have a philosophy of life? Was there a particular attitude you had at that time that guided you or set the tone for your actions?

These questions involve the inner and subjective point of view with which you conducted your life during that Steppingstone Period. Attitudes that we had in the past are elusive and often difficult to remember but it is worthwhile trying to recall them. If we can recreate the subjective attitudes and feelings that we had in an earlier portion of our life, we have a means of reentering our past experience from the inside. We are then not limited to the external events that we hold in memory, but we can eventually reach into the seed-potentials that have been trying, often with great difficulty and frustration, to unfold in the course of our life.

These attitudes and images of life are fundamental to our experience, but it may not be easy for us to recall them and describe them when we are beginning to recreate a Steppingstone Period. Many of us will find that it is easier for us to remember the specific contents and events of an earlier time in our life when we are asked about them directly. Then, as a by-product of many cumulative memories, the feeling-tone of our underlying attitudes will come together and the composite picture of our life will reestablish itself.

With this in mind, our next step is to follow the checklist of the Journal sections as we did in the Period Log so as to stimulate our memories with respect to the specific contents of the period. When we have done that, we may wish to return to these general and yet basic questions regarding the subjective attitudes we had in the past. At that point, also, having reconnected ourselves with our past by reactivating our memory of specific events, we will find that we have a much fuller awareness of our earlier attitudes. After we have worked in the detailed contents of the period, therefore, we will be stimulated to return and enlarge our original descriptions of the Steppingstone Period.

JOURNAL CHECKLIST

We turn now to our checklist of Journal sections, which serves as our basic guideline for recapitulating and exploring the time-units of our life. We follow the same procedure in using it as we did when we worked in our Period Log. At this point, we may work with the Journal checklist more closely and in greater detail, using it also as preparation for the dialogue exercises to which we shall come shortly as an important part of our Journal Feedback work. It will, as a matter of fact, be very helpful for us to return to this phase of the Time-Stretching exercises after we have carried through the sequence of dialogue feedback exercises as they are described in later chapters. At that point, having more experience in the use of Journal Feedback techniques, we shall be able to work in greater detail and to expand the range of our work in the Steppingstone Periods. But it is good to begin and set the base for our later work by following the outline of the Journal checklist with respect to the particular Steppingstones Period we have chosen as our present focus. We may answer the following questions briefly at first and progressively expand them. Later we may cross-reference them in the Journal section for which they are relevant.

1) *Dialogue with Persons.* During this Steppingstone Period were there significant events or relationships with persons who have an inner importance to us in the unfoldment of our life? It is easy to recall in this regard the dramatic encounters of love or anger or abrupt changes that took place; but we should not overlook the more prosaic, everyday relationships that continued through the period.

2) *Dialogue with Works.* Were there any outer activities that became a focus for our energies in a way that held an inner meaning for us? These artworks may be of many kinds, and may include works that were carried through to completion during the period, works that were begun and were life incomplete, and also works that were conceived and planned but were not actually started or given an external form.

3) *Dialogue with the Body.* Were there occurrences or situations during this period that were especially concerned with your relation to the physical aspect of your life? This may include illness, health programs, sensory pleasures, contact with nature, sexuality, athletics, drugs, indulgences and addictions of any kind.

4) *Dialogue with Society.* Was this a period in your life when you were deepening or changing your relation to groups or institutions that have a fundamental connection to your existence? Were you recon-

sidering old allegiances to country or religion or political party? Were you redefining your identification with your race or your family or social group? Was it a time when events took place in history that involved you in serious questions of personal commitment? Did you find yourself during this time deeply involved in literary or artistic works of past or present time, the artworks of others that brought you into profound consideration of the nature of human existence?

5) *Dialogue with Events.* Was this a time when unexpected, and often unexplained, events took place in your life? Were there situations in which it seemed that life was testing you either with pain, as with physical accidents, or with pleasure, as with unusual good fortune? Were there especially difficult or challenging circumstances during this period, outer and inner pressures that forced you to come to closer grips with the riddles of human existence?

6) *Dream Log.* Do you remember having dreams during this period that stood forth with special force and had striking impact on you? The strength of these might be great enough to cause you to remember them even if you did not record them at the time. On the other hand, many people have kept an unstructured diary at various points in their life in which their dreams are recorded. If you kept such a diary, it may be valuable to consult it now when you are working on your Steppingstone Periods, especially with respect to your dreams.

7) *Twilight Imagery Log.* During this period do you recall having waking visions or other experiences at the twilight level of consciousness? Were there any that had a major impact upon you and influenced your decisions or other actions at the time? As you consider these experiences in the retrospect of the events that have taken place in your life since that time, do any of them seem to have had a prophetic quality, or a symbolic meaning for your life which now suggests itself to you? Consider their *inner correlation* to the movement of your life.

8) *Inner Wisdom Dialogue.* What experiences do you recall in which you recognized a profound truth of human existence that was new to you at that time? Perhaps you did not reach an ultimate answer then, but the question has continued to stir inside of you. Who were the

persons who played the largest role in stimulating and deepening your thoughts and feelings at that time? Were they individuals with whom you had direct contact in your life? Were they persons from history whose books you read or whose lifeworks you studied? Or were they persons whose reality lies beyond history in the symbolism and teachings of a great religion or philosophy?

9) *Intersections: Roads Taken & Not Taken.* During this period of your life did you come to crossroads of decision that affected the course of future events in a fundamental way? Perhaps it was an intersection in your life path that depended upon an act of decision which you yourself made. Or perhaps it was an action which you failed to take, which was to that degree a decision made by omission. Perhaps it was an intersection in your life in which the decisive factor was not left within your discretion but was forced upon you. In either case it was a crossroad in your life and the fact that one road was actually taken for whatever reason meant that another road was not taken. Has that untaken road remained a possibility of life that has not been lived?

As you consider these situations of intersection in your life, it is especially important that you perceive them and describe them without judgment. It is beside the point in recording the contents of a Steppingstone Period to give either criticism or praise for the actions you took or for the circumstances that were forced upon you. There is an especial value, however, in recognizing them and in describing as objectively as possible the ambiguities of life that were contained in them. To be able to reenter the intersections of past periods of our lives gives us access to the unlived possibilities of our existence which the future may still give us an opportunity to fulfill, albeit in a different form. When we are writing these basic statements of the contents of a Steppingstone Period, it is best that we describe the Intersections briefly at first, but that we call upon as much quiet awareness as we can muster to enable us to recognize their existence in our life. We wish simply to perceive and to list as many crossroad situations in the Steppingstone Period as we can, but we do not amplify them here. We leave that to the next phase of the Time-Stretching exercise for which they provide a main starting point.

When you have made the entries in the Steppingstone section that follow this checklist of Journal sections, you will have covered the main factors in the period. Do not at this point review or edit what you have written. Let yourself, rather, sit in quietness and continue to feel with increasing depth the atmosphere of the period, as we prepare to continue our work with the Life/Time dimension of our experiences.

Chapter **10**

The Hinge of
Memory and Possibility

Having begun the detailed exploration of our Steppingstones, we can now take a further step in our Time-Stretching work. The entries we have made in the Steppingstone section become a center point from which we move in two directions of Life/Time. We move back into our past, recalling and recapitulating varieties of experiences that have occurred in our lives and drawing them together without restriction into a self-forming collage that reconstructs our life-history. At the same time that we recapitulate our past, we also explore the possibilities that are contained in the unlived aspects of our lives. Thus we open avenues to our future while we are reentering the experiences of our past. It is in this sense that our Steppingstone entries serve as a hinge for us, a life-hinge by which we swing back and forth between our past and our future, expanding our inner relation to our Life/Time as we do so.

This is the heart of the Time-Stretching work which plays so important a role in enabling an individual to reposition himself in the movement of his life. We carry it through by working simultaneously in two sections of the Journal: The Life History Log and Intersections: Roads Taken and Not Taken, using the Steppingstone entries as our base point. We shall first describe the qualities and contents of these Journal sections, and then proceed to the steps by which we use them in the Time-Stretching exercises.

THE LIFE HISTORY LOG

The *Life History Log* is the section of the *Intensive Journal* in which we gather all the facts of the past of our lives.

Whatever recalls itself to our minds we record here without censorship and without making judgments. We describe whatever took place as we remember it, sometimes letting our descriptions be brief as the memories spontaneously come to us, and at other times describing the events of the past in great detail.

Because it is the place where we collect memories and progressively explore their contents, this section was called "Recapitulations and Rememberings" in the original version of the *Intensive Journal*. As the use of the Journal developed, however, it became increasingly clear that this section was serving a predominantly Log function as it was collecting information from all parts of a person's life history. It was thus renamed the *Life History Log*.

In practice, the value of the *Life History Log* increases with a person's use of the *Intensive Journal*. The more he works with it and re-enters the various periods of his life, the greater the number of memories reactivated.

The Life History Log is the place for collecting all these memories. Without judgment or interpretation, we record here all the past experiences as they return to our minds whenever we are working in the Journal. Whether they are events or feelings, situations or facts of experience, we record them in the Life History Log. We may describe them in some detail, or we may merely mention them briefly and indicate with only a few phrases what is involved in them. Often, when we are working in the feedback exercises, we find that memories are stimulated that call our attention to areas of our life which had lain buried and hidden within us. Memories which people have felt to be "blocked" and beyond recall are quite frequently activated by the interior movement that is generated by our active Journal work. They are spontaneously remembered while we are in the midst of a Journal Feedback exercise that deals with some other aspect of our life.

At such times we do not wish to be sidetracked and drawn away from the work in which we are engaged, but we also wish to retain the memory that we have inadvertently unearthed. The Life History Log serves as the section where we can record the memory briefly, while being free to continue with the exercise in which we are working. At a later time, we can return to it and enlarge our description of that past experience, reentering it and extending it in further feedback exercises.

This is part of the active interplay of our Journal contents by which we multiply and cross-fertilize the various aspects of our lives. It is a dynamic factor in the Journal Feedback process that becomes much more visible at a later stage of our Journal work when its cumulative effects change our perception of our lives in unexpected ways. At this point, however, as we are engaged in the basic exercise of Time-Stretching and are gathering the essential data of our life experience, our use of the Life History Log is more elementary. Here we use it for the particular task of recalling and collecting memories of events and relationships and circumstances as they occurred in the Steppingstone Periods.

All these happenings of our life, which were experienced by us subjectively when they took place, we report as objectively as we can without judgment or editorial comment. We simply record them and gather them together here in the Life History Log, letting the pieces fit themselves together as we make the varieties of entries of our memories through the continuity of our Journal work. It is thus that our past progressively reconstructs and draws itself into focus in relation to the present moment. The Life History Log plays an important fact-gathering role in this.

INTERSECTIONS: ROADS TAKEN AND NOT TAKEN

The work we do in this section of the Journal takes us into the very midst of the movement of our lives. With it, we place ourselves back in those experiences that brought us to a point of transition, to an intersection in our lives, where a change of some kind became inevitable.

Some of those changes took place because of decisions which we ourselves made. Others took place because of decisions that were made by others, or that were forced upon us by the impersonal circumstances of life. However they occurred, they were particular experiences which determined the direction and shaped the contents of our lives from that point onwards. Their effects were felt throughout that unit of Life/Time, the period which began at that crossroad and continued at least until we came to a further point of intersection. Now we reenter those moments of crossroad, not to judge them by hindsight but to reconnect ourselves with the inner movement of our lives and thus to give ourselves access to the possibilities which they contain for our future.

Underlying the exercises of this section is the image of the road. Our individual life is like a road that passes through many environments. As conditions change, it varies its style of movement. It takes detours. When necessary, it moves very slowly and cautiously on a broken roadbed. It shifts its direction or moves in circular paths in order to avoid mountains and other obstacles. Through all its changes, however, the road remains itself; so does our life maintain its identity by sustaining the inner continuity of its movement despite all the variations and cycles through which it must pass.

Working in the dimension of Life/Time, especially as we use the Steppingstones, we place ourselves back on the road of our life so that we can develop an inner perspective of its movement. Retracing our Steppingstones has the effect of marking off the lines of continuity in our development. We can see where we are, and we can follow the succession of events by which we came to the present situation of our life. We also recognize the points along the road of our life where we came to intersections, and where we had to choose which road to follow. Very often, at those moments of choice the signposts were unclear. The information available to us was very limited, and we had no way of knowing what sort of terrain lay further along the road we would choose. Very often, also, we had to make our decisions in the midst of the pressures of events, while travelling at full speed and without an opportunity to stop and study the alternate possibilities. Of necessity, then, we have all made many blind choices at the intersections of our life.

As we pause now to consider our life in retrospect, we recognize that the choices we made at those intersections left many potentialities untouched and unexplored. We discern that there are, in general, two kinds of roads in our life: the roads we have actually travelled and the roads we did not take. What we found on the roads that we travelled is now known to us, for it is this that has comprised the contents of our life. What was to be found on the roads that we did not take, however, is not known to us. Those untaken roads contain the experiences of our life that have remained unlived. In one sense they are now beyond us, like river water that has flown out to sea. But in a deeper sense they still contain many possibilities of life that are still present and available to us; it is these that we must explore.

These unlived possibilities of life have never been given their chance; yet many of them have been carried silently in the depth of us year after year waiting for a new opportunity. They are capacities of life that were by-passed because of the pressures of our existence, but many of them retain the strength of life and await the *appropriate moment* for being given form and expression. Any new life they are to have, however, is dependent upon our remembering them and finding them in the depth of ourselves, so that they can be reactivated now in a new context. The primary purpose of working in *Intersections* is to give us the means of doing this.

Considering the unlived potentials of our life is reminiscent of an event that took place in the nineteenth century when an ancient Egyptian tomb was opened. In that tomb a portion of a tree was found, and imbedded in the wood was a seed. The scientists involved in the expedition planted the seed out of curiosity, merely to see if anything would happen. Behold, after three thousand years the seed grew! It had missed its chance to grow in ancient Egypt, but its strength of life had remained intact, dormant and waiting for its next opportunity.

The parallel is clear between the Egyptian seed and those capacities that have remained unlived on the roads not taken in our lives. Because time has passed them by, we assume that the choices we rejected or waived are now dead, and that there is no longer any potentiality in them. We have, on the other hand, many indications that projects which we planned but could not carry through at an early point in our life became ripe for fulfillment at a later time. As the author of *The Cloud of Unknowing* states it, "We grow by delays," and for this reason the later expressions of our plans are often more productive and meaningful than they could possibly have been at the earlier time.

It is a question of the appropriate moment. There are often painful feelings of frustration associated with our letting a potentiality of life remain behind us on a road not taken. But that potentiality is not necessarily lost to us forever. It retains its energy and its capacity for expression, waiting for the right time and the right circumstances. Often, however, because of the painful feelings of frustration, we try to erase the memory of them from our minds so that we will not think of them after we have left them on the road that was not taken. By doing that, however, we permanently deprive ourselves of the energies and the possibilities they held for us.

The natural wisdom of the depth dimension has its own way of reminding us of the unfulfilled potentials we have left stranded behind us. One of these is by our dreaming. It is not uncommon to have a dream that takes us back to a time and to circumstances in our life which now seem to be altogether irrelevant to us. Very often a dream focuses its attention on a person who no longer holds any interest for us and about whom we have not thought for a long time. We may assume that such dreams have no significance, that they are only the pointless replay of old memories; and we may ignore them. But the fact is that dreams of this kind are seeking to call our attention to an earlier period of our life in order to make us aware of some significant fact that we are overlooking. The dream is expressing the nonconscious awareness in the depth of us that intuitively knows that something of great importance for our present situation is hidden in those forgotten events.

It usually turns out to be very fruitful for us to follow the lead of the dream and return to that time in the past to explore the possibilities and the implications of the events that took place then. When we place ourselves back in the period to which the dream is recalling us, we often find that a decision was made at that time, knowingly or not, in which we chose one path and left another untaken. Some aspect of that unlived experience may now be relevant for our consideration, and the dream is calling our attention to that possibility. If it does this in an ambiguous way that is easily misunderstood, that is only because the dreaming process has no other means of speaking than by indirect and symbolic allusions. Though we may not be able to recognize immediately what dreams are trying to say to us, we can at least follow in the direction that they are pointing. When we go back to the earlier times that these dreams are indicating to us, we often find an intersection with an unlived possibility that is relevant to explore at the present time in our life. Doing this is facilitated by the interplay exercises of Journal Feedback, as we shall see at a later point in our Journal work.

Similar to dreams, the experiences we have in Twilight Imaging often draw us back in their symbolic style to crossroads in our life history where significant decisions were made. In this way also, the nonconscious cognition that is inherent in the depth of us directs us to areas of our life where our conscious minds would not ordinarily think to go. When we have become sensitive to these deeper-than-conscious directives and can follow them with an open, nonjudgmental attitude, we find that we have given ourselves access to an important additional source of knowledge for the conduct of our life.

The principle that underlies the Intersections section of the Journal is that we are simulating the time-guidance which our dreams and Twilight Imagery seek to give us as expressions of our own deep psychic nature. We are stimulating the movement of these depth processes and providing exercises by which an equivalent intuitive cognition can become available to us through our Journal work whether or not we remember our dreams. Just as dreams and Twilight Imaging take us back down the time track of our life history, so also do the time-stretching exercises. They make it possible for us to explore afresh the decisions and choices we made in the past so that we can recoup the valuable parts of them which we had rejected earlier.

We use the section, *Intersections: Roads Taken and Not Taken* as a vehicle by which we are able to go back over the road of our life looking for unlived possibilities. We can retravel that road in our Journal work because we gain access to it through the varied exercises we do in the Steppingstones section and in the Life History Log. As we retravel it, we mark off each of the crossroad situations that we are able to recognize.

It may be that, at the time when the actual events took place, we were not aware that we were making a choice, for we did not see the alternatives that were hidden just around the corner. We went to this school, entered that career, took this job, married that person, not being aware of the variety of additional options that were also, though implicitly, available to us. Now we can reenter those situations of the past and explore the possibilities of the roads not taken. We do not let ourselves become entangled in idly thinking about what might have been, but we place ourselves actively upon the road of our life and we reapproach each crossroad situation.

Those potentialities of our life which were not able to find an avenue of expression at that earlier time may be at a further stage of development now. When we first felt them as a possibility and had to reject them as roads not to be taken, they may have been premature intimations of capacities or talents which were actually present but needed more time to mature. Or perhaps the external situation was not favorable at that time. Being rejected, those roads that were not taken may have gone underground. They may have remained out of view, not dead but inactive, resting in a time of latency, forgotten and unobserved, incubating beneath the surface of events. Abilities, projects and relationships which were roads that could not be taken in earlier years may become feasible in a much richer way with the passage of time. It may be that we have developed as persons so that we are more knowledgeable now, and more capable. It may be that the potentiality we felt in ourselves has matured and is now more viable. It may be that external circumstances have changed so that the moment is now more opportune.

For many possible reasons, the road that could not be taken earlier in our life may now be taken, both more appropriately and more successfully. It may be that the original project will now be in a greatly altered form as it will have moved to another phase of its development. It may have ripened from within, or it may have changed in order to respond to the needs of the environment. In any case it is clear to us that the roads not taken at an earlier time in our life are not necessarily dead ends. We see in them the first tangible expressions of the deep stirrings and potentialities of our personal nature. Rather than bury and forget them, we wish to open them to the light of fresh experience.

We do this by exploring equally without judgment and without self-recrimination decisions made by ourselves and made for us by others, choices made and left unmade, roads taken and not taken. We wish to reenter our experiences of the past so that we can reacquaint ourselves with the potentialities that have stirred within us in earlier days but have not yet been able to reach their full expression. By going back to the various intersections of our life and treating them as new starting points, especially by following the roads not taken so that they can indicate the destinations that are possible for us, we draw from our life history those seeds that have not grown in our past but can grow very meaningfully in our future.

Chapter **11**

Time-Stretching

MOVING BACK AND FORWARD
IN OUR LIFE HISTORY

Now that we have an understanding of these two sections, the Life History Log and Intersections, we can proceed with the Time-Stretching exercises. At this point the physical structure of the *Intensive Journal* plays a very helpful role because it embodies in a tangible way the inner space of our lives. It enables us to move about within ourselves not only exploring but changing things. Moving around in the sections of the Journal corresponds to our travelling back and forth through the inner time and space of our life experience. This capacity and freedom for inner movement is the essence of our Time-Stretching work.

We begin by sitting with our Journal open to the Steppingstone entries. This section is at the center between the other two that are important in the Time-Stretching work, and that is why it serves as the hinge for our inner movement. When we turn back to the section preceding it, we come to the Life History Log where we recall the experiences of our past. When we move forward to the section that follows Steppingstones, we come to Intersections where we consider not only the roads we have taken in our past, but the roads that we have not yet taken and that may still hold possibilities for our future. The descriptions we made of the Steppingstone Period provide the base point from which we move back and forth into the past and into the potentials that are still before us.

This is the sense in which it can be said that we are stretching time like a rubber band that is being pulled at each end. We pull it back to encompass the past, and forward to reach into the future. The rubber band itself is the unit of Life/Time that is our Now Moment. It is an atom of time, a unit of Now, whether it is a period of the present taken from our Period Log, or whether it is a period of the past taken from our Steppingstones. As we draw the rubber band back into the time preceding the period, and as we draw it forward to reach into the time that lies ahead of it, we are stretching the unit of Life/Time that is our focus, and we are including past and future in the atom of Now. Thus we help ourselves reach by degrees a unitary inner experience of the movement of time in our lives.

Our first steps in this direction lay in working with our Steppingstones. We listed them. We indicated their contents in general terms. Most importantly, we followed our Journal checklist in guiding ourselves to recall specific events, situations, and relationships that occurred during that unit of time. We described these briefly in the Steppingstone section, recording them only in sufficient detail to enable us to direct our memory to them. We try first to remember the facts of the Steppingstone Period more clearly so that we can reenter the experiences that actually took place. Then, from the inside, we can proceed with them to see where they wish to lead us.

With our Journal open to the Steppingstone section, we see our checklist descriptions of the Steppingstone Period. We reread what we have written. As we review our entries, more of the circumstances of that period of our life are brought to our mind. Soon we are able to recall additional details of specific situations. Our strength of memory grows, and increasingly these occurrences of the past become clear to us. They are not only becoming clearer to us in terms of memory, but our emotions are becoming more flexible and freer to write of the past without judgment.

As we reread the checklist entries that we made for the Steppingstone Period, we encourage ourselves to recall the details of any events that took place at that time. As one comes to mind we turn back to the Life History Log, the section where we record the events of the past. There we describe the event as we remember it. It may be a memory of a house where we lived as a child, or an incident that took place there. It may be a quarrel, or an act of love, or a situation that gradually developed during the Steppingstone Period.

As you recall it, let yourself slide back into the atmosphere of the actual occurrence. As much as possible, feel yourself to be there. For the purpose of describing it in your Journal, let that past become your present, although only momentarily. We wish to recreate for ourselves the quality of life of our past so that we can be there for the moment and capture it in the Life History Log. We feel again the smells and the sights, the pains and the joys that were part of those experiences in all their variety. We recall the feelings and the sensations, and we record them without judgment.

One of the main purposes behind our Time-Stretching work is to give ourselves a very large awareness of what was contained and what was implicit in each of the units of our Life/Time. Thus we begin by turning our attention to the Steppingstone Period, steeping ourselves in its feelings and atmosphere until a memory is recalled to us. Then we turn to the Life History Log to describe our recollection.

When we have completed our entry, we return to the Steppingstone section to reread what we have written there, reentering its atmosphere until another memory comes to us from that period. Again we turn to the Life History Log to make our entry. We do this several times, each time opening up another vault of memory and describing as much as we can.

Sometimes the entries we make in this way are brief recollections. Others are lengthy descriptions and may require many pages before we are satisfied that we have dealt with them adequately. The criterion lies within ourselves. We write enough to permit ourselves to remember and describe all that is relevant to the event. We must satisfy ourselves to know that we have not left something hidden, and that there is nothing that we have censored or falsified. Once again, since the *Intensive Journal* is for ourselves alone and the entries are for our own scrutiny, we are the only judge of whether any particular entry we have made in the Life History Log is complete and truthful.

We can assume that, since our entries in the Life History Log involve a calling back of memories from the past, we will not necessarily remember everything at once. Very often we find that after we have completed an entry and have gone on to another section of the Journal, an additional memory will come to us. We should have no hesitancy about adding that to the original entry. We want to collect as much of the raw material of memory as we can in our Life History Log. Whenever a memory is recalled to us, whatever we are doing at the time or whatever section of the Journal we are writing in, we make a note of it for the Life History Log.

These spontaneous rememberings can also decide at that time whether it is a memory that will be appropriate to use as a base for a feedback exercise in another section of the Journal. From whichever Steppingstone Period we draw them, we consider all the entries that we make in the Life History Log as potential starting points for further feedback exercises that will enable us to deepen or extend our experience of our lives. In this sense, the Life History Log is a gathering place where we collect as much of the raw data of our lives as our memory can provide, so that we can draw upon it as a factual source for our active feedback experiences as we continue our Journal work.

In the Time-Stretching exercise in which we are now engaged, our attention is focused on the one Steppingstone Period that we have chosen. Up to this point, we have described that period in general, and we have filled in many of the details of our description by following the Journal checklist. We have thus already recorded considerable material regarding that period in our lives. This data now becomes the base for us from which we call up memories of events and situations that occurred during the Steppingstone Period. It is these that we record in the Life History Log.

At the same time that we are doing this, we also wish to open up our past experiences from another point of view. As we are involved in thinking about this period and as we are recalling the meaningful incidents that took place in it, we seek also to become aware of any turning points or crossroads of decision that took place during that time. It is, in fact, not always easy to recognize these intersections in our lives because we are often not aware of their being intersections at the time when they occur. We merely take them for granted and we proceed with the events of our life without considering that alternate paths of experience may also be available to us. It is only in retrospect that we can realize that we were actually at a crossroad of decision and did not know it.

One of the goals of the Time-Stretching exercises is to open out our past experiences so that we can see the latent possibilities contained in them. Toward this purpose it is very helpful to include the type of recollection in our Life History Log that will have the effect of drawing us back into the total atmosphere of that time in our life. To place ourselves *there* so that we can feel it again, even in a sensory way, tends to facilitate the movement of memories. It becomes easier for us then to reexperience the events that occurred in that earlier time and to recognize the intersections and alternate possibilities that were present but hidden in the midst of the pressures of our life.

For example, suppose that the Steppingstone Period that we are exploring is the time in our childhood when we moved to a new neighborhood. The specific Steppingstone is probably our memory of the actual move that our family made. The Steppingstone Period refers to the surrounding period as a whole, including some of the years preceding it and the time after it. The memories which we record in the Life History Log for this period will thus cover a variety of activities.

It is good to begin the process of recollection with a memory that draws us back into the atmosphere of that time, perhaps by recalling the locale in which we lived or a definite event that places us there. We may begin, for example, by describing the old house or the neighborhood from which we moved, and then by describing the new one. We may place ourselves back into the moment of moving to reexperience the feelings we had as we left our old place and friends; we may relive the emotions and events that happened when we began life in the new place.

When we make entries like these in the Life History Log, it is helpful to let our minds and our pen move freely, recording whatever comes to us without our censoring what is unpleasant and without being self-judgmental. This free, unhindered movement has the effect of drawing us into crannies of experience that would otherwise be inaccessible to us. We find that events that were hidden from memory in small corners of our life now recall themselves to us. There is a cumulative movement in this. One memory begets another. The important first step in making this possible is that we begin our work in the Life History Log by describing past experiences that have the effect of taking us back into the climate of that earlier period in our lives. In that atmosphere, the process of nonjudgmental remembering unfolds progressively. Each entry that we record further loosens the nonconscious levels of our psyche, and thus we increase the fluidity of our memory.

As we do this, continuing in terms of our illustration, we make varied entries in the Life History Log in the course of exploring the Steppingstone event of our having moved to a new area. We will describe memories of places and events and emotions as they occurred in the unit of time just before and just after the actual move. As we write these, our descriptions transport us back into that Steppingstone Period as a whole. While we are doing this, we also let a special kind of memory come to us, the memory of a crossroad in our life experience when we took one path and left the other untaken.

Many different types of such Intersection memories may now be recalled to us out of that Steppingstone period. Some will seem to be of minor significance in themselves, and yet, in retrospect, may speak to us with great significance for subsequent periods of our life. For example, we may have neglected to say goodbye to an old man who was a friend of ours in the neighborhood. That was a small oversight in itself, that road not taken. But in the perspective of our life as a whole it may speak to us of a type of oversight that has recurred in our life from time to time. Now that we recall it, we realize that this *road not taken* has left a painful void within us. It needs to be remedied, but how can we do so now that time has passed? Having recorded it in Intersections: Roads Taken and Not Taken, we now contain it in our Journal and will be able to work with it actively later on. We will be able to carry it to another level of awareness by means of subsequent Journal Feedback exercises.

Other crossroad experiences that may be recalled to us from that Steppingstone Period may have had much greater and more obvious consequences on the practical level of our lives. It may be, for example, that we needed to find new friends and that we formed our friendships with very little information to guide us. We had to choose this individual and not that one, this group and not that one. Whichever we chose, we did so without knowing the consequences in advance. Now, in retrospect, we can see the multiplicity of events and subsequent developments in our life that began at that crossroad.

Perhaps the individual or the group with whom we allied ourselves at that time turned out to be hard working and to have special interests that added to our knowledge. Perhaps it was because of that friendship that we were stimulated to move into the career we eventually chose. Perhaps they were socially very congenial to us and knowing them led to our meeting the person we later married. The consequences may be exceedingly varied, as wide-ranging in their ultimate consequences as they were unpredictable at the time. Now, as we draw ourselves back into the atmosphere of that time in our lives, we turn our attention anew to the road we took at that time. We reconsider it as deeply and as fully as we can. We describe it, and open ourselves to its varied consequences and implications, which the perspective of time now enables us to recognize.

Reflecting upon it, we find numerous overtones and levels of meaning implicit in the decisions we made at the points of intersection in our life. We recognize the results of having chosen the path that we followed; we also consider the unlived experiences that may have lain in store for us upon the road that we did not take. There are Journal Feedback exercises for us to use later in our work if we wish to explore the possibilities of the roads not taken.

In the Steppingstone Period when we moved to a new neighborhood, the choices we made may have had constructive consequences, and we are content with them; but the course of our life could just as easily have moved in another direction. It could have been that fortune would not be favorable to us in the decisions we made at the crossroad.

Suppose that the group we chose as our friends was one that led us along destructive or frivolous paths. In league with them, we may have neglected our studies, or developed an addiction, gone afoul of the law, and perhaps dropped out of school prematurely. Now, in the context of our life as a whole, we place ourselves back at that crossroad. We recall and describe as much as we can of what transpired then. We know what we found on the road that was actually taken. Now we explore the road that was not taken.

Even though we cannot know how the course of our life would have unfolded had we taken the road-not-taken, there are in most situations a limited number of alternatives that can reasonably be considered to be among the possibilities. We can explore these possibilities and describe them with a degree of objectivity. For example, we can consider the developments that would have followed if, when we were at the crossroad, we had pursued a particular course of study, or if we had entered a particular field of business, or if we had chosen to spend our social time with one group instead of another. Up to a point, the range of the possible consequences of our following each of those paths is foreseeable by us. Barring chance factors, we can project what they might be and describe them objectively in our Journal as the possibilities of our life that lay along the roads not taken.

Chance factors are, however, inherent in our lives, and that is ultimately why it is impossible for us to know what would actually have happened if we had taken those other paths. A large part of each individual's destiny is brought about by factors that are of a chance, or at least an unpredictable, nature. Often it is the combination, or synchronicity, of events that are unrelated that determines the special quality of an individual's fortune. These cannot be known objectively, but they can be explored, even if only in subjective ways and on nonconscious levels.

Twilight Imagery gives us a means of travelling along the roads we have not taken. It enables us to explore in a hypothetical and intuitive way the unlived potentialities of our lives. In effect, the use of Twilight Imagery in the Intersections section of the Journal gives us an active feedback procedure with which to extend the material we gather in the Life History Log.

In using Twilight Imagery in relation to Roads Taken and Not Taken in our lives, it is important not to use it too early in our Time-Stretching exercises. Sufficient groundwork should be done first so that the context of a life-perspective will have been established. When you are working with an Intersection in a Steppingstone Period, the best way to begin is to delineate the circumstances of the situation as you experienced them at the crossroads. Set all the facts down as simply and as nonjudgmentally as you can. When you have done that, describe the path that you actually took with emphasis upon its beginnings and the early stages of its development. At this point, we want to keep our emphasis and focus close to the time when we were actually at the crossroad, thus holding ourselves well within the boundaries of the Steppingstone Period. We want to retrace our movement along the road we have taken just far enough to indicate how events turned out there, but not far enough to become involved in the complicated interrelationships of chance and other factors that entered the picture later on.

Having described our decision at the crossroads and its early consequences, we may proceed to the roads not taken. This is inherently a subjective exercise since we are speaking of events that have not actually transpired. We are dealing with possibilities and especially with our desires and inclinations. There is a significant truth in the saying that "the wish is father to the act." But, when we speak of "roads not taken," we are often dealing with wishes that did not lead to an action. At least they have not led to one yet. One of the reasons we are interested in exploring our roads not taken is that they may involve wishes that are valid but whose time had not yet come. Their moment of actuality may be in our future. We are therefore dealing with possibilities that are real to the degree that they reflect wishes or inclinations that have an organic root in the depth of our being. Those seedlings of potentiality may eventually come to full growth if we nurture them patiently and with a sensitivity to the rhythms of our inner development.

We begin by calling to our mind the various roads not taken that we can reasonably believe were feasible at the time. These are the roads not taken that may still be taken in some new form in new circumstances. We list and describe these possibilities briefly. These are all based on our conscious knowledge and our intellectual appraisal of the circumstances at the time. Now we take a further step beyond what we cerebrally know to have been possible. We project intuitively and imaginatively the varieties of possibilities, even those that went beyond our immediate vision of practicality. Perhaps they were not actually available to us in the reality of our life, but our imagination projects us onto that road. Perhaps it was not a possibility at the time; perhaps in being a road not taken it was a road that could not possibly have been taken at all at that time. But it speaks to us now as a deep desire, perhaps as a symbol of some other possibility of life that we might follow. Therefore we let ourselves explore it.

We close our eyes in quietness and place ourselves out on the road of our life, specifically on each of the roads not taken. We project ourselves forward on each of the roads into the type of situations in which those pathways of experience would likely place us. We let the imagery form and present itself to us on the twilight level. We do not guide or deliberately direct the movement of this imagery. We merely place ourselves in the atmosphere of a road not taken as that now suggests itself to us. And we let the process of Twilight Imagery take it from there, shaping its script with its symbolism of person and action out of itself without our conscious guidance.

By Twilight Imagery we can move along the road of our life through and beyond the intersections. It becomes a vehicle by which we can go in more than one direction at once, exploring the possibilities both of the roads taken and of the roads not taken. We can use it to reopen crossroads that occurred in the past, and it can also guide us in making decisions in the midst of conflict or crisis at the present moment of our lives. While our conscious minds often balk at making decisions and acting upon them no matter how clearly indicated they may be, we possess a deeper-than-conscious resource that strengthens not only our understanding but our will to action. Twilight Imagery places us in contact with this resource, allowing us to experience it directly and draw upon it as a support of our actions and as a source of energy and will power.

In the context of our Journal work, many situations arise in which Twilight Imagery facilitates a difficult decision at an intersection. Using it in conjunction with the Period Log and the Dialogue sections of the

Journal, it can be very helpful in adding its dimension of knowledge of facilitating the decision-making process. A simple example concerns a young woman on the verge of dropping out of high school. She was at a crossroad with two clearly marked roads from which to choose, to continue or not to continue with her education.

On the conscious level she knew the negative consequences of dropping out of school, but for various emotional reasons she seemed determined to do so nonetheless. She was a person who was very much in protest against the advice that others gave her, even when she agreed with it. As is often the case with young people who are in a conflict of transition, she was especially in protest against the guidance of older people. The more her conscious mind perceived the reasonableness of what was being suggested to her, the more rigidly her will became set against it. It was necessary, therefore, to have a means of reaching beyond her conscious mind so that her life decisions would not be based merely on her negative reaction to friendly advisors. We needed to reach the deeper-than-conscious levels of her self, not only in such a way as to give her information and insight, but so as to engender an energy and a conviction within her that would carry through her decision by its own power. In the context of her work in Journal Dyad, Twilight Imaging provided such a vehicle.

Sitting in quietness she closed her eyes, looked inward to the twilight level, and placed herself on the road of her life. Presently she came to an intersection. One road went to the left, the other to the right. They were the alternate roads of dropping out of school or staying in.

"Go down one of the roads to see where it leads and observe what you find along the way. Then you can come back to the intersection and go up the other road. When you have seen what is on both roads, you will be able to make your decision. See if you can do this." Those were her instructions.

The young woman first took the road to the left. This was the road she preferred, the road on which she would be freed from having to go to school. She saw herself walking along that road, laughing and at ease, "having fun." She continued up the road when suddenly the scene changed. It became a street in a deteriorated part of town, and there were slum buildings on it. She saw herself in one of the apartments of these buildings. It was a dingy apartment. Apparently she had several children, small ones. She was trying to feed them, but they were noisy, crying, disobeying her, not eating, but pulling down the wet laundry she had hung out to dry in the kitchen. The scene was bedlam for she had become a young harrassed mother. She hated it.

Now she left the apartment and returned down the street. It became once again the road on which she had been walking, and it took her back to the intersection. This time she took the other road. It also became a city street, but now it was Park Avenue in New York City. She had apparently continued in school and had eventually become an interior decorator. Her office was in a fashionable store on Park Avenue. Now she herself was emerging in the image. She saw herself opening the door of her store. Elegantly dressed, she was coming out of her store.

Where was she going? "Oh yes," she said, "parked at the curb there was a limousine." She saw her chauffeur holding the door of it open for her so that she could enter and be driven to her next appointment.

With imagery like that coming spontaneously from within herself, there was no need for interpretation, nor for any discussion to help her make a decision. Its meaning was obvious to her. But the imagery did more than give her guidance. Coming from the depth of herself, it carried an *inner knowing* that was self-generated from its own private, integral source. It did not come from others but from within herself. For that reason, it could not be reacted against in the style of her old pattern of behavior. It could only be affirmed. The affirmation, we should note, was not only of a particular decision, but it was an affirmation of her existence as a person in whom decisions could naturally form themselves. The energy and resolution with which to carry it out was inherent in the decision itself. Since it came from within her depths, it was organic for her to follow through with it.

The drawing up of energy from the organic depths of our life is one of the major capacities of the Twilight Imagery process. Coming from the nonconscious levels, it is not inhibited by selfconsciousness, nor by our previous attitudes. It merely presents itself, speaking out of its own nature. It uses symbolic forms much as dreams do, but these eventually become self-disclosing. They explain themselves to us without analytical interpretation but simply by their intimate correlation with the actuality of our lives. When we are working in the depth and the continuity of our life history in the Journal process, the symbolic message which the imagery carries for our life becomes self-evident. That is why, when the young lady saw the chauffeur holding the door open to her limousine, she did not take it literally. She did not assume it was an imagery-guarantee that promised her success and affluence if she stayed in school. She understood the message of her imagery rather as a metaphoric way of being told by the depths of her psyche that life will go better for her if she takes one path than if she takes another.

In this unprepossessing way, the Twilight Imaging process gives us guidance with a conviction that enables us to do what our inner nature tells us. It is moving organically from our depths, and therefore we feel no reason not to pay heed to it. The movement of imagery is especially reflective of the potentials of our life and the possibilities of our future. It enables us to see how the future is trying to unfold. For this reason Twilight Imaging is a method that is especially helpful to us in exploring the roads not taken in our lives.

We may use it in the present moment of our life if we are at a crossroad or a crisis where a difficult decision has to be made, and especially when we require the energy and inner resolution with which to follow through in action. It provides one means of opening out an impasse in a current situation; but it can equally be used to explore the roads not taken in a past situation to see whether they have a relevance for our future as roads that we have not yet taken. In this part of our Journal experience, working with the Life History Log, Steppingstones, and Intersections, the use of Twilight Imagery provides a bridge between the Depth and the Life/Time dimensions of Journal Feedback. It expands the range of possibilities available to our life. By stretching our contact with the past and future in a fluid and symbolic way, it draws us into an intensive experience of the unity of the Now moment in which all of our life history, what is past and what is still to come, has its immediate focus.

RECONSTRUCTING OUR AUTOBIOGRAPHY

It is apparent that the Time-Stretching exercises which we carry out in the Life/Time sections of the Journal have the capacity to reach into little noticed corners of our lives. Events that have been by-passed by our memory are called back to us so that we can consider them from a new point of view. While we are moving back and forward in the Journal, we are also moving about in the past experiences and the future possibilities of our life. Our entries reflect the varieties of action and circumstance that have combined to form our individual existence up to this point in time.

As we work in the Life/Time sections, we progressively reconstruct our life histories. We do not do this all at once, but a segment at a time. We begin with the generalized outline of our life movement when we list our Steppingstones. Then we fill in the details of the past, but always with an active methodology that treats the past as part of the present and opens it toward the future.

Whether we are doing the Time-Stretching exercises at a Journal Workshop or in our own privacy, we necessarily have to focus on particular segments of our life in order to proceed. Each time-unit of our life comprises an atom of experience containing within its own context the relationships and activities of that period in our life. As we reenter these Steppingstone periods describing and exploring their contents, we reconstruct our lives one atom at a time. It would in fact be more accurate to say that our lives are reconstructing themselves as we are doing this. Progressively events fit together in a way that not only gives us an intellectual perspective but generates an energy that carries us forward and shapes our future. Working with the Time-Stretching procedures gives us a self-expanding methodology with which to draw our autobiographies together. Many persons, especially those in retirement, have used these techniques as a systematic format for recapturing and recording the story of their lives.

We begin the work of Time-Stretching by drawing ourselves into an atmosphere of stillness. Our eyes closed, we let ourselves inwardly feel the movement of our life. We try to keep our judgments and our opinions out of the way. Without commentary, we simply let the movement of our life present itself to us in whatever forms and divisions it wishes. That is how we get the basic listing of Steppingstones that gives us our framework and starting point.

Our first step is to list the Steppingstones of our life, bringing them together concisely and spontaneously. Our next step is to feed them back into the process of our inner experience. We do this by reading the list as a whole first to ourselves in silence. Then we read it aloud. If we are at a Journal Workshop, it is good to read it aloud in the presence of the group, not in order to communicate our lives to others, but to share in the feeling of movement, the *elan vital,* of our life and the lives of others. We each read the list of Steppingstones as a whole so that we can experience the inner continuity that underlies and connects the various changes and cycles of each person's life.

With the Steppingstones as our frame of reference, we begin the work of drawing ourselves deeper into the specific contents of our existence. We describe more fully each of the Steppingstones that we have listed. We do this as preparation for the expansive work of opening out the details and contents of the individual Steppingstone periods.

For this next step we return again to silence so that the process of life-recollection will be carried out in a deepened atmosphere of stillness. We sit in stillness with our Journal open to the entries we have made in the Steppingstone section. With our attention directed to a particular Steppingstone Period, we let memories come to us. These will be recollections of our past experiences, and they will also be recognitions of intersections in our life. We become progressively more aware of those earlier circumstances in which, whether by our own decisions or the pressure of events, the course of our life was drawn in one direction rather than another.

We describe these memories and awarenesses as they come to us, writing about them as fully as we can. We then return to the center, to the hinge of our experience in the Steppingstone section, and we sit in quietness again. Always we return to stillness so that our Steppingstones can provide a fresh point of departure from which we can move both back and forward in our Journal, back into the Life History Log to record a memory, and forward into Intersections to describe an experience that we recognize as a time when we were at a crossroads in our life. Thus the contents and potentials of our life become increasingly accessible to us.

We begin the Time-Stretching work by focusing on a single Steppingstone Period, but eventually we proceed to all the time-units of our life. At a Journal Workshop, we have to concentrate our attention on one period because of the limitations of time. After a workshop, however, when we are working in our privacy, we have the time and opportunity to explore all the other time-units on our list of Steppingstones. Though the task may seem to be a large one, we find that the details fill themselves in gradually and cumulatively, and that they tend to set themselves into place as though guided by a self-integrating principle.

A good way to proceed is to carry out the first basic steps of Time-Stretching for each of the Steppingstone Periods that are meaningful to you. Begin by writing a general description of the period in the Steppingstone section. Then move back into the Life History Log to record some basic memories of that time, while also going forward into Intersections to describe whatever crossroad experiences come to your mind. It is not necessary to make full and detailed entries when you are beginning to work in a particular Steppingstone Period. You need only take the first steps by making a few basic entries. The additional material will suggest itself to you as you proceed with other phases of the Journal Feedback work.

We find that, as we carry out the feedback exercises in the other sections of the Journal, our attention is called back to events of the past that would not otherwise have occurred to us. The active reentry into our lives which is stimulated by the Journal Feedback procedures draws out memories that have been covered by layers of past experience. As we proceed in our own Journal work, especially as we follow the various steps in the exercises of the dialogue and depth dimensions, forgotten contents of our lives are progressively evoked as a by-product of our Journal work. It is the Interplay procedures of Journal Feedback that make this possible and they have cumulative results in the continuity of our total Journal work.

The procedures of *Journal Interplay* begin to operate after we have worked in all the sections of the *Intensive Journal*. We have then completed one full cycle in using it and have adapted the sections and their accompanying procedures to the specific context of our individual existence. The work of active inner interrelationship among the contents of our life as carried by the Journal sections can then begin. Once we have become accustomed to its procedures, we find that the work of Journal Interplay is cumulative and that it has a multiple, cross-fertilizing effect.

The exercises that we carry out in one section of the Journal serve as a starting point and stimulant for exercises that we carry out elsewhere. In this way we find that we are progressively opening out more and more of our life history, and at the same time we are reconstructing our autobiography.

It is a self-enlarging process drawing more and more into itself as it proceeds. When, for example, we are working in the various sections of the Dialogue Dimension, we shall be dealing with the details of our relations with other persons, our work activities and the contents of physical and spiritual experiences. As we are describing these and are deepening our relationship to them, we shall also be reactivating many memories that are adjacent to them in our minds. When we move one box on the shelf of memory, we cannot help but jar the box next to it. And what is more as we do that we also jar our curiosity so that we cannot help but look into that box as well. Consequently, as we proceed with the various Journal Feedback procedures throughout our Journal work, we find that a side-effect of what we are doing plays a major role in accelerating the total work. But that is inherent in the indirect method of our process. Journal work that we do in one aspect of our life has multiple reverberating effects in other sections of the Journal and therefore in other areas of our life. Specifically, the active exercises which we shall soon begin in the Dialogue and Depth dimension of the Journal, will feed back to the Life/Time sections additional memories and awarenesses. These will become a continuous source of new factual information to be fed into the Journal Feedback process to further expand the inner perspective of our lives.

Whatever the source of this additional life-data, we enter it in the Life History Log as it comes to us. We record the entries briefly and without judgment or interpretation, especially since we do not wish to interrupt the feedback exercise in which we are engaged at the time. We make a concise entry at the moment that the memory is recalled to us. Afterwards, when we have sufficient time and opportunity we describe it as fully as it requires. We pursue its further feedback implications. In this way, working indirectly and cumulatively, we gradually draw together, while working in the various feedback exercises of the Journal, the memory data that will fill in our Steppingstone Period and provide the necessary basic information for our biographies.

The process by which we reconstruct our life histories moves in two directions. On the one hand we gather in our Life History Log the facts of memory that are recalled to us while we are working in the feedback sections. We later expand these as life-recollections and increase their contents. We use them to provide the details of each of the Stepping-stone Periods and to make us aware of intersections in our lives when we followed certain paths and left other roads not taken. This is the way we fill in the sections of the Life/Time dimension, thus recapitulating the movement of our lives.

On the other hand, as we gather the data of the Life/Time sections we are also providing ourselves with materials that will serve as starting points for the active exercises we carry out in the feedback sections. This, in fact, is a fundamental aspect of the structure of the Journal Feedback method. All the facts of memory and experience that we collect in the log sections of the Journal, and especially the data that we draw together by our entries in the Life/Time sections, serve as raw material which we extend and explore in our active Journal work. Having begun the process of recording this data, and bearing in mind that we shall continue to gather it all through our active Journal Feedback work with additional entries that are by-products of that work, we are ready now to turn to the feedback procedures themselves.

Chapter 12

Toward Inner Relationship: Dialogue with Persons

We are ready now to enter the dialogue phase of the Journal Feedback process. Having begun by recording and exploring much of the contents of our life history, we now take the next step of deepening our relationship to them and letting them speak to us. The various procedures with which we work in the dialogue sections give us a means of doing this. Taking as our empirical base the factual data of our past as we have assembled it in the Life/Time sections, we move toward a dialogue relationship with the meaningful components of our life. We shall find that it is not necessary for us to force any of the contents of our life to speak to us. As we work in our life history and learn the dialogue procedures, we provide a context in which dialogue relationships can establish themselves whenever they are ready. Thus we open an avenue for interior contact in the midst of the ongoing movement of our lives.

The work we do in the dialogue sections of the Journal combines the specific dialogue procedures with all the additional techniques that are available to us from the other dimensions of experiential feedback. Together they have a cumulative effect, activating potentials and crystallizing decisions at a level that bypasses psychological analysis. The momentum and continuity of the Journal Feedback process evokes an awareness of inner direction that is deeper than conscious, and this is articulated in the dialogue scripts as the work proceeds. Rereading our dialogue scripts, it is not uncommon to find that information that is significantly new to us has been stated in them or to recognize that attitudes of long standing have been transformed in them—and in our own handwriting. These cumulative results do not arise of themselves, however, but are the outcome of a definite sequence of procedures in our use of the various dialogue sections. It is important that we follow these carefully and that we prepare for our dialogue work by establishing a deep enough base in each of the areas where we use it. Then we can reap the benefit of the cumulative feedback effect.

As part of this preparation we should recognize that the term, "dialogue," has several levels of meaning in the context of the *Intensive Journal*. Its most obvious reference is to the specific technique of the *dialogue script* in which we write a dialogue in our Journal; or, more accurately stated, we make it possible for a dialogue to be written. Underlying these written dialogues, however, is the more fundamental sense of dialogue not as a technique but as a *way of relationship*. The dialogue relationship is a mutual meeting of persons, each accepting, speaking to, and most important, listening to the other. This is the I-Thou relationship of which Martin Buber spoke. It is the deeper, more satisfying aspect of relationship between persons in society.

Beyond such outer dialogue, there is the further step of inner dialogue within a person's life. This involves the inner relationship between the separate aspects of an individual's life. Often the various aspects of a person's life proceed as though they were out of contact with one another. In the colloquial phrase, it is as though the left hand does not know what the right hand is doing. One of the important functions of the *Intensive Journal* as an integrative instrument is that it provides a unifying field and numerous techniques by which the diverse aspects of a person's life can be brought into relation to one another. This is the condition of wholeness, the integral relation of the parts to the whole of the life. It is a quality of *inner relationship* that enables the varied facets of an individual existence to change and move and develop in relation to each other. It is, in fact, a multiple dialogue taking place within the unfoldment of a life.

This is the broadest sense in which the term "Dialogue" may be used. As a major goal of our work, it refers to the encompassing dialogue which we seek to establish between our inner self and the whole unfolding movement of our life. This is an ongoing dialogue which we seek to maintain through all our daily experiences. As we become attuned to it, it enables us to deal with our immediate and pressing problems in a large and open-ended context. It becomes an intimate inner communication carried on continuously in a variety of forms between our conscious self and the nonconscious mini-processes of our individual unfoldment.

As we turn now to work in the dialogue sections of the Journal, we are beginning the large process of establishing an inner relationship with all the significant areas of our lives. We shall do this a step at a time, first drawing upon the facts of our life history as we have described them in our entries in the Life/Time sections, and then proceeding with the additional entries we make on a current basis as we continue with our daily use of the Journal. We draw upon our past experiences and upon our unfolding present for the life material that we feed into our dialogue process. We take the facts of our life experience as our starting point, and by means of the exercises of our Journal work, we reenter those experiences so that from various vantage points they can speak to us and guide us with respect to the future conduct of our life. Section by Journal section we shall establish a working relationship with each of the aspects of our life as we carry out the basic dialogue exercises and as we learn the procedures for continuing them. We begin this active work of Journal Feedback by turning to the section *Dialogue with Persons*.

This is the aspect of our Journal work in which we focus our attention upon our relationships with other people. We do not do this in order to analyze our interpersonal relationships, but to open them and to draw forth what is potential in them. We are already familiar with the external aspect of our relationships, but our dialogue exercises enable us to reenter them from an interior point of view. This places us on the inside of the life situations in our life so that we can help them open out from within, as a bud unfolds. Thus we establish an inner relationship to the people who are significant in our life as we work in *Dialogue with Persons*.

As we proceed in our Journal work, the persons with whom it is meaningful and necessary for us to carry out dialogue exercises will be indicated to us by the events and circumstances that arise in our life. As we start our dialogue work, however, it may be difficult for us to decide who should be given priority. Who are the persons with whom it would be most beneficial for us to meet in dialogue? Who should come first? The primary criterion as to the persons whom we choose for our dialogue exercises is that they be individuals whose existence, as well as actions, has an important bearing on our life *as we experience it from an interior point of view.* Our relation to them may be one in which we are actively engaged in the present, or one that took place in the past. It may have been a relationship that was difficult and brought problems into our life, or one that was pleasant and fulfilling.

The main factor to consider is not whether there is a problem involved in the relationship, but whether we feel that the relationship itself plays a role of inner importance in our life. The measure for this is altogether subjective, but it is definite enough. We know by the strength of our feelings, by our intuitive and emotional perceptions, whether our relation to a particular individual has an inner importance for our life. Especially we know by the magnetic way that we are drawn into the relationship, and by the degree to which we find ourselves thinking about the other person, either with pleasure or anxiety, when we want our mind to be on other things.

Whatever our opinion of that person, whether we love them or like them or merely respect them or do not like or respect them at all, our nonconscious feelings make it clear that their existence matters to us, inwardly if not outwardly. Our emotions give us criterion enough to judge their inner importance for our life. Mostly these relationships are with people who are close to us in our life, parents, children, brothers and sisters, husband and wife, or close, longtime friends. It may also happen, however, that a particular relationship feels important to us when our only basis for that feeling is a hunch or an intuition. Very little may have transpired in the relationship up to that point, but we sense that something of value is present as a potentiality. This may be the case with someone whom we have newly met, or it may, at the opposite extreme, apply to an older relative, as an uncle or a grandparent, or a teacher with whom we have had only a passing contact in the past. Although those relationships may have remained largely unlived, our intuition tells us that if it were possible to extend the contact, to do so would be meaningful. One of the important uses of Dialogue with Persons is to enable us to experience the inner possibilities of relationships which, like these, have remained unexplored because of the outer circumstances of our lives.

What do we mean when we say that a person has an *inner importance* for our lives? It may or may not include actual time that we have spent or will spend with them on the external level of life. But it does mean that we feel that that person has an internal significance for us with respect to aspects of our lives that are still seeking to unfold. That person whom we meet externally represents to us something that is still to come to fruition within ourselves. Therefore, he or she awakens intimations of greater meaning in our life and we are drawn to them.

Relationships that are based on direct and intuitive attractions may easily be analyzed away in terms of *projection,* or *transference,* or some other interpretive category. Those analyses are correct as far as they go; but it is important for us to recognize that when a person is drawn to another by a strong attractive force, the seed of the person is reaching out to a new avenue of experience. Beyond the analytical factors which are obviously there, the relationship contains possibilities which his growth requires him to explore. The attraction which he feels expresses his intimation of the fact that the person to whom he is drawn embodies an aspect of his life experience which his future growth requires in some form.

Whether it is to be an harmonious relationship or one that will eventually be painful, we feel drawn to add this further experience to our existence. There is an inner urge in this that reaches beyond pleasure or pain, and beyond prudence or folly. It is the direct sensing that this new experience is in some to-be-discovered way an integral part of our unfolding life. We know that we shall have to live it regardless of consequences. Using the exercises of Dialogue with Persons, however, we can enter into such relationships within the context of the Journal so that, without analyzing them away, we can explore their possibilities and at least prepare ourselves for what life has in store while determining whether we actually wish to take the plunge.

Probably the largest proportion of relationships that have an inner importance for an individual's life are those between persons who are in close and constant contact, especially where the relationship has an objective as well as an emotional content. This is the case between parent and child, between siblings, or between relatives within a larger family unit as uncles and cousins. It is also true for persons who have had a close friendship over a long period of time, especially where the roots of the friendship reach back into the adolescent period of development. In such extended relationships between persons, the closeness of the repeated contact—the frictions as well as the harmonies—give the relationship an inherent and unavoidable importance in the individual's life. It becomes an integral part of the house of one's existence, like the walls and the windows. They may not be large in relation to the whole, but if they are allowed to fall into disrepair, rainwater will leak into the whole building.

Relationships of this kind have an inner importance in a person's life and must be given serious consideration. Whichever way we act toward them, whether affirmatively or negatively, they will have a large emotional impact upon us. This, in fact, is the primary criterion for the inner importance of any of the contents of our lives. Because of their integral position, they have an impact upon us whether we say yea or nay to them.

In every individual's life there is a wide range of personal relationships that have this quality. They have their greatest intensity when they are actively being experienced as current relationships, since that is when the intensity of the emotions is felt with the greatest immediacy. But when one person's relation to another has an inner and emotional importance to him through having become imbedded in his life experience, its psychic force as an inner relationship remains strong even after many years. We thus find that the personal relationships which call themselves forth to be explored and extended in the section *Dialogue with Persons* are often relationships that reach back into our past, and are not in the forefront of the current involvements of which we are aware. The persons who become the subjects of the most fruitful exercises in this section are often individuals whom we have not seen in many years.

Quite often, also, they are persons who are deceased, and that fact places no limitation on the importance and the vitality of our inner relation to them.

Persons who have been an integral part of our inner life retain that importance whether or not we were fully aware of their meaning to us at the time of our close contact with them. Often we find that such relationships have opened a possibility within us, but that their promise has not been fulfilled in the course of our lives. Consequently we all carry around within ourselves the traces of relationships that have unfulfilled potentialities.

In the motion picture, *I Never Sang for My Father*, there is a line that expresses the essence of the work that is done in Dialogue with Persons in this regard. At the point in the story where his father dies, the main character says, "Death ends a life, but it does not end a relationship." The implication of this, which we experience as a fact in our Journal Feedback work, is that relationships between persons have a life of their own. They carry potentialities which press us from within until, either inwardly or outwardly, they are resolved or fulfilled or completed. The fact of relationship is its own reality.

We begin our work in the section, Dialogue with Persons, by drawing together a list of those individuals with whom we feel our relationship, past, present, or future, warrants further exploration. There are two primary criteria for those whose names we place on this list. They are, in the first place, persons with whom we feel a connection of inner importance in our lives. And, in the second place, they are persons with whom we feel our relationship has some further step of development or clarification that needs to be taken. Our Journal exercises make it possible to take that next step and to explore the future possibilities and implications of the relationship.

Relationships of inner importance to an individual's life are often elusive and difficult to define, but we feel their emotional pull and their meaning to us in a way that is more than casual. Such relationships should have an opportunity to move forward and to unfold their possibilities in our lives. That is what our dialogue exercises make possible. Since we are primarily interested in the potentialities for meaning that lie in a relationship, the question of whether it has been pleasant and satisfying, or has been tense and difficult, is beside the point. Whatever it has been, there is something else that it can become. Our primary criterion in choosing the persons for the dialogue exercise is our feeling that there is something potential in our relationship greater than what the relationship has so far produced. Of even greater consequence is the possibility that whatever has been inadequate or conflicted in the relationship in the past, will be resolved and drawn toward its next step when we work with it on the dialogue dimension.

We now compile our list of persons with whom we feel it will be meaningful to carry out the dialogue exercises. At Journal Workshops we make it a practice to draw together a full list of such individuals. At the workshop itself we usually carry out the dialogue exercises only with respect to one or two of them, but we extend the list to six or eight or ten persons. By listing them, we have their names before us for future reference so that we can carry out the dialogue exercises with them at a later time when we are working with the Journal by ourselves after the workshop is over.

The persons we place on our list may come from various corners of time. They may be persons with whom we are currently involved in the present activities of our lives. They may also be persons with whom we have been involved in the past but with whom we are no longer in contact. They may be persons who have in the past been important or meaningful in our lives, but whom we have not seen in many years. This category of persons may include both those who are living and those not living. What is central for us is the possibility of establishing a dialogue relationship by means of the Journal exercises, in which the reality of the relationship is not limited by the physical fact of death.

It is helpful while we are drawing up this list of persons to refresh our minds by going back over the entries we have already made in the Journal. When we were working with our Steppingstones, we were already laying the foundation for this feedback exercise. As we elaborated the Steppingstone Periods of our past, we made special note of those individuals who played a meaningful role in our lives at that time, and now we can draw upon those entries in preparation for our Dialogue with Persons.

Some of those individuals whom we recalled in describing our

Steppingstone periods may no longer seem to be significant to us. We may feel that, at this point in our lives, it would not be fruitful to enter into Journal dialogue with them. Others, on the other hand, who were important to us in the past and have been absent from our lives since then, may have left a seed of meaning in our experience which we now wish to nurture and explore. These are persons with whom it will be valuable to do the dialogue exercise. In addition, there may be others who were important to us in the past but who are now not living, and whose passing left the potentials of a relationship unfulfilled. On the dimension of dialogue, that relationship may still be pursued.

For the persons who have an inner importance in our life at the present time, we draw upon the entries we have made in the Period Log and Daily Log. For the persons from the past, living and not living, who hold the potentials of an inner relationship with us that may now be carried to a further point of development, we draw upon the entries we have made in the various Steppingstone Periods.

With these resources from our earlier work in the Journal to draw upon, we sit in quietness to prepare for our dialogue experience. We go back over the panorama of our lives, by means of memory and by reviewing the entries we have written in our Journal, to fill out our list of potential persons for future dialogue. We shall have three categories on this list, present relationships, past relationships, and persons who are not now living. This list may be as long or as short as we wish it to be. It need not be exhaustive. We can always add to it. In fact, as we continue to work in the Journal Feedback process, our life experiences will themselves add persons to our list of dialogue relationships.

Now we are working in our silence and in our privacy. When our list is ready, we shall choose for our first exercise a person from the list either from the past or the present, either living or not living. Eventually, as we continue in our Journal experience, we shall enter into dialogue with several of the persons on our list, but let us choose as our first subject a person whom we spontaneously feel to be of current significance in our lives. This may be a person whom we have not seen in many years, or a person who is not living. The current relevance of that person does not depend on the time when they were actually part of our lives, but rather on the quality of that person and the nature of the relationship between us. For our first dialogue let us choose a person with whom we feel it would be desirable and valuable, even in some cases urgent, to make contact.

When we have decided upon the person with whom we will conduct our dialogue, from whichever category we have chosen them, we begin by sitting in stillness. We are nurturing a quiet readiness for the inward speech of the dialogue experience. We write the name of the person we have chosen at the head of a fresh page. Now we are concentrating on that person and our attention is focused on the relationship between us as we perceive it. We let ourselves consider the situation in a general way, not thinking of the details, but feeling its tone and quality. Now we write a brief and direct statement describing the essence of the whole relationship. We want to make this a forthright and spontaneous statement that sets forth without embellishment just where things are, how the situation is at its core, between the other person and ourselves.

This statement should be direct and written with a minimum of conscious deliberation. It should reflect our thoughts but also, and more importantly, our feelings. It should be brief, perhaps two or three or four paragraphs, but it should contain the heart of the matter. It should indicate, though without the details, what is affirmative and negative in the relationship, what is satisfying and frustrating, what has been freely expressed and hidden. If possible, it should also indicate the movement of the relationship. The various phases through which the relationship has passed should be mentioned to show how it has arrived at the present situation. We should freely state where things are now between us, even including some hopes and possibilities as well as anxieties and misgivings.

We describe the relationship *where it is now* even if the person in question is someone whom we have not seen in many years, or if it is a person who has died. Our statement places the situation where it is now. We are presenting the factuality of the present moment as objectively as we can, including in that statement our own subjective feelings and the subjective feelings of the other person as far as we know them. We state it all briefly and in a neutral way, making no judgment. Here it is. This is how the situation and the relationship between us reflects itself when I hold a mirror up to it. Our statement will be such a mirror if we write it spontaneously. It will reflect the essence of just what is seen through our eyes at the moment when we write it. Then it can serve as a base and starting point from which our dialogue can proceed.

Write your statement now, briefly and directly. Remember that it is not to be an exhaustive essay, and it is not to be interpretive. It is to state the heart of the matter concisely. Literary flourishes are not necessary. In fact, it is usually better to avoid them since they may divert you from your primary purpose.

Remember to mark down the date on which you are writing your statement. That can become a very important piece of information, as it may be very meaningful to you at a later time.

When you have finished writing your statement, read it to yourself. As you do so, you may feel that you wish to make some changes in it. That is good to do, but do not make the changes by editing what you have written. Let the original stand, but make your changes as additions to what you have written. In that way you will preserve the record of your spontaneous feelings and perceptions, and you will also give yourself a valuable reference point for further feedback experiences.

Writing the statement of *where it is* in our relationship and reading it back to ourselves begins to carry us into the atmosphere where the dialogue can take place. This preliminary feedback enables us to make any additions that we feel to be necessary in order to give a truer picture of the situation. More important, it enables us to make whatever adjustments we find to be necessary within ourselves. To make these inner adjustments is an essential part of the preparation for the dialogue exercises. We have to recognize the fact, however, that when we write a spontaneous and uncensored description of our subjective feelings, we are taking ourselves into an area of our inner self that may be strange country to us in which we may feel both unfamiliar and uncomfortable.

The fact is that when we write our statement of the situation, our statement of the actuality of our relationship as objectively as we can see it, we have given tangible embodiment to subjective feelings that may be very delicate. We may be very sensitive about them, much more sensitive than we have realized. It may be that we have been guarding them privately for a long time, even hiding them from ourselves. When for the first time we let ourselves give written expression to emotions which we have been concealing both from ourselves and from others, why should we not expect to feel deeply moved, perhaps shaken, unsettled and even disturbed to some degree?

These emotions are an integral part of the process in which we are working, the process of loosening the soil of our inner lives. Having stirred them, we must now recognize them, give them space and time to be felt, and then record them as part of our Journal Feedback work. As we read the statement back to ourselves we take note of whatever feelings now arise in us. It may be that we were quiet and objective when we wrote our description, but that strong emotions stir in us as we read it. Or it may be that our emotions were churning as we wrote it, and that we are calm now as we read it back to ourselves. Many combinations are possible. Whatever our experience, we accept it. We leave room for it to move through its full cycle. We observe our subjective responses, and we record them as objectively as we can. In this way, we *feed into* the Journal the raw, empirical data of our inner experience, cumulatively gathering it so that it can feed itself back to us at progressive levels of reintegration as we proceed with the Journal Feedback process.

We come now to a very important step in our dialogue work. Our goal is to establish a deep quality of dialogue so that we can open out the full possibilities and implications of our relationship. To do that, we cannot let ourselves fall back into the old patterns of communication—or non-communication—that have characterized the relationship in the past. We wish to reach a level that we have not reached before, not the superficiality of old conversations that have skirted the issues, and not the repetitious arguments that carry so many relationships in angry circles. We want to get beyond the outer mask to the inner person so that we can speak from an authentic depth in ourselves to the deep core of being in the other. To paraphrase the words of the Prophet, when depth speaks to depth between persons, that is dialogue. The question is, how can we make it possible for dialogue *truly* to take place in the actuality of our experience?

Our first step is to reach through beyond the accustomed patterns of our relationship to the essence of the other person as he is living his life. We do this by placing ourselves inside the actuality of his life as though we were participating in it from within. Once we feel the other person's life from the inside, we can be aware of what it is secretly seeking to become. Then we can enter into deep dialogue with that person.

To achieve an inner perspective of our own personhood in an earlier exercise, we listed the Steppingstones of our life. Now, to reach a comparable interior view of the person with whom we wish to establish a dialogue relationship, we shall list their Steppingstones as we did our own.

To do this, we begin by sitting in quietness and letting ourselves feel the movement of their life as much as we know of it. We may not be familiar with all the details of the other person's life, but it is the outline of the main direction that is of primary importance to us. We place ourselves within their life and we reconstruct the movement of their life just as we did our own. As we did for ourselves, we record their Steppingstones in the first person. The first Steppingstone for them, as for us, begins with the phrase, "I was born." And then. And then...

We let the list form itself, and we record it under the statement of the situation that we have written in preparing for the dialogue.

Just as we did for ourselves, we list about a dozen Steppingstones for the other person. When we listed the Steppingstones for our own life, the most important factors were the subjectivity of our intimate memories. The spontaneity with which we drew the list together, and especially our inner knowledge of the events by which our life has unfolded so far. It is probably not possible for one person to have a full intimate knowledge of the contents of another person's life, no matter how closely related they have been. But it is possible for us to feel an empathy for the hopes and the frustrations, the successes and the emotions, the times of wondering and fearing and summoning up courage. To do this we let ourselves sit in stillness and gradually feel ourselves to be present within that other person's life. In the old phrase, we are walking in the other Indian's moccasins. We are walking with their feet over the road their life has taken. Thus we write on their behalf, "I was born." And then we recapitulate the next important event in their life that we know of, and the next, and the next until we come to the present time.

You will probably find that in reconstructing another person's life it is more difficult to limit the number of Steppingstones to a dozen. That is because the factors of selectivity and spontaneity are less effective here. Do not let this become an obstacle to you. If you find yourself listing a large number of events or marking points in the other person's life, as many as twenty or thirty, do not restrict yourself. List as many as suggest themselves to you, and as are helpful in drawing you into the movement of that other life. List them briefly and simply. A word or a phrase will suffice, just as when you drew up the list of your own Steppingstones. It is the thread of continuity in the movement of the life that is important here, not the details. At a later time, if you wish, you can describe the details of those Steppingstone periods in the other person's life with which you are familiar. That will be a further step in building your dialogue relationship.

When we have completed our list of the Steppingstones of the other person's life, we settle back into quietness. We close our eyes. We breathe slowly, softly, maintaining a gentle and regular rhythm. Our eyes are closed, and we are looking inward. Our consciousness is directed toward the person of whom we have written. Now we are letting images come to us. These may be images that we see on the screen before our mind's eye; they may be sounds or words that we hear spoken; they may be memories that are brought back to us, body feelings, emotions, or intuitions, that come to us when our eyes are closed in stillness and when our awareness is turned inward and moving around this particular person.

For some minutes we give ourselves over to this spontaneous movement of Twilight Imagery, letting the images take their own form and carry themselves by their own momentum. The immediate focus of the images is the person and the relationship of our exercise, but we do not suggest the content of the images nor guide their movement. We let them direct their own movement and take themselves where they will. As we observe them proceeding within us, whether visually, by sound, or in whatever sensory form, we perceive them inwardly. We behold and record them. We then add our perception of the movement of Twilight Imagery to the listing of the other person's Steppingstones and to the statement that we have written describing *where it is* in our relationship. We began with a statement describing our conscious attitude; we then brought together facts of which we are aware in a more general way; and now we have added perceptions that have come to us from the nonconscious depths of ourselves.

We write these imagery perceptions in the Journal, but we do not let ourselves leave the twilight atmosphere in which they came to us. We remain in that deep and quiet place. We feel the movement of the images in their twilight atmosphere. We feel the soft quality of the inner space in which they, and we, are present.

Now, within that atmosphere and with that quality of feeling, we let ourselves feel the presence of the other person. We may see the image of them before our eyes. We may feel them as being present, though they are not seen. We may feel them as being within us, or as being present in our imagination. In whatever form it takes, we focus our attention toward them, and we become quiet with them. The two of us are alone in our inward place.

As we are together now in our silence, we feel the movement of our life; and especially we feel the movement of the other person's life. In the twilight atmosphere of our imagery we feel the wholeness of life, and the fullness of time in its ongoingness. We place ourselves again within the other person's Steppingstones as we listed them, and we experience the inner continuity of their life history, what their life has been seeking, what it has found, and what it has not been able to find. And we feel again the inner movement of our own life history. We feel the flow of Life/Time as it moves in all of us. Specifically, we feel it moving through the other person, and we feel it moving through ourselves. It carries the person within the process of our lives. It carries the inner person of each of us.

We perceive that inner person and we feel its presence in the soft quietness of the twilight level. We feel that inner person carried on the flow of Life/Time. We feel it in the past and moving toward the future. And especially we are with it in the *place between*, in the Now moment between the past and the future. This *place between* is an open moment in time. It is where the process of a life is fluidly moving, moving out of the conditioning of its past and into a future that is not yet formed. This open moment in our lives is the free space for our inner process. It is the space where the *person within the process* of our lives has its opportunity to give a new shape to our existence. This is therefore the place and the open moment where we can meet with the person within the process of the other's life. In this open moment, the person within them and the person within us can meet and speak with one another without the burdens and without the restrictions either of the past or the future. We meet as we are in our naked being, as we are at the depth of the unfolding process of our lives. There we speak to one another in a totally unconditioned way.

We are in our silence now, feeling the presence of the other person, and letting the dialogue get under way. We speak to them. We greet them. Perhaps we refer to something that was in the statement we have already written. Perhaps we open an altogether new line of discussion. However it happens, without conscious or deliberate thought, we say what comes to us to be said; whatever that is, we write it in our Journal.

As we write, our inner attention is directed to the other person. We feel their presence, and thus they speak to us. Perhaps we inwardly hear their voice in the silence: perhaps they speak to us via our pen. However it takes place, we let it all be written, whatever is spoken by each of us. We speak and we listen. The other speaks, and we record it as it comes to us. A *dialogue script* is forming itself.

As we proceed with it, we find that the dialogue writes itself. We may begin by thinking about what is being written, but increasingly we realize that the dialogue is merely using our pen as its vehicle. We freely allow it to do that. We let our pen become the means by which speech takes place between the person within ourselves and the person within the other. We do not guide it. We do not create the dialogue script. We do not think about it and deliberately write it. We let it come forth of itself. And we let it continue to move along its own path wherever it wishes to go. Even when it says things that do not seem to be rational, things with which our conscious mind does not agree, we let it continue. We trust the dialogue script to find its own way and to bring us unpredictable awarenesses.

That is the general approach we follow in enabling the dialogue scripts to be written. With practice they will come more fluidly and will take us more quickly to deep levels of experience. As we work in other dialogue sections of the Journal and become more accustomed to the Journal Feedback process as a whole, many nuances of dialogue will become apparent to us and it will become an increasingly effective technique for us. But the basic steps in the exercise as they have been outlined here are sufficient if we follow them and practice them. Let us at this point, therefore, pause in our reading, go back over the steps of preparing for dialogue, and let a dialogue script be written with the person we have chosen.

After we have written our dialogue script we return to stillness. We let ourselves become aware of the emotions we felt while the dialogue was being written. Whatever these were, we record them now as an addition to the dialogue. We make no judgment and no interpretation of them, but we describe as objectively as we can the subjective feelings that accompanied our dialogue exercise from the time that we began it by choosing the person for the dialogue and writing our statement of the situation through our writing of the dialogue script itself. To record this interior movement is an important part of our work.

When we have rested from this, we begin to read the dialogue script back to ourselves. We do this in silence, taking note of the emotions that arise in us as we read it. Are they different from the emotions we felt when it was being written? We record our observations.

Having experienced the feedback effect of reading the dialogue in silence, we may now wish to take the further step of reading it aloud, and especially of hearing ourselves read it.

If you are at a Journal Workshop, especially if you are participating in an ongoing Journal group, you will have an opportunity to read it in the presence of others. But you may not wish to. It may be that the material contained in your dialogue is of too confidential a nature, or that you feel the need to keep this part of your life within your own privacy. In that case, you have two paths open to you. One is to read the dialogue aloud to yourself when you are in your own privacy. Another is to read it into a cassette recorder, and then to play it back to yourself. The latter method has the double advantage of enabling you both to read it aloud and to hear it read, and these are valuable aspects of Journal Feedback. Whether you use the cassette or not, it is important to observe the emotions that arise in you as you are reading the dialogue and hearing it read. All this should be added to the continuity of your Journal entry.

As a matter of practice, the best procedure seems to be to use the set of dialogue exercises which we have now carried through as the base of a sub-section in this part of the Journal. Here we can build and maintain an ongoing relationship with the person who was the subject of our dialogue script. We have laid the foundation for a deepening ongoing relationship by the work we have already done. Our statement of the situation between us, our recapitulation of the Steppingstones of their life, our Twilight Imaging about them, and especially our writing the dialogue script are all steps in our establishing a dialogue relationship that will be strengthened and extended by experiences both within the *Intensive Journal* and by our further external meetings in life.

Let us consider some examples and possibilities of how we can continue to work with such sub-sections within Dialogue with Persons after our basic workshop experience. At the beginning of the exercise we listed persons in three categories who have an inner importance in our lives and are meaningful for our dialogue work. These are: persons with whom we are presently engaged in an active relationship of some kind; persons who have played a role in our lives in the past but with whom we are not now in contact; and thirdly, persons who have been significant in our lives but who are no longer living. How would we work with each of these in extending our dialogue relationship after the workshop?

If our dialogue is with a person who is part of our current experience, the possibility is good that we will soon have contact with them in actuality. If the relationship in which we were working is with our parents, or our children, our husband or wife, or a close friend we shall very possibly be seeing them or speaking with them when the workshop is over. Whatever transpires at that time should be recorded in a Journal entry, directly following our dialogue experience. We would ordinarily record experiences of this kind in the Daily Log section, for that is where we describe the events that comprise the ongoing movement of our life. Now, however, we record it directly in the sub-section of Dialogue with Persons in order to focus on our relationship with that particular individual.

In this sub-section we record the full range of contacts that we have with them, both outer and inner contacts. After the workshop, for example, we meet them again and perhaps we lapse into the type of circular uncommunicating conversation that had been customary in the past. We are still dissatisfied with them, but now we are aware of additional possibilities. We enter in the Journal a description of our meeting and our conversation, and we add to it a statement of the feelings and thoughts that arise in us with respect to it. Perhaps also as time passes during the next few days, we find ourselves thinking further about that person and the nature of our relationship. These thoughts should also be entered in the sub-section.

When enough time has passed after the workshop to give you distance from the dialogue script, it is good to read it again. You may perceive it in another perspective now. As you reread the script, the atmosphere in which you wrote it will reestablish itself. You may find yourself back in the dialogue, feeling the other person to be present as at the workshop. Now the dialogue script can pick up where it left off before. It may continue the line of discussion that was followed in the original dialogue, or it may proceed in another direction and open a new subject matter. In either case, let the dialogue script be free to move as it wishes, extending itself out of its own atmosphere and momentum without your censorship or conscious direction. Let it continue in this way as much as it wishes, and then be free to stop. You can always pick it up again and let it continue when it is ready to move further out of itself. Make sure, however, that you remember to record the date of each of these entries and dialogues so that you can reconstruct the continuity of your experiences when you read them back at a later time.

If we maintain a separate sub-section within the Dialogue with Persons section, we soon find that a full picture of a relationship-in-motion has begun to take shape. This is particularly true if the individual is one with whom we are currently in contact. Then, in addition to the basic steps of preparation for the dialogue script and the recurrent additions to the script, we make a number of other types of entries, all of which are gathered together in the sub-section. We make the entries regarding current meetings, conversations, and events involving that other person. We record also the stream of our thought and feelings and the variations in our emotions with respect to them. Sometimes, when we let our thoughts go free as we record them it does not take the form of a dialogue but is more of a Journal soliloquy. Such monologues often carry the movement of our thoughts in a very effective way, and thus the work we do with them within the Journal helps us deepen the level of the relationship.

All of these entries, exercises, inner experiences, and outer events which we record in the subsections of Dialogue with Persons contribute to the dialogue relationship as a whole. It is this that we are seeking to develop with our work in the dialogue sections of the Journal. It is not merely the dialogue scripts that are important, but all the forms of our contact with the other person, inner and outer. As we record these in all their variety, and as we work with them by means of the various Journal exercises, our inner connection to the other individual deepens and strengthens. This is the dialogue relationship. We fill it in with the flesh and blood of daily reality as we work with it in the continuity of our Journal entries and exercises. Working progressively in the interior dimension of our actual life, we may establish deep dialogue relationships not only with those persons who are actively present in our current life, but also those who belong to our past but who are kept alive by our inner experience of them. In Dialogue with Persons and its sub-sections we work in manifold, ongoing ways to deepen our dialogue relationships with those persons who play or have played a meaningful role in our life.

Chapter 13

Dialogue with Works

As our work in the Journal proceeds, a pattern of back-and-forth movement becomes apparent. Sometimes we begin at the surface of our life, starting with external events and taking them inward to explore and enlarge them. At other times we begin with our interior experiences which are indefinite and elusive as images and ideas, and we carry them outward in order to give them form and expression. We are constantly engaged in an inner-outer movement, working in the actualities of our lives and then moving to the depth levels for imagination and inner awareness. We go from one opposite to the other. Thus we gradually bring our lives into balance, filling in the empty spaces of potentiality.

This dialectical movement expresses an underlying principle in human development, and it is especially important for the person who is actively involved in creativity. Our growth as persons is an inner process. It proceeds from within us as the seed-potentials of our life unfold and seek to realize themselves; but it can barely proceed at all if it does not possess a specific and tangible task, an artwork, to serve as its external point of focus. The movement of energies, both physical and psychic, comes from within. An outer work, however, is necessary in order to activate it, to stimulate it, to draw it forth, and give it direction.

In this respect, the life of the artist provides a prototype by which we can recognize the necessary movement of energies in an individual's life. The artist is a person who directs his energies toward an outer work with the goal of carrying that work to a significant level of fulfillment. The interesting fact is that, as long as the artist is able to work well in relation to the outer object of his work, he feels harmonious with it and continues to grow inwardly. When his relation to his artwork breaks down, however, his interior life also falls into disorder. That is why there is a profound significance in Otto Rank's description of the "neurotic" person as an artist who has been blocked and frustrated in carrying through his artwork. Our ultimate artwork is our life itself, but it helps a great deal if we have a good relationship with the specific works in which we are engaged. A major goal of the exercises we carry through in the *Dialogue with Works* section is to enable us to maintain a strong inner relationship with the varied outer works that are meaningful to us in the context of our lives as a whole. In this way we may hope to become in the largest sense of the term, artists-in-life.

Dialogue with Works is the section in which we apply the Journal Feedback procedures to those activities in our lives in which our energies are directed outward toward specific projects and goals.

The conception of *works* has a special meaning in the context of the *Intensive Journal*. It does not refer merely to a job that you have to do, nor to a task that is placed as a burden upon you. Having a *work* implies a strong and warm caring, a special interest and concern. It means to be engaged in an activity which you value as something meaningful and valuable in your life, and which you are seeking to enlarge and to strengthen.

A work is a specific project that emerges as an outer activity drawn from an inner source in a person's life. It takes a definite external form, but its meaning and direction come from within the person. It also draws its main energy and inspiration from inner personal sources while serving in a balancing way as the continuing outer focus for the person's activities. In this sense, a work begins in the depth of a human being. It begins as an idea, a hunch, and especially as an urge to bring something new into existence. The basis for a work is always a deep desire, not in the sense of an egoistic or sensual desire, but in the sense of a desire to create something and to bring it to fruition. To have a work is firstly, to have a feeling or a vision of possibilities that may be brought to fulfillment; secondly, to devote oneself to bringing those possibilities into actuality in a way that is as authentic for the work and as satisfying for oneself as may be possible.

The process of growth in a human being, the process out of which a *person* emerges, is essentially an inward process. It involves an inner balancing, an integration, a strengthening of inward capacities, and an unfolding of the Self. As we observe the process of unfoldment in a person, however, we recognize that it is not altogether inward. It begins within the person, as the growth of a tree begins in its seed, but then it moves outward. The inward process of growth moves in an external direction in order to fulfill itself. It does this because it needs to be embodied in a tangible content in order to fulfill itself in the actuality of life.

The artist cannot simply be an artist in the abstract. He has to have a field of work in which he can do his art, be it music or sculpture or drama or architecture or science, or the practice of medicine or politics, whatever it may be. He needs to have a field of art, and he needs to have specific works of art in which he can place the image of himself as a specific type of artist. In doing this, it becomes possible for his image to take form in his life, and for him to grow as a person.

The process moves first from within outward, from the seed-image of the artist to external works. But, as this is taking place, we find that the opposite is also happening. We see also that this second step is taking place simultaneously with the first. As the artist is giving form to his artwork externally, something is also taking form within him. The image of himself as a special type of artist is taking shape in the form of a person. In that sense we can say that, since the person who is doing the work acquires fuller form and strength in the course of completing his artwork, it is the person himself who is the ultimate artwork of the creative process of life.

We perceive in this also that the process of growth in a human being proceeds by a multiplicity of effects. In order to grow within himself, an individual needs to conceive and carry out works outside of himself.

These outer works thus derive their motive power from a source that is within the person; but the person draws the strength for his future growth from the very process by which he completes his work in a satisfying way. The work and the person, the artwork and the artist, in every field of activity, are thus in a mutually creative relation to each other. Each requires the other. Each has something to give to the other. Each has something to communicate to the other. The relation between a person and his work is thus a living expression of dialogue.

The format and exercises of the section, *Dialogue with Works*, are specifically designed to assist the mutuality of dialogue that is inherent in this relationship. Our goal is to enable each individual to focus more clearly on the works that are possible in his life, and to give him tangible means of fulfilling them in a way that will extend the inner process of his growth as a person.

As we follow the inner relationship between a person and his work, we observe two main phases of energy movement. The first is an inward movement of energy that activates the image within the person on which the work will be based. This provides the inner vision that sees the possibility and sets the goal. The second phase of movement is outward, and it extends over a longer period of time. This is the continuing process of focused activity by which the seed of possibility that is present at the outset of the work is nurtured through the cycles of its growth, and is progressively brought to fruition in the form that is most appropriate for it.

In this second phase, the phase of *doing the work*, there is an implicit criterion guiding the work, drawing it onward, and setting the standards for its goal. This criterion is the original image, and it calls for fulfilling the inner possibility of the work, to make the work as effective, as esthetic, as satisfying, and especially, as *whole unto its inherent nature*, as can be.

In this sense, what we are speaking of as a work might indeed more accurately be described as an *art*work, since it involves not merely physical work but work that measures itself by a standard of inner excellence. This is the essence of art. We would, however, prefer to avoid the impression that we are dealing with works that are primarily in fields that are usually classified within the creative arts.

The process of which we are speaking is found, of course, in the fine arts, in literature, in music, and in all other fields of artistic endeavor. But it also expresses a general principle which is found throughout the activities of human life. In its use in the *Intensive Journal*, the term *work* has the meaning of *artwork* and includes all those activities in which a person moves with an inner interest and concern to direct his energies into a particular object or activity. Thus, a business man establishing a business and conducting his business affairs is engaged in a work that has the qualities of an artwork. Seen from within the unfoldment of his life, it is a focusing of his life energies outward into an activity that carries a great inner meaning for him, and which he is seeking to carry out as well as he can. In the same way, we consider as works with the quality of an artwork, all those projects and involvements that we carry out in our craft or profession, our participation in social or community programs, wherever we are inwardly involved in an outer activity that is meaningful to us. The molding of a career in any area, the raising of a child, the maintenance of a household, all constitute artworks. Each combines an inner image which carries the goal of the work, and an external focusing of energies directed toward giving the goal an outer form and bringing it to fulfillment.

A good first step to take in preparing for the feedback exercises in the Dialogue with Works section is to draw together a listing of the varied works that have been meaningful to us in the course of our life. A convenient way to gather these is to turn ahead in our Journal to the Steppingstone section and reread the descriptions we have written for each of the Steppingstone periods. For each period we ask ourselves the question: During the length of time covered by this period, what were the projects and activities that were especially meaningful to me and that had an inner importance for my life?

As we ask ourselves this question, we must bear in mind that the works which we are seeking to identify are activities and goals to which we feel an emotional commitment. We *care* about them as we invest our energies in them. Therefore we are not carefree nor haphazard when we are engaged in these works. We do them as well as we are able up to the limit of our emotional commitment and our capacities. To the degree that we care about them in this way and that we seek to fulfill them as well as we can up to their highest possibilities, we are treating these works as artworks, regardless of whether their content is in the fine arts or in the more prosaic aspects of our lives.

As we go back over the Steppingstones to remind ourselves of works that were meaningful to us in the past, we find that our list becomes exceedingly varied. During the childhood periods of our life, the works we undertook were multiple and we quickly lost interest in them. Some, however, left a stronger imprint upon our minds, either because we remained with them for a long time, or because we felt drawn to them and were prevented by the circumstances of our childhood environment from pursuing them further. These works that have made the stronger imprint on our minds are the ones that we should place on our list so that we can explore the possibilities they open for us, lived and unlived.

It is helpful to include on our list projects and goals from earlier years that now have passed altogether out of our range of interest. We merely jot them down, briefly adding a phrase to describe them. When we have drawn our list together, covering the various Steppingstone periods, we find that reading the list as a whole opens a larger perspective for us of the interests and commitments we have had in the course of our life.

As we draw our list together, we should bear in mind as our criterion the definition of works that we are using. By works we mean the outer activities in which we place our energies as goals or commitments that have an inner meaning for our life. Studying music as a child may be such a work, and stopping it, by necessity or desire, may also be a significant entry in the Journal. So also are our plans of being an athletic star, including the commitment of time and effort, and the success or failure that came with it. Sometimes hobbies that we pursue casually in our earlier years become meaningful work commitments which we treat as artworks. Photography and the childhood experimentations in science are examples of this. Farming and gardening and the care of animals are instances of meaningful works in early years.

In some cases your work will cover an entire field of study or interest, a profession or career as a whole; at other times, it will be limited to a specific task or artwork. It may be farming or horse-racing as a whole; or it may be taking care of a particular stallion. It may be the fields of writing or art as a whole; or simply a particular story or painting. In each case it will depend on how we subjectively perceive our own relation to the work. If you find that the field of work as a whole is of great meaning to you and that a particular artwork within that field is also important, there is no need to make a choice. Record them both on your list. As you proceed with the feedback exercises, they will draw your entries into balance and indicate the best way to proceed with them.

As you go over your list of Steppingstone Periods, many works may come to your attention. Choose those that seem to be the most meaningful in terms of the possibilities of your future. In this regard, your emotions and intuitions can be a valuable guide to the areas of work that have significance for your life. It is good, therefore, to look closely at those work activities of the past that awaken a twinge of sentiment in you when you recall them. Sometimes this sentiment is only wistfulness, but that, in itself, may be an important sign for you. It may be calling your attention to possibilities that are still present in activities which you began in your earlier years, but which you did not carry to completion. The energy of emotion that is attached to these old, unfinished works indicates that they still are alive and relevant. Works of the past which we have neglected or discarded often have very valuable suggestions to make to us with respect to our current work activities.

We often find that when we go back over our Steppingstone Periods to recall the meaningful works of our past, we make ourselves aware of roads not taken in our life that now have come to a new point beyond their earlier detour. We now have new possibilities because, as we have travelled the road of our life we have arrived at a new intersection. We thus often find that we are opening a productive new situation as we recall and reactivate memories of our earlier work activities. New circumstances now provide a new context, and they open potentialities of experience that were not present before. It often is exceedingly fruitful to explore the possibilities of these new developments of old projects by using exercises that involve the other feedback dimensions of the Journal, especially when we work in the Intersections section and use the techniques of Twilight Imagery.

The interplay among the Journal sections based upon past works stimulates the Journal Feedback process and often opens unexpected possibilities for the future. We find that roads that were not taken in the past now become available to us in a fresh context. We were not capable of meeting their requirements at that earlier time, but now, as we have the benefit of our additional life experiences, we can approach them anew. This is one reason why the basic exercise of recalling and listing in our Journals the outer activities that have had an inner meaning to us in the past often leads to valuable new projects. What was old and rejected becomes the seed of future works. The cumulative movement of the exercises of Feedback Interplay enables us to draw them to fruitful, and often to very unexpected, results.

As we continue with our listing of the meaningful works in our life, we find ourselves touching all phases of time, works of the past, the present, and the future. From our Steppingstone Periods we draw our works of the past, the works in which we are no longer actively engaged. From our entries in the Period Log and in the Daily Log, we identify our current work involvements. These are our present works, the works which we began in the past and which are still the focus of our energies. From all of these come the works of our future. Future works are those for which a seed has already been planted in the form of an idea or an image or a plan, but which still remain to be acted upon. Such works are already present within us, but they have not yet been activated and given a tangible form.

When we have drawn together our listing of meaningful works, we sit in quietness. It is good to read the list through as a unit so that we can have a feeling and a recognition of the range and variation of the works that have been important to us in the course of our life. As we read, we may be reminded of additional works which we briefly began, or toward which we had a strong impulse and which we "always wanted to do." We may add these also to our list.

Now, for a second time, we read the list through to ourselves, this time amplifying it. We add brief comments, a word, a phrase, expressing an emotion that is aroused in us or a memory that is recalled. As we reread our list, we will be taking ourselves back into the circumstances of our lives at the time when we were engaged in each of our various works. Our minds will be stimulated to remember the events and the feelings of those times, and we may now wish to add some further comments and descriptions regarding them.

Some of these new thoughts that arise in us will lead us to make entries in other sections of the Journal. We will especially be stimulated to describe our recollections in the Life History Log as further memories come to us. These memories may be called back to us by our thoughts of earlier work interests, but they may also lead us to valuable rememberings regarding all phases of our life. Similarly, as we reread the list of our work involvements, we may evoke in ourselves very meaningful realizations regarding the roads taken and the roads not taken at various points in the course of our life. These insights may reach far beyond our involvement in work activities since we often find that our reflections on the works of the past become the occasion for important rememberings in all phases of our life experience.

As these memories, thoughts, and additional realizations are stimulated in us, it is advisable to make the entry immediately in the appropriate section. We write our description and our comments in the Life History Log, in Intersections, or whichever is the relevant section. As we do this, it is also good to make a cross-reference in Dialogue with Works so that we will have a record for ourselves of the way that our thought processes were stimulated to move in interplay through the various aspects of our life experience.

The entries that we make in these other sections of the Journal may extend to considerable length, especially when they involve full descriptions of our circumstances in the past. We may not complete these longer entries when the thought of them first occurs to us, but we should at least write sufficiently to indicate the tone and direction of the entry so that we will recollect it easily when we return at a later time to write the rest of it.

These derivative entries may be lengthy in contrast to the brevity of the entries which we make at this point in the Dialogue with Works section. Now we are merely listing the works that have been and are still meaningful to us. We are recalling them to our minds, describing them succinctly, and adding brief comments or specific remembrances of them. Later, we shall choose from our list of works the few that are most significant to us, and we shall direct our attention to these in a full and active way. Now, as we have reread to ourselves twice or even three times our listing of meaningful works, as we have reflected on their contents and on their movement in our lives, and as we have made whatever additional entries occur to us at this time, we are ready to take a further step.

We begin by choosing one of the works on our list as the subject of our first dialogue script. Eventually, as we continue to use the Journal, we will find ourselves drawn by the interplay and the momentum of the feedback method to carry out our dialogue experiences also with a number of the other works on our list. But now, to begin, we choose a work, whether past or present, or a work that we are contemplating for the future, a work which we feel has something further to say to us and a work with which we wish to speak.

It has been my observation that, in these exercises at Journal Workshops, people frequently concentrate their attention on the works and activities in which they are presently engaged and whose problems are preoccupying their minds. They also give preference to projects they are planning for the future, works that are still in an embryonic stage waiting for guidance as to how they can be brought to birth. These are very important, and the dialogues with them are very valuable. We should not, however, overlook our relation to works of our past, especially those works that have been carried to partial fulfillment but still have a greater potential. Our primary criterion in choosing the work on which we shall focus our attention in establishing a dialogue relationship is not that it contains problems that we wish to resolve. We choose it, rather, because it is a work that seems to contain meanings and potentialities greater than those that we have so far recognized and understood. We choose a work that has a further possibility of development. It will then in all probability also be a work that has something to teach us. When we choose the work for our first dialogue exercise, we bear in mind that this is only the first of a series of exercises by which we shall establish contact with the various works that are meaningful in our life.

Whichever work we choose, whether it is a work from the present, the past, or the future, we begin by making a statement of the situation in which we find ourselves with respect to that work. If it is a piano that we have not touched in twenty years, if it is an ambition that we have repressed since adolescence, that is the fact of the situation which we begin by saying in our statement. If, on the other hand, it is a difficult set of circumstances in our business or at our job, we express that also in our basic opening statement. Our purpose at this point in establishing our relationship with the work is to place ourselves in an honest and realistic position with respect to the facts as we perceive them at the present moment.

In writing the statement, we are essentially describing the present period in our relationship with the work, whatever that work may be, whether it is running an organization, rearing a child, completing a piece of sculpture, maintaining a household, conducting a business, carrying out a research project. Whatever the particular work may be, this brief statement draws our thoughts into focus with respect to the present relationship between ourselves and the work.

In the structure of the Journal Feedback method, writing this statement to focus our relationship in the present is the equivalent of our working in the Period Log as the opening exercise in a Journal Workshop. It has the purpose of placing us at the mid-point in the movement of time, as this Now moment is between the past and the future. The effect of positioning ourselves in this way is to enable us to move back into the past in order to establish a context of continuity in terms of which we can move forward organically into the future. The way we do this in the structure of our Journal Workshop is to follow our work in the Period Log by working in the Time-Stretching exercises, especially our Steppingstones.

We take a comparable step in establishing our dialogue with works. Having made our statement of the situation as it is at the present with respect to the work that we have chosen, we now go back over the steps by which the work has developed. We are interested in all the important aspects of the work and our relation to it. Thus we recapitulate the Steppingstones that have formed the life history of the work. We list them briefly. Just a word or a phrase with a minimum of embellishment is sufficient. Our purpose at this point is to establish contact with the inner continuity by which the work has been trying to unfold and fulfill the potential of its own unique existence. We are seeking to identify and to meet the person within the process of the life of the work. We therefore begin by listing its Steppingstones as we listed the Steppingstones of our own life, and of the lives of the other persons with whom we conduct our dialogues.

In doing this, however, we do not restrict ourselves to any specific number of Steppingstones. This list need not be a short one. It should be long enough to reflect the full chronological development of the work, and for this purpose it is usually better to include more material rather than less. In this regard, we follow a slightly different procedure in drawing together the Steppingstones of a work than in listing the Steppingstones of our own life where the factor of selective subjectivity is important. For the purposes of reaching the person within the process of the work, we recall all the information we can to mark off the various stages and phases in its development.

We ask ourselves, for example, when did it begin? And we record our answer as a Steppingstone. What led to the idea or inspiration that brought this work into being? Was some other person instrumental in bringing it about? Did it come from a dream or some other interior experience of ours? Once the idea was formed, what were the events that enabled it to continue? What difficulties did it encounter? How did it manage to continue? What variations and compromises did it make? Did it have long pauses when the work was at a standstill? What was taking place during those seemingly silent times? What feelings have you had about the work and your relationship to it? How has it proceeded in the recent period? What is the situation now?

These questions may serve as your general guide in reconstructing the life history of the work. We must take care, however, not to list the answers to these questions merely as an intellectual exercise. It is important that when we list the Steppingstones we do so not as outsiders to the work, but from a position that is *inside* its life.

To make this interior connection, it is good to stop the movement of our conscious thoughts. We sit in stillness and close our eyes. We let our breathing become slower, softer. We relax our body and let our concerns drop away. Breathing slow, our minds emptied in the stillness, we let our attention turn to the life of the work. We recall its beginnings, its sources, its possibilities, its phases of development, its difficulties. As these present themselves to us, we record them. Thus we gather events and situations that comprise the Steppingstones of the life of the work. They may not come to us at first in their correct chronological order, but we record them as we recall them. Later, as we read them back, we can renumber the individual Steppingstones so that the list will reflect the inner unity of movement in the development of the work.

Having drawn together the Steppingstones of the work we perceive the continuity of its life history, and thus we can recognize the reality of the person unfolding within it. It is this person with whom we wish to communicate in dialogue. We set the atmosphere for this dialogue by loosening our conscious thoughts and going to the twilight level of imagery. We sit in stillness with our eyes closed, feeling the presence of the work as a person. We do not think about it, but we let ourselves feel the work and our relation to it. Now we let images come. We do not direct these images. We do not make suggestions to them. We simply let them come of themselves, totally unguided, and we observe the symbolic forms which they take.

Our Twilight Imagery may take many varied symbolic forms. It may come to us in the image of an individual with qualities that represent the work; or it may come to us as a series of changing Twilight Images that reflect the movement in the life of the work, its past and its future. Whatever these images may be, we take note of them and we record them as part of the continuity of our entries here in the Dialogue with Works section.

We record these Twilight Images reflecting the life of the work, but we do not leave the state of stillness. When the images are recorded, we close our eyes again and sit in quietness. We feel the presence of the work. We feel the images that have come to us. We feel the quality of the work. We feel the quality of the continuity of its life, and especially we feel the inner existence of the work, its goals and its life history. We feel the work as a person.

We remain within this atmosphere of quietness, letting it deepen around us. Since we now perceive and feel the work as a person, there can be a relationship of equals between us. We can actually dialogue with the work. Sitting in stillness and feeling the presence of the work as a person, we speak to it. We address it, greet it, and speak to it with whatever words come to us. Very probably we shall soon find ourselves speaking to it of the things we have written in our basic statement. This is the essential subject matter. But the relationship between ourselves and the work is person to person. It comes out of the quietness, and it proceeds out of itself, reflecting its own nature and its own needs.

We speak to the work and it speaks to us. We record the words as they come to us, as we say them and as we hear them. We do not think about them nor contrive them, but we let them come of themselves and write themselves through our pen. We speak and the work speaks, and we record what is said as the words come to us. It is thus that the dialogue script builds its momentum and continues itself. Once it has begun and has established its movement in this way, we serve merely as the vehicle for the dialogue. We hold the pen by which it writes itself. The person in the work speaks and we speak, and the dialogue carries itself onward. We enable it to be written until it has said all that wishes to be said at this time.

When the dialogue script has gone as far as feels right to us, we return to our stillness. We take note of the feelings we had while the dialogue was being written, and the feelings that come to us as we sit in silence now that the dialogue is completed. We record these in the Journal as objective reportings following the dialogue script.

When we have added these entries, we may go back over the dialogue and read it silently to ourselves. We do not edit or change what has been written, we merely read it to ourselves. If further thoughts or feelings come to us, or if we wish to add a comment, we do not insert it within the dialogue script. Rather we add it as an afterword. We also describe the feelings that led us to make this additional entry. Having recorded the series of our thoughts and feelings in this way, it will be clear to us when we reread the series of entries at a later time what the actual movement of our experience has been.

When we have read the dialogue back to ourselves, there may be some substantial comment, thought, or feeling that comes to us. Perhaps it will be a further awareness about what is involved in our relationship with the work. Perhaps we are making a new resolution or a resolve that will form in us as to a course of action that we wish to take in the future. Whatever it is, we add that as a further entry.

As we make these additional entries, it becomes evident that the *dialogue relationship* between ourselves and the work is not limited to the actual spoken and written dialogue. The dialogue relationship involves much more than the dialogue script itself. It includes all the events and feelings, thoughts, hunches, and decisions that form the active continuity of our relationship. It includes also the intensity and the intimacy of the involvement between two equal persons. That makes it a dialogue. The dialogue script is part of this larger dialogue, together with the recording of the outer events and the inner thoughts and feelings that continue to occur in the relationship. All of these entries in the Journal are part of the enlargement of the total dialogue relationship.

After reading the dialogue script to yourself, and having entered your further comments in the Journal, you may find that the dialogue with the work now wants to extend itself. By all means enable it to do so. We very often find that the first segments of a dialogue script serve primarily as an introductory warm-up exercise. Their halting and uncertain movement clears the way so that freer and fuller dialogue experiences can follow. When we find ourselves impelled, after re-reading our dialogue script, to make additions to it and to extend it, it is good to follow that impulse. Those extensions which we add to the basic entry are very often the most valuable parts of the dialogue script because they carry the fruitage of the whole experience.

A certain part of what has been described of the above exercise and experiences can be carried out at a Journal Workshop. The atmosphere of the group is of great help in deepening the level at which the dialogue script can be written.

To draw out and clarify our relationship to our meaningful works, however, may be a very large task. It will require more time for writing, reflection, and inner experiencing, more time than the duration of a workshop permits. In addition, since the works in which we are currently engaged involve us in an ongoing activity, they constantly require new Journal entries and exercises. The writing that we do at a Journal Workshop serves, therefore, to lay the foundation for the further entries and exercises that we carry through as our experience continues. Especially in this section, the Journal work that we do after the workshop is of the greatest importance. For many people the Dialogue with Works section provides the ongoing laboratory in which the contents of their productive activities can be progressively formed, tested, and reshaped.

When a workshop is over, the momentum that has been generated often continues into the days that immediately follow it. That is a good time to make the additional entries in the exercises which we began but left incomplete at the workshop. For the most part these entries involve further background material, descriptions and elaborations of the life history of our works.

With respect to the dialogue script, however, it is good to allow a lapse of time before we reapproach it and seek to continue the dialogue. Let a few days or a week pass before you reread the dialogue script. Then, if sufficient time has passed to give you some distance and a fresh vantage point, it may be productive to reenter the relationship and let the dialogue carry itself further if it wishes to do so.

Chapter 14

Dialogue with the Body

Having established a Journal relationship with the persons who are significant in our life and with the work activities that are meaningful to us, we turn our attention now to the physical side of our existence. In the *Dialogue with the Body* section of the Journal we seek to deepen our relationship with the physical world in all its aspects, especially those relationships to life that come to us by means of our body.

While the meaningful contents of our lives are expressed in our emotions, our aspirations, and our deep inner experiences, they all are carried by our body. To that degree, our personal existence is dependent on our body. In a further sense, we make our contact with the world of nature, with music, the physical arts of dance and sports, sexuality and the realm of the senses all by means of our body. The body of a human being is the primary instrument of connection between his personal life and the fullness of the physical universe. It is with our bodies in this large sense as open-ended instruments of connection with the world that we seek to establish a deep relationship in this section of our Journal work.

We are familiar with the phrase, "The wisdom of the body." Many of us have had the opportunity to experience the presence of that wisdom in our lives in a variety of situations, as when our body has given us warning signals, or when it has spontaneously healed itself. In the state of nature animals possess this wisdom as their instinctual heritage, and they rely on it. It serves as a self-regulating mechanism for them, telling them when they have eaten enough and copulated enough, when they are to be active, and when they need to rest. It guides their basic biological functions. The complications of living in modern civilization, however, tend to blur this natural wisdom so that not only modern man but even his domesticated pets lose their contact with this primordial source of guidance. One of our goals in building a dialogue relationship with our body is to reestablish our access to its natural wisdom, and to provide the means for this wisdom to articulate itself in forms that can be directly applied in our lives.

The body of a human being functions by principles that are universal in the species, but each individual body is unique. Each begins with a different seed-nature unfolding by its own timing in its particular environment. Each body builds through the years its own life history with its unique combination of growth and illness and activity. Each physical body has its past, lives in a present moment, and moves toward a future of its own. The combination of these for each is unique. Each body has its special continuity of life, just as a person does. And this is the key to our dialogue relationship with the body. The essence of the life history of a body is an *inner person*, a person at the core of the process of the body's ongoing life. This person within the body carries the wisdom of the organic depths, and also carries the direction of the needs of each body's development. When, therefore, we are able to establish a dialogue at a deep level between the person in ourselves and the person in the process of the body, the result may have very profound effects in integrating our life experience.

As we consider the unfoldment of our individual existence, we realize that our body is the physical counterpart of our whole life history. Our inner life, our creative and spiritual growth, our problems and our pleasures, all are accompanied by the life of our body. Our experiences of exaltation as well as of pain come to us through our body, and that is one main reason why we are accustomed to think of our body as supremely private. Our body is the instrument for our most intimate relationships and our most meaningful participation in the life process as a whole.

The life of our body parallels the movement of our personal life. To a degree they are distinct in the sense that each has its own principle of unfoldment, the physical and the psychological. But they share one another's experience, so that the successes or frustrations of one are reflected in the strengths or illnesses of the other. The life history of our inner, personal existence and the life history of our body are mirrors of one another, but they each have their own style of speech and their own perspective.

To establish a dialogue relationship with our body, we have to make contact with the inner continuity of its life history. In that way we shall be able to meet the person within the process of our physical life.

Our first step is to recreate as much as we can of the life history of our body. Another way to say this is that we are now going to list the Steppingstones of our physical life in as full and far-ranging a way as we
. can.

Listing the Steppingstones of our body is a very similar exercise to the listing we made of the Steppingstones of our life at an earlier point in our work. But it has certain differences. This listing is not limited to a small number as in the case of our Life-Steppingstones. In drawing together the Steppingstones of the body our purpose is to give ourselves as broad a view as possible of the continuity and unfoldment of our physical life in all its many-sidedness. We are not interested here in pin-pointing the main markers that outline the movement of our life, but in calling to our awareness the richness and variety of experiences, pleasant and painful, that comprise the whole life of our body.

To do this, we let ourselves go back into memory and recall spontaneously past experiences that relate to any aspect of our physical life. We let these recollections come to us of themselves. We sit in stillness, opening the doors of memory, and letting earlier experiences of our physical life return to our mind. As they come to us, we record them briefly. A single word or a phrase is sufficient at this point if it will indicate to us the contents of the memory. At a later time we can fill in the details of those memories that are meaningful to us, and perhaps even extend them in the Life History Log and other sections of the Journal.

Now we go back in time and recall the numerous Steppingstones of the life of our body, jotting them down on our list. They may not come to us in chronological order, but that does not matter at this point. Later we can set them in order by numbering them so that we can reread them in continuity. But now we merely record them as they come to us.

These Steppingstone memories of the body may be of many kinds. It may be a memory of standing in a crib crying. Or being tossed in the air by a playful father or a visiting uncle. Perhaps a memory of looking up at a tall adult and thinking how small we are. Or being ill as a child with a high fever. The feeling of thinking you would die of illness. The memory of running in the snow, playing games, breaking a leg, seeing a sunset, being frightened by thunder, discovering your sexual difference, dancing, sweating, swimming, fighting, making love, being in a car accident, seeing a dead person, climbing a mountain. All the varieties of physical experience may be among these memories, and we draw them together from all the years of our life, from early childhood through adolescence and maturity to the present.

At a Journal Workshop we have found it to be a helpful procedure to speak out our body memories as they come to us. We do not elaborate upon them, nor describe them in detail, nor expect a comment from anyone else. We merely speak them out into the air as they come to us, and we add them to our list. Speaking them into the air of the workshop while we are in the act of recalling and recording them seems to help us loosen the hard soil of memory.

It is, in fact, a general principle in the work of Journal Feedback that to articulate an inner experience in words that can be heard outwardly stimulates the flow of the inner movement. We find this to be true also at certain points of our Twilight Imagery experiences.

In drawing up the Steppingstones of the body we find also that as we hear other persons speak out memories that are similar to ours, our restraints are relaxed. We are freed then to dig deep into ourselves to draw up experiences that may have been tightly packed and hidden beneath layers of inhibition and repression. As others speak, we also are reinforced in accepting the experiences that we have had as being the "normal" contents of a human existence. Thus we can be assured that we will not be judged or diagnosed for those experiences of which we may have been ashamed. We are free then to draw up memories of the life of our body without any self-imposed reservations, without censorship or self-reproach.

We now sit in quietness and turn our attention back into memory to draw up key recollections of our physical life. As at a Journal Workshop, we speak our recollections out into the air as they come to us, and we record them on our list in the Dialogue with the Body section. As we are writing, others are speaking too.

"I remember being fat as a kid."

"I fell and broke my arm. The bone was curved when I took off my coat and looked at it."

"Running fingers through the muddy sand at the beach."

"We played 'Doctor,' and my grandfather caught us. I felt foolish."

"I had a high fever and I thought I was going to die."

"Playing football in high school. Sometimes I was afraid but I loved the contact."

"I started to menstruate."

"Driving a car fast when I first learned to drive."

"The first dead person I saw at a car accident."

"Blisters on my feet but I kept on dancing."

"The dentist drilling."

"Locked in a dark closet. My father yelling."

"Climbing a mountain. A feeling of exhilaration. And some fear too when I looked down."

"Seeing the autumn leaves and feeling connected to their colors."

"Making love for the first time. Confused."

"Turning cartwheels."

"Having headaches day after day."

"Enjoying sex after many years. A great discovery."

"Realizing I was getting old. Walking slower."

"Necking in a car."

"Jumping on a hayloft."

"Being massaged."

"Sitting quietly in the park. The sun is very warm."

"Smoking a good cigar."

"Childbirth. Some I forget; some I remember and feel again."

"Fasting. It's unpleasant but it feels good to be doing it."

"A hangover."

"Being at one with the waves of the ocean."

"Cuddling a baby."

"Awaking from anaesthesia."

"Walking out of a hospital."

Those are some of the Steppingstones of our physical life that we hear spoken around us at the workshop. We hear them only with our outer ear, for our inner ear is attuned to our own experiences. We continue listing these until we have about fifteen or twenty, sufficient to give us a sense of the phases and changes through which the life of our body has passed. The entries we make are brief. A single word may be enough in some cases, like skating, or swimming, or flying. Sometimes a simple phrase will suffice, but at the most a sentence or two. It is important to keep the Steppingstones of the body in the form of a list so that we can have the feedback experience of reading our entries back to ourselves in continuity at the proper time. If there are entries that we wish to elaborate, the best practice is to copy them on another sheet so that we can enlarge our descriptions as fully as we feel is necessary while keeping our list open for additional Steppingstones of our body experience. After the workshop as additional memories come to us, it is valuable to add them to this list on a continuous basis, then amplifying them in a separate entry.

Now we continue in silence recording our body memories until our list is long enough. Before we stop we should check to make sure that we have at least one or two entries from each of the major time periods in our life, childhood, adolescence, maturity, including the present. As much as possible but without straining, it is best if our list of body Steppingstones is representative of the movement of our life as a whole. We draw it together and sit in silence.

In a little while, allowing enough time so that we can feel some distance from our list, we read the memories back to ourselves in continuity. It is good if the list is in chronological order, but that is not essential. The composite effect is sufficient. As we read the list to ourselves, perhaps rereading it two or three times, we let ourselves feel the fullness, the variety, and the ongoingness of the life of our body. Especially in our rereading of the list, we experience the inner connections among the various entries. In all their diversity, the events of our physical life come together as the varying phases of a single line of development. A process of unfoldment has been taking place within the life history of our body. As we reread our list, we perceive this process to be a single continuity of life. It is as though a specific person is present, unfolding the continuity of his experience through the life history of our body. This person within the process of our body's life is the one whom we shall now meet in dialogue.

In the course of carrying out this exercise up to this point, as we are rereading our list and as we are feeling the presence of the person within the continuity of the life of our body, we are necessarily recapitulating the relationship between ourselves and our body as it has been taking place over the years. As a next step in establishing a dialogue relationship with our physical life, we now write a summary statement of this relationship. What is the situation as it has been and as it is now between ourselves and our body? We write a brief, objective, nonjudgmental statement describing our attitudes and actions in relation to our physical life as they have been and as they are now.

A few sentences will be sufficient. Depending on what the circumstances of our physical life have been, however, several paragraphs will not be too much for this basic statement. It should be as short or as long as is necessary to enable us to draw into focus the essentials of our relationship to our body and to the physical world as a whole in whatever aspects we have experienced it.

This statement may contain a great deal, or it may include very little. It should be a spontaneous statement of our feelings and perceptions at this moment of writing. Allow it to be whatever it is so that it will be an honest reflection of the actual situation within you. Do not compose it as an essay, or edit it with judgments and standards of what you think "should" be your attitudes, or what the situation "should" be. Let it be whatever it is. It is important to be truthful and factual with respect to the situation. Bear in mind that, after all, this statement is not the ultimate achievement of your relation to the body, but it is only intended to be the starting point from which we can proceed.

When that statement has been written, we can take a further step toward our dialogue relationship. We sit in quietness and close our eyes. We turn the focus of our attention inward and we feel the inner continuity of the life of our body. We feel its presence as a person, the person within the process of the life of our body. Feeling this with our eyes closed, Twilight Images may come to us. If they do, we take note of them. We observe them, and we record them in the continuity of our entry.

We remain in quietness with our eyes closed, now progressively feeling the presence of a person, a being who personifies the inner continuity of the life of our body. We feel the presence of the person within the process of our physical life, and we speak to it. We greet it as a person. We address it, saying what comes to us to be spoken. Whatever we say, we write in the Journal.

The *person within the body* responds, and we record this also. Then we speak and the person speaks, and thus our dialogue script is under way. Perhaps we begin by discussing the subject matter of the basic statement that we wrote. Perhaps something altogether different, altogether unexpected becomes the subject of discussion. We do not direct it. We let the dialogue script compose itself as it moves. It writes itself through our pen. We speak and the person in the body speaks. The dialogue takes shape by itself out of its own nature. We let the inner speaking proceed now in the silence.

When the dialogue script has gone as far as it wishes, we let it rest.

Many persons have found that when they let a dialogue come to a stop without trying to prod it forward, that stoppage becomes merely a natural pause. Soon it resumes by itself. For this reason it is good to remain in silence for some time after a dialogue script seems to be finished. It may merely be resting before it moves ahead to further statements.

We sit in silence for a while. When we are satisfied that the dialogue is finished for the present, we go back and read it to ourselves. At that point, also, it may be restimulated and resume its movement. If it does, we give it an opportunity to continue. If not, we take the further step of recording the reactions that were stirred in us as we read it back to ourselves.

Were we moved by it, or surprised, or disturbed, or interested to explore it further? Does the content of the dialogue script suggest to us another line of approach that we can follow elsewhere in the Journal? If so, we should make note of these *dialogue leads* that may be given us. They provide the kind of inner guidance that eventually produces very valuable Journal Feedback experiences.

At a Journal Workshop some of the participants will read aloud their Dialogue with the Body. These scripts have the greatest variety, and often take unexpected turns. Sometimes they seem to be facetious, but their humor is mainly unpremeditated and is an unanswerable means of responding to some of the dilemnas of human existence. One college student, for example, turned his dialogue script into a poetic exaltation of the grandeurs of the human mind. He waxed poetic about the marvels of philosophy and science which the human mind has achieved. In contrast, he told his body that it plays only an insignificant role in his life. Thereupon the body responded in the dialogue script and said, "That's all very well. Your mind is high and mighty. But try going to the toilet without me!"

And the young man added as he read it at the workshop, "I don't know how that got to be written. It wasn't what I was thinking at all."

Or again there are the several occasions when priests and monks at workshops have understood the Dialogue with the Body in the context of the tradition of St. Francis who addressed his body as "Brother Ass," and engaged in friendly dialogue with it. The two approaches fit together naturally, all the more because St. Francis' conception of the body parallels the definition that we follow in these exercises, namely, that the body is each individual's instrument of connection to the whole of the physical world. It is not at all surprising, then, that sisters and priests as well as monks have found this to be a congenial way of working with intimate personal problems in a modern framework.

We often find that when persons with a religious background take the "Brother Ass" approach to the Dialogue with the Body, as has been done spontaneously on a number of occasions, the dialogue scripts tend to begin with a tone that is gentle and often humorous. When they are read at the workshop, they may evoke strong laughter at the beginning. As these dialogues proceed, however, and especially as the person's dialogues with "Brother Ass" continue in the active context of Journal Feedback, they display a marked capacity for toughmindedness. Beginning with gentle humor, they move progressively into realistic confrontation with the difficult issues of physical life that are inherent in the experience of persons who are living under religious vows.

This pattern of Journal experience is characteristic of the progressive development that takes place when the Dialogue with the Body exercises are used by diverse types of persons. At the outset the experiences tend to be light and somewhat self-conscious, possibly because it seems strange to be speaking with our body as with a separate person. After a while, however, as we become more accustomed to the dialogue relationship, it feels natural to us and we are able to reach deeply into the physical realities of our life. Thus, when a business man or professional man of middle years carries through his first dialogue with his body, it may take the form of a self-conscious recital of guilt confessing all the sweets he eats, the alcohol he drinks, and the tobacco he smokes. In the dialogue he will very likely apologize to his body for abusing it and promise to treat it better in the future. That promise, of course, is as valid as a New Year's resolution, and it usually lasts just as long.

If he continues to work in the dialogue relationship with his body, however, an integrating development soon takes place. As the Journal Feedback process continues to build, the dialogue scripts move beyond the surface level of concern with food and drink and good behavior, and they turn to the more fundamental questions of a person's way of life. At that point the business man finds himself considering how much longer he can expect his body to continue functioning well for him. He finds himself discussing with his body the prospect of death, and with that comes the question of the meaning of his life. Soon the conduct of his whole existence has become the subject of his dialogue with the body. Not infrequently, in situations of this kind, the body becomes the spokesman for a profound wisdom and guidance that relates not only to the physical, but to the whole conduct of a person's life. At such times, also, the dialogue opens issues that can very profitably be explored in other sections of the Journal. These dialogue leads can be very valuable and should not be overlooked.

A similar deepening in the Dialogue with the Body seems to take place when it is carried through by individuals who have had to live with serious physical limitations. It may be that a person has a congenital heart weakness, or be lame from childhood polio, or blind. Writing the basic statement of the situation at the start of the exercise provides an excellent opportunity to lay all the facts on the table. Unfortunately, however, at that early point in the work a person may not yet be psychologically able to recognize and articulate all that is relevant and necessary to say. Much more of the Journal Feedback process may need to take place before a full focusing statement can be made. That is what the dialogue scripts do.

The first dialogues may express the pain, the anguish and the resentment that often accompany a major infirmity. It is good, in fact, for those unpleasant emotions to be given space where they can be stated tangibly, reread, and referred to again and again. With that as the base point, the Journal Feedback process is set in motion. As the person proceeds with its exercises, it expands the context in which he experiences his life and makes it possible to *live in relation to the illness* rather than merely cursing it. Having deepened the level of awareness, the life as a whole is perceived in a new way with important practical consequences.

The movement of the continuity of the dialogues over a period of time is a major factor in bringing about change through the Journal Feedback process. The first dialogues with the body of a person who is physically handicapped may be mainly expressions of anger and the resentment of an unjust fate that placed this difficulty in the life of a person who had done nothing to deserve it. When these things have been said and responded to in the dialogue, it begins to be possible for the relationship to move to a deeper level. After a person has articulated his resentments it is common to feel emotional fatigue; that becomes a time when he falls silent and therefore can listen.

At that point the body can speak more fully. Specifically, that is the point at which the illness can speak for itself, can describe its genesis, its purpose, place, and meaning in the individual's life. Questions can be asked and dialogue can proceed at deep levels, moving toward trans-personal understanding of the ultimate conditions of life and its suffering. I think in this regard of the blind woman at our Journal Workshops who struggled long with the unfairness of her blindness until it described to her the kinds of inner vision that her lack of outer vision made possible. She had not been asked whether she wished to pay the price, but having paid it anyway and having her blindness explain it to her from its own depth, the angry waves could become calm in her and she could begin to see from within.

Sometimes it is not a dramatic illness or physical incapacity that carries the dialogue to a deepening awareness, but the universal fact of aging from which none of us is immune. I recall the West Indian lady at one of our Ghetto workshops who began her Dialogue with the Body in a laughing, teasing way. "It used to be," she told her body, "that any old rag I had would look beautiful on you. But now I can hardly find a dress big enough to fit you."

As we might guess, the body of such a lady was not daunted by her chiding remarks, but it spoke up for itself. It called her attention to her eating habits, and as the dialogue proceeded it made some other crit-icisms as well. At a certain point, however, the tone of the discussion changed. The fact was, they both agreed, that the two of them were getting older together. Their children were grown, the mid-point of life was past, and all the manifestations of their life were changing. "If you still want to be beautiful," her body told her, "you can't count on me. You'll have to find some other way to be beautiful." And with that wisdom to guide her, laughing and serious, she could say YES to the transitions of her age.

Wherever we are in our life, the deepening of the quality of consciousness within us is our most important attainment. Whatever contributes to this inner atmosphere is of value to us, especially if it enlarges our awareness in relation to the actualities of our life. This is the goal of our Journal Feedback exercises, and our experience up to this point has indicated that it involves a continuous and cumulative process. No single dialogue script, however exciting and revealing it may seem to us at the moment when we write it, carries the entire process. In principle it cannot, for the very definition of *process* implies a *series in motion*, with variations and changes and developments as part of its continuity. We therefore expect that all the experiences of our life will move through a continuity of changes, and our Journal procedures are designed as vehicles to carry these movements and variations.

When we write our dialogue script with the body, we recognize that it is one step in a process. The process as a whole is the ongoing dialogue relationship which we are establishing with the various aspects of our physical life. We have noticed that the writing of the Dialogue with the Body itself moves through a process of variation. It begins at the surface where its style is often self-conscious and its subject matter very generalized. As the dialogues proceed, however, the process of the work seems to take over so that the dialogue scripts write themselves spontaneously at deeper than conscious levels. That is the point at which the wisdom of the body enters the dialogues, often showing itself to be a large wisdom of life. It also shifts the subject of discussion to the specific problems and situations that require our attention.

We try in our dialogue exercises, whether we are at a Journal Workshop or in our privacy, to allow the dialogue script to move as far as it wishes and then come to a natural stop. The important next step in extending our dialogue relationship is what we do when the script itself is no longer in motion. We read it back to ourselves and we record the feedback experiences that come to us. By that time, the dialogue process will have become specific, and it will be directing our attention to our body's particular interests and requirements.

How do we proceed in the Dialogue with the Body section after the basic dialogue script has been written?

Our goal is to extend our dialogue relationship to the body in such a way as to position ourselves for solving whatever problems arise. One of the results of our dialogue script is that it enables us to draw into sharper focus those aspects of our physical life that require our attention. Very often these are issues that we have by-passed and tried to ignore, but the dialogue articulates them so that we have to give them recognition.

Perhaps there is an illness with which we must deal, or the danger of one to protect against. There may be a decision we have to make as to the approach to treatment we shall follow and the doctor we shall choose. We may be considering a new type of diet or a new physical regimen that will give us a constructive approach to health. Our dialogue with the body may have called our attention to the need of altering our style of life, perhaps changing our habits of personal conduct. It may involve our attitudes toward drugs or alcohol or other tendencies to addiction to which we are vulnerable. Perhaps our attitudes toward sexuality have had some questions raised or new light brought to them so that there are new approaches to our social behavior for us to consider. It may be also that our relationship to sports is changing both as participant and observer, or that we find ourselves developing a new approach to the world of nature.

In sub-sections within the Dialogue with the Body section we continue to work with whatever issues have been brought to the fore by our dialogue script. We work with them on a current and ongoing basis and thus draw them toward new resolutions and awarenesses.

It may be, for example, that your dialogue script raised questions about your physical treatment of yourself in some particular area, perhaps food or drink, work habits or sexuality. One way of approach is to keep a particularized Daily Log within the Dialogue with the Body section. Brief daily entries should be sufficient to enable you to form a perspective of what is actually taking place. Bear in mind, however, that you cannot gain a new perspective without working for a *continuity of time*. One insightful entry is not enough. A series, brief though the individual entries may be, but extended over a sufficient length of time will enable a perspective to form naturally out of itself. When you are groping your way toward new decisions, there is a valuable protection in taking sufficient time to accumulate a number of entries. The series enables a self-balancing principle to operate, and thus your entries can self-adjust themselves if you are being led off overenthusiastically in an unwarranted direction.

As you are making your daily entries in your Dialogue with the Body sub-section, you may find that your mind is stimulated to move strongly in exploring a particular line of thought. Let it be free to do that. Let its stream of thought and associations range as far as it feels impelled to go. Only make sure that you record the flow of it in this section without censoring or judging it. Let it move fully and freely, and record it as it comes to you.

It may be that when you read it back to yourself, this activated flow of thought will stir you to reopen your dialogue. Then, with that monologue of thought as your starting point, you can set another dialogue script into motion. Let it go as far as it wishes, and then resume your daily entries. Or let another monologue pick up the movement of your thoughts and associations.

From time to time it is good to check your entries by asking the question of where else in the Journal they can be explored. Perhaps they awaken memories that should be described in the Life History Log. Perhaps they open the recognition of a crossroad of decision where you chose one path and left another road not taken without realizing at the time that you were by-passing or eliminating a possibility of life. That can be described and reexamined now in the Intersections section. In the course of making these various entries, the individuals who were involved with you in these phases of your life may also be recalled to your mind. It may then be valuable for you to reopen your contact with them in the Dialogue with Persons section.

Interplay of this kind that moves back and forth among the various sections of the Journal stimulates the energies of our inner life. As we move from the Dialogue with the Body to the Life History Log to the Intersections and the others, we are reactivating the various phases of our life and relating them to one another. This is the larger aspect of the dialogue process, of which the dialogue scripts that we write are one part. So also are the daily entries and the monologues of thought. The interplay of exercises that carries us from one section of the Journal to another, forming out of diversity one integrated being, is also part of the dialogue process. In all their variations, they are building ongoing dialogue relationships between our deep self and each of the aspects of our life. Ultimately they are placing us in a dialogue relationship with the inner unity and the unfolding meaning of our life as a whole.

Chapter 15

Dialogue with Events, Situations and Circumstances

We come now to the section of the Journal where we establish dialogue relationships with the specific events and situations of our life. As we learn to work with the exercises that become available to us here, we find that the circumstances in which we live no longer exert a cold, hard force upon us. They are no longer fixed and opaque, but they become accessible to us as persons with whom we can communicate. Thus they can speak to us and indicate what their requirements are, and potentials of life can be opened to us by means of them. Aspects of our life to which we had resigned ourselves with feelings of futility may then be renewed with hope. Situations we had thought to be inflexible and therefore not subject to change may even be softened until they give us a message that guides us to next steps in new directions.

The events of our lives take many forms; we tend to respond to them in the immediacy of the moment in terms of pain or pleasure. Some we rejoice in, some we treat as disasters, others we merely endure. Beyond the outer form in which we experience them, however, there is an inner principle of movement in the events of our life. This interior factor is the key to the dynamic that forms our individual destiny, and the exercises in this section of the Journal give us a means of establishing contact with it.

When we speak of *events* in the context of Journal Feedback, the term has two levels of meaning. One is broad and generalized, referring to the underlying factors of change in our life. Its other usage is more limited, referring to the specific occurrences that take place within each individual existence. It is, in fact, the interplay between these two levels of meaning that enables us to discover what the varied events of our lives are trying to say to us. One sequence of events is taking place on the surface of life and another is happening at hidden levels. If we are attentive we can discern the relationship between the two within the context of our individual lives. There are large implications, both of universal and personal import, in the fact that the point at which the underlying flow of events coincides with and becomes an individual event is the point where human destiny is shaped. One of the purposes of the Journal Feedback approach as a whole is to provide practical methods of enabling individuals to relate their personal lives to the larger flow of events.

The *Dialogue with Events* section plays a particularly sensitive role in reaching that goal, and it does so in several ways. One is that it is the section where we work with those aspects of our life the meaning of which is elusive and ambiguous, those events in which we feel, not knowing why, that the hand of fate or destiny, good or bad, is touching us. At certain points we become engaged therefore in unraveling the mysteries of our personal existence.

Secondly, the exercises in this section of the Journal serve to complement and augment the dialogue relationships that we have begun to establish in other areas of our life. When we come to blockages in our life experience, or when we have difficulties in working in other dialogue sections of the Journal, the procedures we use here give us an additional vantage point that enables us to break through the impasse. Further, these procedures serve to stimulate the interplay among the other Journal sections so as to give us access to advanced levels of techniques and experience. At this time, however, we shall work with the fundamental exercises of the Dialogue with Events section as they feed into the basic integrative experience of a Journal Workshop.

When we use the term *events* in its larger, encompassing sense, it refers to all the varieties of occurrences that emerge out of the flux and flow of human experience. Every event that occurs in an individual's life is an outcropping of an ongoing process that is moving at the depth of his existence. It is an interior process, and the events that take place on the surface of experience at any moment are its external manifestations. They are embodiments of the fundamental principle by which growth and change take place in our lives. This underlying and encompassing process carries the inner dynamic of experience. It creates the specific contexts of life, the situations in which our life experiences can move forward, and then it breaks these situations apart by bringing forth additional events which establish ever new sets of circumstance. It is with this inner process of perpetual life transformation that we seek to establish our contact through our dialogues and other exercises in this section of the Journal. We wish to build a continuing inner relationship with the process of movement and the goals that are unfolding through the multitude of events that shape our individual lives.

This is the general sense in which we speak of events as including all the experiences that feed our interior process. But there is another, more specific meaning of events in the context of the Journal Feedback process.

For the specific purpose of our feedback exercises, we define events as the particular occurrences that take place with meaningful impact on the movement of our lives. Events of this kind call attention to themselves by their dramatic quality, by the questions they raise about the mysterious movement of human existence, and especially by the effect they have on other aspects of our experience. Sometimes they are specific happenings that mark themselves off by the sharpness of their impact, their unexpectedness, their irony, or their pathos. At other times, they are less dramatic and take the form of *situations* that have established themselves over a period of time without our realizing they were happening, and they now are present as facts of our lives. They may also take the form of *sets of circumstance* brought about by factors external to us but which provide the context for important parts of our life experience. In these varied forms they comprise the content of our *Dialogue with Events, Situations and Circumstances.*

A main criterion of the events that we choose as the focus for our exercises is that they are experiences that have had a strong emotional impact upon us, whether in the past or in the present. This is an indication that they have an inner importance for the movement of our lives and that our entering them in the feedback exercises will be valuable for additional areas of our experience. They are outer events that have an inner importance.

They may be events that have occurred unexpectedly or dramatically and have substantially altered the conditions of our lives. For example, a well-to-do man experiences a major reversal in his business, altering his financial situation with the result that all the members of his family undergo a change in their style of life. It is an event that will speak to each of them in a different way, each in the context of his life. Outwardly it will be the same event, but inwardly it will be a different event for each of them.

In general, regardless of their specific content, what we are dealing with here are events that life has presented to us. They come unbidden, unexpected, and mostly undesired by us. Often they carry a paradox of life, express an irony of existence, and present us with a dilemma. It may be, for example, that all has been going well in our lives when suddenly we are brought low by an illness. Or by a car accident. Or our career is progressing well when unexpectedly the company that employs us loses its contracts and we are left without a job. Or we have been careless and committed an error in judgment that has resulted in a sharp interruption of our career. Many people in the modern world have experienced rude breaks in their lives because of political events or natural catastrophes over which they have had no control. Other people experience the impact of events in more personal terms, through a change in the composition of their family or divorce or remarriage or the birth or death of a member of the household. For each it is an event that sharply effects the situation and circumstances of life. Some may react to such events with anger or frustration. The question, however, is whether these occurrences have a larger meaning for us, whether we can find their message and learn from it.

We require a perspective that reaches beyond the particularity of events and encompasses our life as a whole. Since all the events that we experience are part of the moving process of our life, they reflect something of our past and they also carry the possibilities of our future. Those events that we perceive as adversities may be experienced as painful, and we may wish that they had been avoided; but they may also be the vehicles by which an expanded awareness of the meaning of our life is being opened to us. There are mysterious questions of personal destiny that are difficult to answer, and we know that they often reveal themselves to us in circumstances which we initially regard as catastrophes.

The choice we have before us whenever a striking event takes place in our life is whether we shall react directly to the event itself, or whether we shall place it in the context of the movement of our life and let it speak to us. In general, it is more usual for setbacks or other painful occurrences to serve as the events that have a message for us. These are very often the events that have the most to say to us when we engage them in dialogue, but the same may be true for any event that has a strong impact upon us.

Successes may be as meaningful as failures. Favorable events may have as much to say to us as disasters. It is especially important that we speak with them in order that we may discover what lies behind them. Sometimes a striking success carries a particular danger because it leads us to drop our guard in enthusiasm and assume that other successes will follow. This brings a loss of perspective and may lead to carelessness or thoughtlessness in the conduct of our lives. Whether an event comes to us in a form that is pleasant or painful, it is important that we place it in the context of the moving cycles of our ongoing experience. Whatever it is, it is subject to change in terms of the larger process that is unfolding in our existence. Behind each event some effective element in our life process is at work. It is with this that we wish to establish an *inner relationship* by means of dialogue.

Once we have learned to perceive our lives in the context of the moving cycles of experience, we realize that the question of whether an event is pleasant or painful is secondary. The primary criterion is whether its subjective impact upon us leads us to feel that it has an inner importance for the further development of our lives.

The expressions of this may be exceedingly variable. Sometimes it is simply that an event occurs without apparent meaning or reason, and yet it has a strong effect upon us. We feel, then, that there must be something behind it that we need to explore. To open it, we enter into dialogue. Sometimes an event leads us to a conundrum about our life, an inexplicable situation about which we can make no decision. Such life-riddles suggest to us that the events which brought them about contain a hidden message for us.

Sometimes, also, events that are meaningful for our lives occur as coincidences, or as "synchronistic" events with no apparent cause. These coincidences often seem to have an uncanny quality so that it is common for people to feel that there is a more–than–human agency directing them. They therefore treat such occurrences as "signs" and often base far-reaching decisions upon them. The emotional impact that accompanies these events indicates that they do indeed have a message for us. Whether that message is demonic or providential, or whether its source is the inner wisdom of our organic depths, it will be valuable for us to establish a dialogue relationship with it. We can then extend our contact with it and discover what the nature of its guidance is, whether it is valid for us to follow it, or whether its message for us is what we had earlier assumed its meaning to be.

Not all the events that have an inner importance for our lives take place with striking and dramatic impact. Some do not occur visibly and are not brought about by a definite set of actions. They do not come into existence at any single moment but only gradually establish themselves. Suddenly we realize that a particular set of circumstances has become a fact of our lives without our realizing it. Although it has been a long time in taking shape, the moment when we recognize it is like the discovery of something new that has arrived upon the scene.

The circumstances that have gradually established themselves in particular areas of our lives are events with which we can enter into dialogue. Often these provide not only the background, but the key to the personal relationships that are most important in our lives, in our friendships, our families, our work relationships. The situations that develop as the contexts in which we live may very well have more to say to us about a relationship than the relationship itself. Where there is a problem, for example, within a marriage, it is very important to establish a dialogue relationship with the marriage itself, as well as with the other person involved in it. The Dialogue with Persons section is the place where the relationship between the two individuals can be worked with directly; but we work with the situation itself in Dialogue with Events.

When we consider the inner quality of such personal situations as a marriage, a friendship, or a close business relationship, we realize that each one has its own life-history. Each situation, with the set of circumstances that lies behind it, has its own past, its inherent seed of potentials, and its own characteristic movement through the present toward its goals. Recognizing this life-history enables us to perceive the presence of a *person* as the essence of the situation. The marriage, the friendship, each relationship, and each set of circumstances, has its own life as a human being does. When we reach this *person within the process* of the situation or the event, and when we establish an inner relationship of dialogue with it, we make it possible for the movement of our life to speak to us with openness and with fluidity. We often find that when we apply this procedure in the Dialogue with Events section we open a channel for deeper contact with the contents of our lives than would be possible with any of the other dialogue sections alone.

This supplementary function of the Dialogue with Events exercises gives them a very important role in building the dynamic of Journal Feedback. Whenever the exercises in other sections of the Journal lead us to an impasse, the procedures we have available here give us a means of breaking through and opening new ground. This is particularly true of the three dialogue sections—Persons, Works, and Body—in which we have just carried out our exercises.

A clear and common example of this occurs in the case of a marriage that is in difficulty. For one reason or another, marked disagreements have developed between husband and wife and whenever they attempt to discuss things amicably, it ends in the same type of argument as in previous attempts. Each seems to be saying the same thing again and again. The usual situation is that these areas of discord have been reinforced by so many previous encounters and have broken down so often into anger or acrimony or a sullen stoppage of communication that patterns of habit have been formed. Whenever a new attempt at discussion is made, it quickly falls into the same old circular grooves. The result is the usual impasse and additional frustration.

In the context of Journal Feedback, the place where we take such a situation is to the Dialogue with Persons section. Since we are aware of the pitfalls inherent in such troubled relationships, we undertake to set an atmosphere that will draw the dialogue to a level deeper than its accustomed conflicts. We do this by moving away from the externals of the immediate situation and invoking a sense of the whole, unfolding life of each of the persons in the relationship. Very often at this deeper level of dialogue it becomes possible for a new quality of understanding to be achieved. In many situations, however, the dialogue with the other person is only a partial first step. It serves to push the door ajar, but it is not sufficient by itself to overcome the repeated angers and frustrations that have accumulated over the years. Very often, dialogues of this kind move a short distance, make a little progress, and then become bogged down in the same, circular misunderstandings of one another that had devastated their actual relationship. Repeated attempts at renewing the dialogue between persons can gradually improve the situation until eventually a breakthrough is achieved. But there is a better way. To reapproach the situation from a different point of view, from a second vantage point, often has the effect of taking the relationship to another level. We achieve this in the context of Dialogue with Events.

After we have carried the Dialogue with Persons as far as it can go, we shift to this other section of the Journal. In the first dialogue, the husband, for example, undertook to speak with his wife and, after a sympathetic beginning, found that he could not move beyond the self-righteousness and the antagonisms that had developed in the relationship. Now he resumes his attempt at dialogue, but this time it is not with his wife. It is with the marriage itself; or, if he prefers, he conducts the dialogue with the relationship as a whole.

To begin this dialogue he goes back over the series of events by which the relationship has grown. He lists the Steppingstones of its life history. He lists the events of its beginning, the first meeting, the later friendship and growth of intimacy, the marriage and the acts done together, homes furnished, children born and reared, experiences of love and anger, warmth as well as antagonism. With all of these he reconstructs the outlines of the life of the marriage, and from it a person emerges. This person is not himself, and it is not his wife. It is the person within the process of the life history of the marriage. It is this third person with whom he conducts his dialogue. This is a neutral person, but one who is intimately involved in the situation. The combination of the two dialogues, coming as they do from different but complementary perspectives, often throws the light of a new awareness on the relationship.

The same procedure of combining the Dialogue with Persons and the Dialogue with Events can be used effectively in the relationship between a parent and a child. Especially when the child is no longer young and the circular patterns of noncommunication have been repeated over many years, it can be very difficult to establish dialogue. I have been present on many occasions when a person tried to dialogue with an elderly or deceased mother or father only to find that their bitterness and blame cut the dialogue short. Often such dialogues open of themselves after sufficient time has passed and repeated new beginnings have been made. To add to that dialogue, however, a dialogue with the event of that relationship, and to converse with the person within the process of the ongoing situation between them, often breaks directly through the circular repetitions of resentment. Many times it has made possible a reconnection by love at the deep level of one another's lives.

In a similar way the Dialogue with Events exercises may be combined with Dialogue with Works to gain an additional perspective. Suppose, for example, that you are in a job situation where you feel yourself being enclosed and cut off from future opportunities. When you dialogue with the job, it tells you that it is limited, that it has nowhere to go, and that it holds no stimulation for you. You feel frustrated and at a dead end. At that point it would be productive to dialogue with other areas of work so as to open other possibilities. The difficulty is that, when a person is in a frustrated work situation, the probability is that their energy level is low and that their emotions and imagination are also in a depressed state. Whatever additional Dialogues with Work they may attempt at that time therefore tend to have a minimum effect.

That is when there is a special value in turning to Dialogue with Events in order to enlarge the perspective and to stimulate additional energies. Each person will approach it in his own way but, however it is phrased, the focus will be placed on the event of being in a dead-ended job, the larger situation that it involves, and the circumstances of life that are its background. With this as the focus of the exercises, we are progressively drawn into a number of areas of our life experience that open additional avenues of approach to our work situation. Also, while we are taking the steps in the exercises to establish our dialogue relationships with the event of our work situation, many feedback leads to other sections of the Journal will suggest themselves to us. As we follow these, we shall thus be generating additional energy by building the momentum of the Journal Feedback process.

Consider how this combination of procedures would operate in the situation of a young man who has been dropped from law school. After he has made his basic Daily Log entries, his next step would be to explore his projected law career in the Dialogue with Works section. Given the mood of the moment, the negatives that would come to the fore might well be overwhelming as the feelings of depression would be multiplied by the angers. Working within the Journal Feedback process, the movement of energy would be turned further inward by these first Journal entries, thus intensifying the unpleasant emotions.

Some additional dialogues with persons involved in the situation might then be indicated. At first these dialogues would further increase the inward energy movement, but as they progressed they would tend to relieve the pressure of anger. This would then be the moment when a larger perspective of life could turn the situation around. It would be the time to dialogue with the event in the context of his life history as a whole. What had been experienced as a disastrous failure would then have its opportunity to disclose its message for the future development of the person.

An indicative example of what is involved in the full cycle of this process is found in the Old Testament. We are familiar with the story of Joseph, the event of his brothers selling him into slavery, his career in Egypt, his imprisonment, his prophetic interpretation of dreams for Pharaoh, his being placed in a position of administrative power, and his finally being the person who could allocate food for his brothers in a time of famine.

We can imagine the thoughts, the inner dialogue, that Joseph had when he saw his brothers and they knew who he was. If we follow the parallel of the depth process as it moves through the *Intensive Journal*, we can project the equivalent of the Dialogue with Persons that Joseph carried out with his brothers in the secrecy of his heart. That dialogue could not have been without anger and bitterness at the painful experiences he had been forced to endure. But there was another important step that Joseph took in his interior work. Parallel to the Journal Feedback process, he established a dialogue relationship with the event of his captivity. In principle, he recapitulated the life history of the event, its past and its future. It then became much more than an episode of a brother betrayed. It included then a long series of events, some of them reaching back before Joseph was born. It included the hard life of the older brothers, the father's favoritism for a younger son, the understandable jealousy of the brothers, the bitter act of selling him into slavery, and then the further unpredictable series of events that gave him a saving role in the social crisis of his time.

The life history of the event of captivity reached far beyond the particular happening itself. In fact, the simple act of his being sold into slavery became a small and necessary event in the larger scenario. Its ultimate meaning was shown to be much different from the personal meaning it had in the moment when it transpired. Reconstructing the whole sequence, it seemed indeed that the event had its own life history as a person unfolding a unique and meaningful destiny. Establishing his dialogue relationship with the person within the process of that whole continuity of events, Joseph could see them in a much larger-than-personal context. When his brothers recognized him and begged his forgiveness, he was therefore able to speak from the full perspective of the situation and say in the language of his day, "You intended it for evil but God intended it for good."

A major role of the exercises in Dialogue with Events is to enable us to experience the movement of life in so broad a vista that we are not enclosed by the emotions of the moment. We perceive the ambiguity that is inherent in events. They may have not one or two but several levels of meaning, and these disclose themselves not at the time of the happening but only at later points in the course of our experience. It becomes essential, then, that we keep ourselves free from fixed conclusions and have a means of holding ourselves open for the further recognitions of meaning that will come to us with the passage of time. The Dialogue with Events becomes a means of positioning ourselves so that we shall be free and able to see the next steps that will become possible for us in the future. In this regard it serves as an active supplement to much of the dialogue work that we do in other sections of the Journal and progressively expands the range of the Journal Feedback process.

With this as our background, let us now prepare to take the steps that will establish open-ended dialogue relationships with the meaningful events, the situations and circumstances of our lives.

We begin by opening our Journals to the Dialogue with Events section. Our first step will be to draw together a flexible listing of the varieties of events and situations which we feel have something more to say to us with respect to the larger movement of our lives. These may be from any area of our experience and from any time-unit, past or present. One criterion of the events that we list here is that they had a striking impact upon us at the time they happened. Another criterion is that we feel there is a further step to be taken in our relationship with them. Especially it may be that we are still contained within the emotions of anger or resentment that accompanied the original occurrence, and we sense that it may be possible for us to reapproach that event now in a larger perspective.

To assist ourselves in recalling events of this kind, it may be helpful to turn to the section where we recorded the Steppingstones of our life. We may not have mentioned such events there specifically, but as our memory moves back over the outline of our life we may be reminded of them. It may also be helpful to check back over the entries that we have made in the Life History Log. In the course of describing some of the past situations of our life, we may also have alluded to events that had a striking impact upon us. A place where it is particularly important for us to look is in the section, Intersections: Roads Taken and Not Taken.

Let us recall instances of events that had a striking impact upon our lives and place them on our list. For example:

The experience of returning from a trip and finding that our father had taken his belongings and left.

An automobile accident that left us with a severe injury. Or perhaps an illness that has had lasting effects.

Receiving a scholarship that opened up opportunities for development which we had not anticipated having available to us.

Being tricked or misled in a business venture. Or in a personal relationship. Feeling that we were betrayed by a friend.

Having an intense religious or conversion experience happen to you, an experience that changed your attitude toward life, and comes as though carried by an external force, like "a bolt from the blue." Such experiences may not be limited to religion, but may extend to political life or to ideologies in general.

Being physically molested or attacked, as by rape. Alternately, the surprising and moving pleasure of an unexpected physical or sexual experience.

These are a few instances of events of striking impact in our lives, events that were significant and also ambiguous in their meaning for our lives. There is, of course, a virtual infinity of the types of such events that we may have encountered in our lives. We wish also to add to our list, however, those situations and circumstances that may hold a message that is larger than what we have so far been able to perceive. What are some examples of these?

The social circumstances of our birth, our being born into poverty, affluence, a persecuted minority, or a dominant majority. Correspondingly, the social circumstances in which we are presently living.

A situation in which we find ourselves, a triangled love affair, a crime or error of our youth being discovered or returning to embarrass us, a commitment or promise we have made that no longer feels valid to us.

We may find ourselves in a situation or relationship that seems to have come into existence by itself. We did not plan or deliberately call it into being, but now, without having chosen it, we find ourselves living in the midst of it. Many questions of the ambiguity of our life open here as we become more aware of the circumstances in which we have inadvertently placed ourselves.

Personal living arrangements that are burdensome but are difficult to change, the relationship of children and parents, the break-up of old friendships, conflicts and mistrusts between business partners, patients seeking the strength to leave their therapist.

Another place to look in seeking to remind ourselves of situations and circumstances of this kind is the other dialogue sections. In the dialogue exercises which we have already carried out with respect to Persons, Works, and Body, we have necessarily indicated a number of such circumstances. In the case of some of them, it will be particularly valuable for us to open an additional road that will enable us to approach them from another direction.

In these other dialogue sections the events and situations that will be called to our attention will be from the present as well as from the past of our life. It is important that we include these. It will also now be helpful to go back over the entries we have made in our Period Log to see what else may be added to our list from the current period of our life experience.

When you feel that your list contains the main items that are meaningful to you, that it is full enough for your present use, draw it to a close, but also leave it open so that you can add further entries to it as they come to your mind. It is good practice to leave lists of this kind open ended in the Journal so that there will always be room for more to be added. To insure this, we begin the next phase of our exercise in this section on a new sheet.

Now, with our list before us, we sit in silence. We consider the entries we have made and the implications they may hold for the past and future movement of our life. Several of them may be meaningful for us to explore in detail, but we shall choose one as the focus of our Dialogue with Events exercise at this Journal Workshop. We bear in mind as we are making our choice that this is not by any means an absolute decision. We are not eliminating any of the others. We are merely choosing one as our immediate point of focus, holding open our option to work with any or all of the others at another time. In fact, the rule holds here as in all the other exercises that when we begin by making a choice of subject and the progress of the exercise indicates that something else on the list would be more productive, we stop and start anew. It is, after all, our own life that we are working in. It is best, however, if we begin by choosing an event or situation that evokes a strong emotion within us when we think of it or read it on our list. That is a sign that it is pertinent for us so that to establish a dialogue relationship with it will be a valuable experience.

We begin by writing a brief description of the event or situation that we have chosen. In placing it on our list, we described it only very briefly. We wrote only a few phrases, just enough so that we ourselves would know which experiences in our life we were thinking of. Now, however, we write a full statement of what is involved in it. In writing this, we want to mention all of the main factors that are relevant, but without losing ourselves in detail. We want to write a focusing statement of the event or situation.

Having made this basic statement to crystallize our awareness of it, we are ready now to reconstruct the life history of the event. What are the Steppingstones of its life? We may go far back in time in recapitulating these Steppingstones, back beyond our own birth. The young man who was dropped from law school, for example, may go back to the fact that his grandfather was a lawyer. He may then list his family's expectation of him to continue a tradition, and his own expectation of himself. Added to that would be other relevant facts and events, like his study habits, his interest in the law, his interest in other fields of study and work, the role of other persons in his life, professors and friends, all as they have contributed to the striking event that finally came to pass.

If it is not a clearly visible event that you are describing, but a situation or relationship that has gradually and imperceptibly established itself, the Steppingstones that you list would be of a more general nature. Your list may begin with the state of mind and emotion in which you were when you first met the other person. And the frame of mind in which they were, their desires and attitudes. From these each Steppingstone will reflect another phase in the development of the relationship, its pleasures and its problems, moving up to the present situation.

Essentially each of the Steppingstones that you list will be briefly described. A sentence or two will be sufficient to indicate the main contents and qualities of each one. Some of them, however, may stimulate you to write a full and detailed description with elaborations and explanations of all that was involved. It is good to do that, but when you write these extensions of the Steppingstones, try to arrange them in your Journal in such a way that it will be possible to read just the heading or top line of each of the Steppingstone entries in consecutive order. In a little while we want to be able to read the Steppingstones back to ourselves as a quick list that will give us a sense of the continuity of movement in the life history of the event. That will be one of the steps by which we prepare for writing our dialogue script. We should bear it in mind while we are gathering the Steppingstones together.

Now let us sit in silence. Our eyes are closed. Our breathing is slower and slower. In the quietness our attention is turned inward. We are feeling the inner movement of our life, and especially we are feeling the particular events and circumstances that we are considering now. We feel that situation inwardly. We perceive it in its wholeness, all sides of it, its varied aspects, all perceived by us now without judgment.

In the silence, our eyes closed as we are looking inward, we let images come to us at the twilight level. Whatever they may be, we make note of them. But mainly in the silence we are letting ourselves go back down the track of time that is the life history of our event or situation. We let ourselves be carried inwardly back down to its very beginnings, and as these memories present themselves to us, we record them. Now in the silence we are listing and describing the Steppingstones of the life history of the event or situation that we have chosen.

We allow as much time as we need to satisfy ourselves that we have described these Steppingstones adequately. When we have finished, we remain in silence. Again we close our eyes and let our breathing become slow. In the stillness we let ourselves drift inwardly down to the level of Twilight Imagery. This time, having completed the writing of the Steppingstones, we let ourselves remain there longer, letting images present themselves to us in whatever form they wish. We record them as they come to us without judgment and without interpretation. They have come to us as part of our listing of the Steppingstones and later we shall read them together, in correlation with one another.

As we are sitting in silence, we read back to ourselves the top line of each of the Steppingstones. It is as though we are reading the given name of each. As we read them in sequence, the consecutive life history of the event forms itself for us and we feel the process that has been moving within, moving in the past, through the present, and into the future. We feel that continuity of the inner movement of life as it has come together and has crystallized in this event. Now we feel that process of life as it has moved into this event, as it moves through it, and as it moves beyond it. We feel the inner process of the event as it moves through all the phases of time, as it has moved through the Stepping-stones of its life. This is the person within the process of its life. We feel the presence of this person.

Now we are ready to write our dialogue script. In the silence, our eyes closed, our breathing slow, we let ourselves feel the presence of this inner person, the person within the process of the unfolding life history of the event. We feel the inner continuity of its life, its past, and its movement into the future. We feel the presence of the person within the process. And we speak to that person. We greet it and speak whatever comes to us to be said. And we write what we say as the start of our dialogue script.

We speak out of our deep silence, and it speaks to us. It speaks out of the deep place where its process has been moving, and its words reflect that movement. We write all that is spoken. We record it as it comes, without editing, without directing it, without censoring it. We let it come, and we let it flow directly into and through our pen. The person within the process speaks out of the deep movement of life, out of the deep movement of our life. It speaks, and we speak. So it continues. It speaks through our pen. It speaks and we speak together in deep, undirected dialogue. It continues on by itself, out of itself. It continues until all that needs to be spoken has been spoken. And has been written. We let it be written, in the silence, in the silence.

When the dialogue script has finished writing itself, we remain in silence. Let the breathing become slow again, for it may have become agitated during the writing. Presently we return to the dialogue script and read it back to ourselves. We take note of how it feels to us as we read it now, and we compare this with the feelings we had while it was being written. As we read it back to ourselves, the dialogue may wish to resume its movement. If so, we let it do as it wishes. When it has finished, we also shall have earned our rest. We set it to one side. Later, some days or a week later, we shall take it up again and read it to ourselves anew.

Then we shall see what new feedback leads it gives us, to which other sections in the Journal it directs us. We shall then let it show us what next step it desires in deepening its dialogue relationship with our life.

Chapter 16

Working with our Dreams

Working with the dialogue exercises for Persons, Works, Body, and Events leads us to a twofold experience. It enables us to explore the circumstances of our lives as they are on the surface, and it also draws us toward the deeper-than-conscious levels underneath. While the dialogues are working with the details of the situations and events that are at the forefront of our consciousness, they tend to call our attention to possibilities and implications of which we were not aware. That is why we often find when we reread our dialogue scripts that we have written information and insights that we did not know we knew. It is a knowledge that is apparently contained at nonconscious levels and the dialogue exercises serve as vehicles for our drawing this knowledge to the surface without our realizing it. The dialogues thus point toward a second level, a deeper level of consciousness, with the implication that as we touch this further depth in ourselves we enlarge our capacities of awareness.

Working on the Dialogue Dimension draws us toward the Depth Dimension, especially because it indicates that the personal aspects of our lives, lead beyond themselves and have implications for the trans-personal meaning of our existence as a whole. We begin by directing our attention to the surface of our lives where our immediate problems and circumstances are visible. Progressively we discover that there are levels of experience beneath the surface, beneath our consciousness, and we realize that these may hold the key both to the problems and the potentialities of our life. We thus turn our attention from the surface to working at levels deeper than consciousness. We wish to move from the purely personal to the deeper than personal level of our experience.

A primary step in this direction is for us to work with our dreams. Dreams are unselfconscious reflectors that express all the various levels of the individual psyche as it is in movement. Dreams express the outward circumstances of a person's life, his current problems and fears, and also the hopes and goals toward which he is consciously planning. In addition, however, dreams reflect the deeper-than-conscious goals that are seeking to unfold in a person's life. These may be the long-range purposes that set the fundamental directives of a life, and yet are not consciously known by the person himself.

Dreams of this kind carry the seed-nature of a person. They serve an especially important role because, as the dreams carry the seed-goals of a person's life, they place them in relationship to the actual circumstances in which he is living. Sometimes, also, there are patterns and purposes working in a person's life of which he is not aware, but which are destructive in their relation to other goals of his life. The dreams bring these to the fore. In addition, dreams reflect the tensions and anxieties that are bound to arise in a person's life out of the conflict between immediate desires and the requirements of the long-range goals of his life. Many of these conflicts are not conscious to the individual, but the dreams express them and carry them further toward resolution. While the difficulties regarding the personal contents of life are being resolved, the dream movement is also making the person aware of the seed-potentials of his life, and is giving him intimations of the more-than-personal content that gives meaning to a human existence. It is thus that the dream process actively mediates between the personal and the transpersonal, leading a person to successive levels of depth experience while working in the current circumstances of his life.

How shall we proceed in working with our dreams?

In the *Intensive Journal* we have two separate sections for our dreamwork, the *Dream Log* and *Dream Enlargements*. The first is the section in which we gather the basic factual data regarding our dreams;

the second is the section in which we use the Journal Feedback procedures to work actively and non-analytically with the dream material so as to see where the dreams are trying to go and what their message may be.

In the *Dream Log*, without interpretation or analysis, and with a neutrality as objective as is possible, we write down all the dreams that we can recall. We record small fragments of dreams when that is all that we remember. Often we find that when we record only a small portion of a dream, perhaps the "tail" of one since that was the only part of it that remained with us when we awakened, the act of writing as little as we remember serves to draw the rest of the dream back to our consciousness. We catch the dream by its "tail," and thus we recover it for our consciousness. Many people who believe that they do not remember their dreams would find that a large proportion of their dreams would return to them if they made a practice of writing down whatever small bits of the dream they retained upon awakening. It requires a regular practice, and a definite place in which the writing may be done. This is one primary purpose of the Dream Log.

No interpretation of the dream is done in the Dream Log. As a Log section, it is merely a place for a succinct recording of basic facts. In the case of dreams, we describe whatever is relevant, not for understanding the dream since that is a more complicated matter, but we write all that will be necessary to enable us to remember what took place in the dream when we read it at a later date. We are gathering our dream data. Later, because of the entries in our Dream Log, we shall be able to retrace the movement of the various processes within our minds by means of the continuity of our dreams. Because of what we have recorded in our Dream Log, we shall be able to put ourselves back into the flow of our dream life and be able to reconnect ourselves with our dreams so that we can go where they are trying to take us.

To make this possible, it is essential that we make a practice for a sufficient period of time of recording our dreams in the Dream Log. We should record them simply as we observe them and as we experience them. If we make any judgments about them as we are recording them, and especially if we undertake to save time by eliminating the "unimportant" dreams, we shall probably lose the dreams that turn out later to have the greatest significance to us. It is important simply to be reporters to ourselves in recording the elements of our dreams in our Dream Log.

The reason we keep a Dream Log distinct from the more general Daily Log is to enable us to build a continuous record of our dreams in the integrity of their own movement. In the Daily Log where we are recording the inner events of our life, it is valuable also to report on our dreams. But it is sufficient there if we make only a brief entry regarding a dream, just enough to identify it, and then we cross-reference it to the Dream Log where we record the dream in detail.

In the Dream Log we have nothing but dreams. We record the date, whatever background material is necessary, and then we describe the details of the dream as we experienced it. We record nothing but the dream in our Dream Log, no interpretations, no analysis, no feelings or thoughts about the dream that followed after it. We record only the dream itself.

By keeping our Dream Log free of everything but the actual dream material, we gradually accumulate a moving picture of the continuity of our dream life. When we read it back to ourselves there are no intrusions of theory or interpretation or reaction to the dreams. There are only the dreams themselves, as much of them as we could retain and as much as were recalled to us after we began to record them. Reading these back to ourselves after a period of time has passed enables us to feel the unity of movement of the dream process working within us. We can then perceive the *seriality* of our dreams, the inner continuity that is establishing itself at the core of their movement. Thus we see the direction, not only of our individual dreams, but of the unfolding process of our dreaming as a whole.

At the point where we read back to ourselves the continuity of dreams that we have collected in our Dream Log, a further step that extends our experience becomes possible. Our purpose in *feeding back* these dreams to ourselves in their consecutive movement is not to enable us to interpret their movement, nor to "understand" them, nor to analyze their "pattern." Our purpose rather is to place ourselves back into the movement of our dream process as a whole so that the process can now freely extend itself. Having come this far, where else do our dreams wish to go? What else are they reaching for? What else do they wish to say to us? In the *Dream Enlargements* section we make it possible for our dreams to indicate their messages to us.

To begin your dream work in the *Intensive Journal* it is good to catch up as best you can with the major dreams you have had in the past. If you have never recorded your dreams before, it is good to begin by describing in your Dream Log the earliest dreams that you remember. Perhaps there are some dreams from childhood years that have remained in your mind. They may be pleasant dreams, or painful dreams that you experienced as nightmares; or, as is often the case, they may be dreams that you remember because they were connected with a dramatic, or traumatic event in your life, as the death of a beloved person or the end of a close relationship. Sometimes dreams of this kind are clairvoyant or telepathic in content, but they are part of our dream process and should be recorded in the Dream Log. They, like all the dreams that we record in the Dream Log, are to be described as objectively as possible. We are merely reporting what we recall as the experience we had in the dream. No analysis, no interpretation, no elaboration of our feelings. We are merely recording as factually as we can the events of the dream.

When we have recorded the dreams of our early past, we come to a middle period between that past and our present during which many dreams may have occurred relating to the changing phase of our life. Give yourself leeway in recalling these dreams. They may not return to your mind all at once, but a dream at a time, or even a piece of a dream at a time. It is good, then, to leave room in your Dream Log so that you can insert these dreams of your past from time to time, as they recall themselves to you. You will very likely find that once you have turned your attention to your dreams, several of them will rush back to your memory. After that, however, as you are trying to remember more of them, the fact that you are trying will impede you. Therefore, after your initial recall of your dreams, let yourself relax, not deliberately seeking to recall them any longer. Go about your other activities, but with the silent resolution that whenever a dream of your past recalls itself to you, you will write it down and enter it in your Dream Log.

There are many of us who have recorded our dreams sporadically in the past in various contexts and situations. It may have been in the course of keeping a personal diary or writing about our inner experiences during a period of emotional difficulty. It may have been as part of a treatment in psychotherapy by one of several analytical techniques. Whatever the occasion for it, if you possess such a record of your dreams from any earlier period in your life, this is a good time to draw the old notebooks out of your files and read those dreams again. You can then transcribe them into the Dream Log of your *Intensive Journal.* If you have recorded a great many dreams in the past, you may prefer now to choose only those that have a special impact and significance as you read them in the present. If you copy into your Dream Log only a selective few of your earlier dreams, that will be the equivalent of recording your past dreams now without reference to an earlier journal, but only relying on your memory. For memory is in many ways a spontaneous selective factor with respect to our personal past, and it can have a great value in that regard.

After you have recorded the main dreams of your early life and also the general range of the past years, turn your attention to your recent dreams. Perhaps there is a dream of recent weeks or months that comes strongly to your mind. Record it in your Dream Log. While you are describing the dreams that return easily to your mind, others that were partially forgotten may also be recalled to you. Record them as they return to your mind, even if it is only a small piece of a dream. While you are writing it, more will be recalled to you. When you find it difficult to remember the contents of a dream, it is often helpful to direct your attention to the elements of movement in the dream. What changes of scene and of action took place in the dream? What shifts in the scenario or plot? Did the themes change, and what variations were there among the participants in the dream? Were there changes in the atmosphere or tone of the dream? Even if you do not remember the specific contents of the dream, questioning yourself about the elements of movement within it will very often serve to reconnect you with the general trend of the dream. That will put you in touch with what is important in the dream, for its interior movement is the essence of the dreaming process.

Let yourself now think of your most recent dreams, dreams of the last few nights, dreams of last night. Describe these in the Dream Log as fully as you can. Now you will have brought your record of your dreaming up to date so that you can work with your dreams actively by the Journal Feedback process.

The first step that we take in working with our dreams is a negative one. It is what we do not do. We deliberately refrain from analyzing them. We refrain from interpreting their symbolic content no matter how profound are the insights into them that we feel we possess. We make no interpretations from the point of view of any special theory, not from Freud's, nor Jung's, nor Adler's, nor any other, nor any eclectic mixture. We do nothing which would in any way make the dream or its symbolism "stand to reason." To do that would, in the first place, have the effect of rationalizing the symbolic material and thus violating the fact that its nature is inherently nonrational.

Of much more serious consequence, however, is the fact that to intellectualize dream material by interpreting it has the effect of lifting it out of the depth flow of the psyche which is its natural habitat. It thus is removed from the environment in which it was formed and on which its continued development depends. To interpret a dream in analytical terms has the effect of neutralizing its power, because it deprives the dream of its ability to continue its movement and to unfold its symbolism within its own terms. For this reason, the first step that we take is to refrain from interpreting our dreams. We allow them to remain on the depth level where they can be continued from within themselves and thus can expand their life.

Our second step, after having recorded our dreams in our Dream Log, is to return to the place in our experience where our dreaming occurred so that we can reenter our dreams and enable them to continue themselves. All our dreams are part of the moving flow of imagery that is continuously present at the depth level of the psyche. Each dream is an excerpt of that large and ongoing movement. It is a bucket of water sent up to us from the underground stream of imagery within us. In order to extend the movement of our dreams, therefore, it is not necessary for us to return to the condition of sleep in which the dreams occurred, but only to place ourselves back in the flow of imagery that is moving within us beneath our conscious minds. This is the flow from which our dreams were drawn.

For this next step in our work, we begin by sitting in quietness. Our Journal is open in front of us, the pages turned to the Dream Log. We close our eyes. In the silence we send our minds back over the movement of our dreams. We do this in a spontaneous and unguided way, not specifying in advance which of our dreams are to be called back to our attention. Rather, we let our minds go back over our dreaming as a whole. We wish to see which of our dreams will recall themselves to us when we place no restraints upon ourselves but merely let our minds roam over the generality of our dreaming.

It may be a dream or dreams from our earlier years that we now find ourselves recalling. Or it may be dreams from the recent past, or a current dream. From whichever period the dreams come, we turn our attention to them and we let ourselves *feel* them again. We do not interpret them, nor do we think now about what their "meaning" was. But we feel them again. We open ourselves to experience the quality and tone of the dreams, but without restricting ourselves as to the kind of feelings that will now come to us. We do not limit ourselves to the feelings that we had when the dream originally occurred.

In this freedom of emotion, we let the atmosphere of the dreams establish itself again. As it does, we deliberately hold ourselves in openness so that we can see without our predetermining it, which dream atmosphere draws us most strongly. We do not hold back but we follow the inner magnet of the dream that draws us to it. In this way we protect ourselves against letting our own preconceptions and opinions get in the way of the depth process that is seeking to unfold in us.

We hold ourselves in quietness, letting a spontaneously chosen group of dreams pass before our mind. We let our feelings move freely with respect to these dreams. We feel the atmosphere of the dreams, and we open ourselves to them so that we can be drawn into whichever dream-atmosphere has the greatest magnetic pull for us at that particular moment. Thus we by-pass whatever analytical or intellectual pre-conception we may have had about which of our dreams is most important for us. We do not let our own opinions interfere, but we leave it to the dream process itself as it is working within us to draw us to the dreams that are important for us now.

When we feel ourselves drawn into the atmosphere of a particular dream, from whichever period of our life it may come, we open our eyes and return to our Dream Log. If we have already recorded that dream, we now go back and read to ourselves the few dreams that immediately preceded the dream. We reread the dream itself, and we continue reading back to ourselves the next few dreams that follow it in the Dream Log. Our purpose in doing this is to enable ourselves to experience the context of the *series* of dreams, the central one being the dream whose atmosphere drew us to it. The seriality of dreams is the key factor with which we build the momentum that enables us to draw the dream process forward.

If the dream that drew us into its atmosphere is not one that we have already recorded in our Dream Log, we should describe it now. The fact that it has called itself to our attention is a sign that it has something meaningful to contribute to our lives and that it will be worth our while to spend some time with it. As we record that dream, we should also try to recall any additional dreams of that period, dreams that preceded and also dreams that immediately followed the dream in question. In that way we can place the dream directly in a series. Whether or not there are additional dreams that we can recall with it, it is good to insert the dream that we are newly recording at the proper chronological point in our Dream Log. Thus we maintain the continuity of our dream movement, and we are able to work with the seriality of our dreams.

Now we are ready to continue with our dream work. Sitting in stillness, we turn in our Dream Log to the dream that drew us back into its atmosphere. We go back a few dreams before it and we begin by reading the record of our dreams. We read them not in order to understand them, but in order to gain entry to them. We wish to get inside the movement of our dreams, as we would wish to be inside a train that is going in the direction we want to go. The train will carry us with it and take us to the next place we are to be in our lives, and so will the movement of our dreams.

There is one important difference that arises in comparing the movement of our dreams and the vehicle of a train. We may know in advance where a train is headed, and we are able to make the decision in advance as to whether that is where we also want to go. But the process of our dreaming has no "destination" printed on a sign at the front of it, and our dreams have no conductor to announce in advance the next station we are reaching.

We never know where our dreams are going. Many of them take us to places that are exceedingly unpleasant and very frightening. When those nightmare dreams come to us, we may wish that we were not travelling on our dream train at all. But that is the time when it becomes most important to remember the comparison between a train and our dream process. The nightmare dream that disturbs us is one of the points along the track. It is a tunnel through which we need to pass along the way, but it is not necessary that we remain there. That is why, when difficult or painful dreams come to us, it is important that we record them in our Dream Log. We thereby add them to the continuity of our dreaming, and we enable our dream process to move beyond them by going *through* them. Thus we can discover the destination of our dreams, and can recognize that that destination often contains the goal and meaning of our life unfoldment as a whole.

In that lies the great experiment and the great wonder of working with our dreams. We do not know in advance where they are taking us, just as we do not know in advance the ultimate outcome of our lives. It is always, therefore, a process of discovery. What we do know is that our dream process is moving out of the seed-potential of our life, and that the direction in which it is heading is already contained in that seed, as the fruit is present in the seed of the tree.

The process of our dreams is moving toward the fulfillment of these potentials. That is its general direction. But the form in which it will arrive there, the specific place where the goals will be located, if indeed they are to be found at a specific place, and the difficulties that will be encountered along the way cannot be known by us in advance. Ultimately to discover what that goal of our life is, is the great experiment of each individual existence. To find it is the adventure of our lives. This is the adventure, or journey, that is depicted in the legends, and fairy tales, and myths of the hero in many forms. We each experience it, and live it, in our own way, supplied and carried by the symbolic process that moves at the depth of us, a main carrier of which is our dreaming.

The movement and unfoldment of this symbolic process is the essential principle we follow in working with our dreams. Especially when we experience the nightmare dreams of anxiety and inner disturbance, we bear in mind that they are part of the ongoing process that underlies our dreaming. The central factor is the continuity of our dreams, and we must avoid breaking that continuity. That is one reason why we do not become involved in the analytical interpretation of our dreams. To analyze stops the movement of the process, and places us in the position of being outsiders who are observing an activity rather than being participants in the midst of it.

When we stop the movement of our dream process by analytic interpretation, we draw it off the track and away from its goal. We thereby prevent ourselves from discovering where the train of our dreams is heading. It is essential that we maintain that movement, regardless of the valleys and the difficult detours through which it passes. It is important also that the movement express each person's own integral dream process, without the insertion of the theories or suggestions of others intended to "help" the process along.

For these reasons as we work in our Dream Log we begin by reading a series of dreams. A single dream by itself may be very interesting and dramatic, but it is also very susceptible to having external meanings and interpretations read into it. A series of dreams, on the other hand, is a large enough segment of a moving process to carry some of the inner momentum of that process. Thus we read to ourselves a series of dreams, focusing on the one that drew us into its atmosphere as we sat in quietness.

We read the series of dreams now, feeling their inner movement. We become aware of the contents of the dreams as we read them to ourselves, but we do not think about them. We do not interpret the content, nor seek to find meaning in them. We simply read the series of dreams and let ourselves become part of their movement. We feel ourselves to be within them. We are inside the dreams, and they are inside us, just as we experienced them when they originally took place.

We let ourselves be drawn into their atmosphere. We are contained by the atmosphere of the movement of the dreams in the series. Gradually the movement of the series as a whole takes over and the separateness of the individual dreams becomes blurred. We read the dreams to ourselves a second and a third time. One technique that we can use at this point to help in the feedback aspect of the work is to read the series of dreams into a cassette recorder. We then play them back as a means of drawing ourselves into the atmosphere of the flow of the dreams.

Now, working alone we read the series of dreams until we feel ourselves to be within their movement. It is a stream that carries us along with it. Our eyes are closed. We are not asleep, but we are not fully awake either. We are in the state of *Twilight Dreaming*.

Now, on the screen of our mind's eye, the dreams continue themselves. Some of the scenes from the dreams may reappear, but not necessarily the scenes nor their contents as they originally took place. It is not our specific dreams that we are continuing, but the inner process of our dreaming as a whole. We are letting it move freely out of its own context so that it can reach and reflect the full range of its possibilities.

Images and feelings and actions continue for us now, just as would be the case in our sleep dreaming. We let the inner movement of our Twilight Dreaming move on by itself. We do not guide it. We do not direct it. We do not restrict it. We encourage it to move on its own and in its own way wherever it wishes to go. Inwardly we follow it. With our emotions and our inner participation, we freely go with it. We let our Twilight Dreaming proceed as fully and as long as it wishes. We behold it, accompany it, and let it carry us as a vehicle driven by its own inner guidance.

As our Twilight Dreaming continues, it is often helpful for us to speak out the experiences that come to us. Even if we are alone, conducting our Twilight Dreaming in privacy, it is good to speak our experiences aloud. Although no one is present to hear them, to articulate them so that they can be heard seems to make them more tangible for us so that we do not lose them in their wispiness but can take hold of them and record them. Once we have described them, we are better able to work with them with additional Journal Feedback procedures.

This is a main reason why in our Journal Workshops, after we have each read to ourselves a series of our dreams and are extending them by Twilight Dreaming, we have a time when we speak aloud into the group the experiences that come to us. Ordinarily, no one responds to what we speak, nor comments upon it. But speaking aloud our experiences of Twilight Dreaming seems to help us invidually to carry our inner process further. Each experience that is spoken seems also to contribute to the atmosphere of the group, thereby strengthening and reinforcing in everyone the contact with the dream level.

After a little while, it will be time to record our experiences. We do not describe them in the Dream Log, since that is reserved for recording our dreams as we originally experienced them. We keep our dreams there in the Dream Log in their pure, unembellished, uninterpreted form so that, when we read them back to ourselves at a later time, the inherent continuity of their movement will be reflected back to us. That will enable us to work with a series of dreams and to place ourselves back within the flow and context of our total dream movement. The inner momentum of our dream process then becomes available to us, and this is a main advantage to working with the seriality of dreams.

We record the experiences that have come to us through Twilight Dreaming in the Dream Enlargement section. While the experience is in process we record it in bits and pieces, just as it comes to us. The Journal entries that we make while we are in the midst of a twilight exercise are brief reportings of the inner events as they are taking place. We learn to write in our Journal with our eyes three quarters closed. Sometimes the atmosphere of our twilight experience is so strong that it holds us for a considerable period before we can break away at all to make even a hazy recording. At those times we have to carry a great deal in our memory while further experiences are coming to us. At other times we make a number of brief, half-legible entries, recording each new perception as it comes to us, and returning quickly to the twilight level. Because Twilight Dreaming is altogether spontaneous and unguided, it occurs in a different form each time we experience it. The practice of it teaches us to be free and flexible in relation to the depth of ourselves.

When our experience on the twilight level has subsided and we have recorded it in the Dream Enlargement section, we can proceed to work further with the material that has come to us. As a unit now, we read back to ourselves the continuation of our dreaming as it took place on the twilight level. As we reread it, we become aware of the feelings and emotions that arose in us as those experiences were taking place. We find that we have additional reactions now as we read them. We add to the continuity of our dream work now by recording all these inner responses in the Dream Enlargements sections.

Making these entries, there are some key questions that can help us focus our inner process so that we can recognize and record what is happening within us. While these experiences were taking place, what feelings were present within us? What was the atmosphere and the tone that accompanied them? And now, as you read them back to yourself in a single continuity, what emotions and awarenesses are stirred in you? As you read the Twilight Dreaming, do you perceive a movement or a direction within it? Do you feel in its symbolism a particular theme or thread suggesting that it has a message to communicate to you? Did you feel that direction or message to be present in the Twilight Dreaming while it was taking place? Or do you only perceive these hints and indications now, after you have recorded it and are reading it back as a unit from your present position in consciousness?

Whatever additional thoughts or feelings, reflections or perceptions of any kind come to you now should be added to your Dream Enlargement section. When we go down, as we just have done, to the twilight level to extend the process of dreaming, we find that many inner awarenesses about our life, our past, and the possibilities of our future, are actively stimulated. Things that we knew, or half-knew, but did not realize we knew, now come to the fore of our mind. While they were vague or inaccessible to us before, once we have recorded them in the Journal, we can think about them lucidly. Now ideas that were merely intimations or hunches before can be considered critically and constructively.

We recognize in this a most significant paradox that is a fact or our deep Journal experience. By working with our dreams and their extensions on the twilight level where the contents are mainly nonconscious, nonrational, and symbolic rather than literal, we experience an unexpected reversal in the quality of our awareness. As we emerge from working within the realm of the unconscious at the deeper than personal levels, we find that our consciousness now possesses a greater acuity. After having opened our psyches to the symbolic material in the twilight depths, our perceptions of the outer world become sharper and clearer, and our thinking processes move more quickly and more relevantly than they did before. Many new thoughts, insights, intuitions, and recognitions of all kinds related to our life in general and to specific projects now come to our mind. Sometimes they come to consciousness in great volume, flooding us with ideas and awarenesses. At such times we have to learn to regulate their flow so that we can retain and record them. Above all, this bounty of new thoughts that come to consciousness in the wake of our twilight experiences should not be lost, but retained in the Journal for our future use.

Let us make sure now that we record in the Dream Enlargement section all the thoughts and feelings, everything that has come to our consciousness after the extended experience of Twilight Dreaming. The content of many of these will relate to other sections of the Journal. It is not necessary, however, for us to be concerned with the question of where in the Journal these entries belong and where we shall work with them. The important task of the moment is to record this new source of material while its momentum is strong and it is still flowing spontaneously. We therefore write it in the Dream Enlargement section regardless of its subject matter, recording it as fully as it comes to us. Later on, when the movement of this material has quieted within us, we can cross-reference its various aspects to other sections of the Journal and there, each in its valid context, explore and extend them with the appropriate Journal Feedback exercises.

One of the most valuable contributions of our dreams lies in the clues and guidance they give us as to which areas of our life we should reexamine. Since they reflect without censorship what is taking place inside of us, our dreams direct us to those sections of the Journal where there is work that needs to be done. These *dream leads* can be especially valuable, and will greatly expedite our Journal work if we learn to follow them. The *dream leads* do not in themselves supply the answer to our problems. In fact, it is important to refrain from reading into our dreams some particular meaning that we infer is giving us specific directions for the conduct of our life. On most occasions when we interpret a dream in such a concrete way that we then say, "My dream told me to do such and such," we find eventually that we imputed to the dream a meaning that it did not necessarily have. It was not necessarily saying what we thought it was saying.

All too often we impute meanings to our dreams either because that is what we wished for or because that is what we were afraid of. Dreams are especially vulnerable to our reading meanings into them which they themselves had no intention of conveying. Dreams are defenseless against our misinterpreting them because their symbolic style is inherently ambiguous, and people have a tendency to see in them either what they are looking for or what they are afraid of finding. Depending on their temperament, many people use their dreams either to diagnose themselves or to encourage themselves by adapting the dreams to reinforce beliefs they already have. Beyond that, as a result of the psychological era in which we have been living, it is difficult for people to become educated in the terms of modern thought without absorbing the concepts of the famous psychoanalysts Freud or Adler or Jung or their numerous derivatives. Without realizing that they are doing so, they inadvertently read their dreams by the light of those particular theories and thus find meanings that may have been valid for Freud's life or Jung's life but not necessarily for their life.

It was Jung himself who remarked that every system of analytical psychological theory is a "subjective confession," including his own, as he was honest enough to say. He also made the very important point, which his particular theory (of the archetypes) frequently prevented him from following in practice, that it is always the context of the individual life as expressed through a series of dreams that holds the key to what the dreams are trying to say. To follow any particular analytical line of interpretation has the effect of entering the dream, and the life, from the outside with a preconceived theory. To that degree it violates the integrity of the individual life.

It is specifically to protect the integrity of each person's inner process that in the Journal Feedback method we avoid the interpretation of dreams. Instead of analyzing our dreams, we encourage their unfoldment by recording them fully and by extending their serial movement through the procedures of Twilight Dreaming. We then draw, both from the dreams themselves and from the dream enlargements, clues and directions as to where in our lives, as reflected in the various sections of the Journal, there is further exploration to be done. These dream leads then provide the starting points for further active exercises of Journal Feedback which we pursue in the appropriate Journal sections.

It is important to understand the principle that is the basis for this non-analytical way of working with dreams. In the first place we recognize that more fundamental than the dreams themselves and more fundamental than the Twilight Imagery is the process that is moving toward life integration at the depth of each person. The dreams are one of the forms by which this process expresses itself, and by which it indicates where it is trying to go, its problems and blockages, and its requirements. It is in order that we may get these messages of inner guidance from the depth of ourselves that we pay attention to our dreams.

Dreams are subject to certain limitations, however. The first of these is the fact that many people do not remember their dreams. The way it often is phrased is, "But, Doctor, I don't dream!" We know, of course, that everyone does dream, since the process of dreaming is an inherent part of the psychic organism. It is true, however, that only a small proportion of our sleep dreaming is recalled in the waking state by anyone. It is further true that a large number of people remember hardly any of their dreams at all, unless the pressure of particular circumstances makes them sensitive to certain "big" dreams of special impact, or unless they practice the discipline of recording their dreams in the middle of the night at the moment when they happen. Most of our sleep dreaming is lost to us, which is the reason that many people believe that they do not dream. This is a serious limitation, particularly if we are relying on dreams as the only or major road, the "royal road" as Freud called it, to the contents of our unconscious levels.

The second, and probably more consequential limitation of dreams is the fact that the language of dreams is exceedingly ambiguous. Dreams do not speak literally in the manner of our rational consciousness. They use a symbolic style, dramatizing their points and making veiled, indirect, allusive references. This is the reason why over the centuries it has been thought to be necessary to analyze and interpret dreams in order to find out what they are trying to say. The language of dreams is not rational and it has therefore been necessary to have some means of making the dreams "stand to reason" if we are to have access to their message for our conscious use in our lives. To find what is rational in the apparent irrationality of the dream's language is the goal that underlies all attempts at dream interpretation, whether it is by God-inspiration as for Joseph in the Old Testament, or whether it is by the analytical concepts of Freud or Jung. The problem is that the analysis of dreams is very susceptible to our subjective reading-in of our wishes, fears, or other preconceptions.

These two limitations of dreams should not be allowed, however, to obscure the more fundamental principle, and goal, of dreaming as an essential fact of our inner lives. There is apparently a primary life process moving at our depth carrying a direct intuitive knowing of the integral needs of each individual existence. When this process expresses itself in dreams, the symbolic language of the nonrational depths which it uses is ambiguous and is vulnerable to misinterpretation; but there are many indications that this fundamental life process is in fact trying to make itself accessible to consciousness and available to our rational understanding. It is stymied by the fact of its symbolism, which is ambiguous not only in dreams, but also in twilight imagery. It is at this point that our use of dream leads provides valuable assistance to the depth process that is expressed in dreaming. It frees that process from the ambiguities of symbolism by enabling it to move through its dreams and imagery to the specific areas of life experience where its messages are needed.

To see how we find and follow a dream lead, let us consider this example. Suppose you have a dream about a person whom you have not seen in many years and who has not been in your conscious thought. You may speculate intellectually about what or who he represents to you, but you run the risk then of making an artificial analysis that will falsify your dream by reading something into it. You will also be stopping the movement of the dream process by cutting it apart with analytical concepts. Instead, we stay directly with the dream contents, but we give them a place and an opportunity to continue to unfold out of themselves.

In the example we are using, a number of options would be available to us as our first step, depending on the feelings that come to us as we reread the dream. In general, it is best to proceed as concretely as possible, staying close to the actual content of the dream. We begin by recalling memories of our relationship with that person, places where we were together, situations, events, emotions that we associate with him. As these memories come to us, we record them in the Life History Log. As we are writing, our descriptions will open outward and enlarge themselves. One memory will beget another.

As we continue with this, we find that additional awarenesses are stimulated in us. We realize, for example, that this person who appeared in our dream was closely identified with a decision we made at an earlier time in our life, a decision that led us to follow one path of action and to reject others. We had not thought of him in that connection before, but the association is now clear to us. Following our dream lead, we now turn to the Journal section, Intersections: Roads Taken and Not Taken. We describe the circumstances at that crossroad of our life. As we unfold our memories and as we reenter the situation of that earlier time, many additional emotions and awarenesses are reactivated. We record these also.

As we make these additional entries, we ask ourselves to which other sections of the Journal we are now being led. Are any new indicators being suggested to us as we proceed? It may be that, as we are describing that earlier intersection in our lives, we are reminded of the choice we made and the various roads not taken while we were under the influence of that friendship. Perhaps it was a choice of a field of study, or a business opportunity, or a change of location that was involved. Following the direction of our Journal work, we might then turn to the Dialogue with Works section to explore the present significance of the avenue of work that was not pursued at that earlier time in our life. We might also turn to the Dialogue with Persons section to reenter our relationship with the person who was in our dream, and perhaps with others who have been called to our attention as we have been following our dream leads.

At this point it is clear that, taking the dream as our starting point, a momentum of exploration and new experience has been generated. We are now being carried in a direction that discloses its next turn to us with each new exercise we carry out. One step leads to the next one as in a chain of continuity. In this sense it can truly be said that the inner movement of our depth process which was reflected in our dream has been enabled to extend itself in an open-ended way. It is unfolding and finding its direction in its own terms within the context of our individual life history.

It is significant to note also that while the dream originally presented us with ambiguous symbolism, the progression of our exercises in the Journal makes its message for us increasingly clear in the context of our everyday experience. Following our dream leads through the interweaving exercises of Journal Feedback enables the organic depth process of our lives to move beyond the symbolic obscurity of dreams toward a greater clarity in communicating its inner messages to us in terms of the actualities of our outer lives.

With this as our perspective, let us now reread our entries to find the dream leads that will be fruitful for us to follow in other Journal Feedback exercises. We go back over the dreams we have described in the Dream Log. Recent dreams are especially valuable in this regard. Now that we are familiar with this procedure, we can look at our new dreams as they come to us to see what leads they give us for further exploration in our lives via the Journal sections. Always we ask the question: Where else in the Journal do these dreams suggest that I work? Thus we find our dream leads. It is good to keep on as current a basis as possible with our new dreams. The sooner we let them lead us to the appropriate sections of the Journal, the sooner they will be able to communicate their inner messages to us, and the greater the momentum of movement in new directions we shall enable them to build in our lives.

While it is important to work with our most current dreams, we should not ignore our old dreams. They may be holding leads that are very valuable for us to follow but which we have overlooked in the past. In fact, even when we are working with our dream leads on a current basis, it is good to go back over our dreams from time to time, browsing through our Dream Log, looking for dream leads that we did not recognize before.

After we have reread our Dream Log, we continue through our entries in the Dream Enlargement section looking for further dream leads. Our experiences in Twilight Dreaming are often particularly fertile in this regard, possibly because they are a step closer to our conscious awareness than the dreams that come in sleep. The same is true of all of our Twilight Imagery experiences. We can find very valuable dream leads not only in the dream sections, but in the *Twilight Imagery Log* and in its follow-up section, *Imagery Extensions*. Drawing our leads from all of these sections and extending them with feedback exercises in other parts of the Journal enables us to channel our deep inner experiences into the activities of outer life. Conversely, it means that the active and available source of our conscious awareness will be in our depth.

Working with dream leads both from the sleep and twilight levels gives us a large resource for discovering and developing the potentials of our life. It is obviously not a type of exercise that is brief and simple. Rather it is open ended and ever expansive. We can work with it as little or as much as we choose, but the more proficient we become in finding our dream leads and following them in other Journal exercises, the greater will be our access to the larger sources of our individual lives.

We have been working with the inward level of reality as it moves on the depth dimension of our experience. Our dreams come from hidden parts of us often in strange symbolic forms, and the extension of our dreaming on the twilight level also proceeds beyond our rational control. We now come to the question of what correlation there may be between the experiences we have had in our inward depths and the experiences that have been taking place on the surface of our lives.

This is an important question, but we should not try to answer it by thinking about it. We can go to it indirectly and let it give us the awareness we desire regarding the inner movement of our lives.

Once again we sit in quietness. We close our eyes and let our breathing become slow. We are letting ourselves slide into the stillness. No thoughts. The slowness of our breathing and the emptiness of our mind enables us to feel the process of our lives as it moves within us. We do not think of what that is. We do not determine it with our minds. We let it present itself to us. We let it show itself and declare itself in its own timing.

As the stillness settles within us with our eyes closed, we draw ourselves back to the original series of dreams with which we began our dream work. As much as we can, we return to them. We see those dreams again and we feel the emotional tone that they carried. More important than the details of the dreams, we feel their movement, and especially the rhythms of their movement. We feel, for example, the energy of flowers growing in our dream, blossoming and then withering. And we feel the movement of the seed breaking in the ground and coming to the surface as new shoots of green. We feel the movement of prolonged submergence in our dream, of angry struggle, chase, escaping, recovery, of tearing down and building up. Whatever it presents to us, we feel the phases of change in the tone and the rhythms of movement in our dreams. We feel that in the silence.

And now we add to the dreams our experiences of the Twilight Dreaming. We draw the two together and feel them as a single continuity moving within us. We feel the unfoldment and ongoingness of their movement as a whole.

When the experience of this is full within us, we hold it. We stop the movement. We hold it where it is, as though we are holding it in our hand. We are holding our inner experience of the depth dimension as a base while we draw together the equivalent movement that has taken place on the outer level of our life as a whole.

With our eyes closed, now, we go back over the sequences of our life. We recapitulate in our minds the outline of events that we listed as our Steppingstones. We feel the rhythms of change and a variation among them, and especially we reexperience the flow and combination of circumstances that carried us into the recent period of our life. In quietness within ourselves, with our eyes closed, we are feeling the entire ongoing movement of our lives up to the present moment of time. Included in this are the external events and the inner events. Mainly we wish to perceive and experience within ourselves the larger outlines of movement in our lives. But we let ourselves feel it all, the plans we have had and the obstacles to fulfilling them, the detours and disappointments, the renewed hopes and fears, the resolutions made, the decisions that we have held off and those that lie ahead.

We draw together the whole movement of our life as it has unfolded up to the present. A great many aspects of our life have opened to us and have been called to our attention in new ways in the course of our working in the various sections of the Journal. We include all of these as they return to our minds now, letting this moment become an experience of total reunification with respect to the movement of our life.

As we do this, it is important to allow sufficient time to enable the process of inward integration to proceed and settle itself in its own timing.

You are sitting in quietness. Your eyes are closed, The atmosphere is one of meditation, even of silence, unarticulated prayer. You are reexperiencing the essential movement of your life, allowing it to integrate itself into a new form as it proceeds.

In a little while as this is happening within you, you will be ready to take the next important step in the process of *life correlation*. Sitting in this stillness with the ongoing flux of your life taking shape within you, let yourself feel the moving unity of it. Maintain your perception of it, feeling the wholeness of it inwardly. You are feeling the reality of your life as a whole. It is taking form. It is tangible enough to touch, definite enough for you to hold it in your hand.

On the symbolic level of imagery, let yourself do that now. Whatever form your life is taking as it presents itself to you, hold it in your hand. Hold it in your right hand. Symbolically this is as though you are placing your life on the right side of your mind. It is your conscious awareness of your life, as your life has been unfolding on the outward level of experience.

Now, still on the twilight level, take in your left hand the combined movement of your sleep dreams and your twilight dreaming as you have already drawn them together. Symbolically within yourself you are holding in your left hand the unified movement of your inner nonconscious life, and you are holding in your right hand the essential continuity of your outer conscious life. Balance one against the other. Balance each in relation to the other. It is as though there is a scale within your mind. Let the two sides equalize themselves so that the interior scale adjusts and places itself in harmonious balance.

When they come into balance, you can ask yourself the question of what the two sides of your life have to say to each other, and what they say to you when you draw them together and set them side by side. As this interior balancing is taking place, let yourself be especially open to any additional images, feelings, thoughts, insights, recognitions, ideas, perceptions, emotions, and especially new inspirations and plans that take shape in you. This is not a time for deliberate thinking but for being especially receptive to the awarenesses of every kind that arise spontaneously within you. The process of *life correlation* that allows the opposites of human experience, the outer and the inner, the conscious and the nonconscious, to establish their relation to one another is especially productive of new understanding. It is a process of inner life-balancing, of nonanalytic self-integration. As it sets the opposites side by side in a neutral, non-interpretive way, new integrative syntheses come forth, as though by themselves.

It is important, therefore, to be receptive and observant as you practice the life correlation of the inner and the outer. Take note of all the new experiences that now present themselves to you, and report them in your *Dream Enlargements* section. Record and describe them as fully as you feel impelled to do. But do not judge or interpret them in the moment that they come to you. Their significance for your life may not be apparent at that time. But describe them in the Journal, and then expand upon them at a later time, recording all the additional considerations they evoke in you. You will very often find as you do this that these experiences provide exceedingly valuable *feedback leads* for you to follow in opening out additional areas of your life in other sections of the Journal.

We can see from the varied procedures that are available to us for working with our dreams that the process of Dream Enlargement has numerous aspects and successive levels of depth to which it can be carried. Working with the seriality of dreams gives us a basic protection against our inadvertently inserting misleading analytical interpretations, and it also preserves the quality of flow that is inherent in the dream process. The procedures of Twilight Dreaming enable us to reenter the dream process, drawing from the depths of sleep the seeds of fresh experiences that can readily be remembered, recorded, and extended. The process of life correlation permits us to move between the opposites of our outer and inner lives so that, as the two meet in a self-sustaining balance, new integrative syntheses are brought forth. Most important of all, however, are the dream leads which we draw from the enlargement of our dreaming, and which feed into the unfolding totality of our life as a whole. These enable us to resupply the Journal Feedback process continuously from the very depths of our being as we carry forward progressive integrations of our outer and inner lives.

Chapter 17

Dialogue with Society

The exercises with which we have worked so far to build our dialogue relationships have been concerned primarily with the personal aspects of our life. They have dealt mainly with what is subjective to our individual existence, the persons with whom we are intimately involved, our work activities, the condition of our body, and the impact of particular events upon our lives. As we have proceeded with these Journal Feedback exercises in the dialogues and especially in the Twilight Imagery and the dream work, it has become increasingly clear that our personal lives have a background that is more than personal. Each of us, in our own way, draws upon history, traditions, the world of nature, the realm of the spirit, and the arts, among other transpersonal resources for the experiences and the potentials of our lives. Sometimes these sources present a problem to us, confusing and filling us with personal conflict where matters of faith and belief are concerned. At other times they become a source of inspiration and enlarged awareness for us. In either case it is clear that these more-than-personal aspects of our life are of profound importance for our growth in wholeness, and that it is of great value for us to have a dialogue relationship with them. This is the work that we do in the *Dialogue with Society* section.

In the original edition of the *Intensive Journal*, this section bore the heading, "Group Experiences." The reference to groups indicated that this was the section in which we would reach beyond our purely personal concerns to the larger aspects of our life that connect us with our fellow human beings. As our experience with the *Intensive Journal* proceeded, however, we recognized that something much larger than group relationship is involved here. We were drawn in the direction of Aristotle's awareness that the human being is inherently social, and our experiences underscored the need for establishing an inner relationship to the social dimension of our existence.

The social aspect of life necessarily involves group situations, but group experiences as such are not of major importance in our *Dialogue with Society.* We are not concerned with transient groups, like those that come together for a weekend, or those that meet for the passing interaction of discussing a common problem, or to enjoy one another's company. We are interested, rather, in those group relationships that play an ongoing role in our lives, especially those that are present before we are born and after our physical death. In this context, our relationship to society is not limited to the direct interpersonal contacts that occur during our lifetime, but it includes the larger units of society that begin before us and extend beyond us.

In the context of this section of the Journal, the term, *Society,* refers to all those aspects of our experience in which we draw upon our cultural and historical rather than our individual sources for the conduct of our life.

For many persons the basic social unit is the family into which they are born and grow to adulthood. We usually find, however, that the specific problems and issues that arise within the family tend to be dealt with in other sections of the Journal. The relationships between individuals within the family become the subject matter for much that is done in Dialogue with Persons. The decisions and situations that are confronted in the course of family life are often dealt with in Dialogue with Events, Situations, Circumstances. In Dialogue with Society, however, we explore the less direct but larger significances of our relationship to our family. Here we deal not so much with the relationships within the family as with the more general contexts of society into which our family has placed us by reason of our birth or the circumstances of our life.

It may be that we have been born into a family with a long lineage and distinguished social position; on the other hand, our family may have only a moderate or a meager social status, or we may have no family at all, or we may have been adopted into a family. Each of these is an authentic fact and circumstance of our life. Whatever our particular situation may be, it is meaningful for us to establish our relationship to it. At various points in our life, it becomes important that we deepen our relation to our cultural background, including the time, place, and group situation into which we were born. This may be a national group, Italian or English or Japanese. It may involve not only biological connections but the geographic ties of living in a particular area, being mountaineers or farmers or city workers, living in the South or West or East of a particular country.

In earlier generations, the units of social identification were often based primarily on biological or on geographical connections among people, but recent times have brought a substantial change in that respect. With the mobility and development of individuals, the sense of group belonging tends to be based increasingly on subjective interests as well as on the more primal factors of blood ties or territorial affinities. We now feel our cultural connection to be not only with people who are related to us physically or who live near us but, even more, those who share the interests of our life involvement. This extends our group identification into a broad variety of areas. We share with others and perceive ourselves to be members of a single social group on the basis of being artists, musicians, scientists, sports enthusiasts, marijuana smokers, rebellious youth, the retired aging, or whatever other bond serves as a means of self-identification and belonging.

Life involvements that are subjective to the individual but are spontaneously shared by many others are a major bond of connection in modern society. They draw together people who would not otherwise be linked by blood ties or cultural background but who have common values and interests. These are particularly important because they enable people to develop their individuality in relation to their inner capacities while giving them external avenues for expression and self-identification. We work with these involvements in Dialogue with Society, and also in other sections of the Journal which deal with the specific concerns and strivings of the individual. Dialogue with Works is especially significant in this regard. It is important that we feel free to reach beyond the boundaries of birth to find group connections in terms of our subjective interests; it is essential also that we not by-pass those areas of our experience that connect us to the more generic units of mankind.

One of the major subjects that is included in Dialogue with Society is the question of our race or our national origin. Especially in countries like the United States where the population is a mixture of peoples, it is important for individuals to have a means of clarifying and maintaining a continuing relationship with their racial or national background. This is particularly true of those groups that are in a minority, or are placed in the position of being socially weaker or less highly regarded than other groups. Where a particular group is regarded as being weaker on the social scale, the individuals in that group often ascribe that stereotype of inferiority to themselves personally, and the integrity of their individual development is thereby undermined.

With this in mind, we work here to establish a dialogue relationship with the larger group units into which we are born. Here we can explore our identification with Black nationalism, or Zionism, or Irish independence, or whatever nation or race is relevant to us. Of special importance is the fact that the dialogue exercises make it possible for these identifications to speak to us and to articulate out of our non-conscious depths the meaning they hold for our life. Beyond this, what holds possibly the greatest value of all for us is that, as we continue to work in the *Intensive Journal* over a period of time, these relationships have an opportunity to grow and change and deepen themselves. Our social identifications are not necessarily fixed, therefore, by a decision or commitment that we make at any particular point in our lives. As our inner experience deepens, our social identifications can be correspondingly deepened and enlarged in their meaning and in the quality of action which they suggest to us.

Sometimes, when working in this section of the Journal, individuals have chosen to do their dialogues not only with the special social groups from which they are descended and with which they have their immediate affiliation, but with mankind as a whole. They are thus expressing their intimation of the fact that the possibilities of a person's social identifications are not limited to the proximate groups of birth or environment. They may reach to larger, universal or global units, such as those envisioned by Teilhard de Chardin, Aurobindo, and other philosophers. By the light of such visions, it may be very relevant to establish a dialogue relationship with One World, a transnational government, or a vision of Utopian society in which humanity is united. By way of strengthening their perception of the wholeness of mankind, some persons have done their Dialogue with Society with the process of evolution by which our species has evolved, or with the seed of humanity that carries the potential of the human species. Such exercises provide a very important channel by which we can establish our relationship with the larger aspects of our humanness. We may achieve this also by means of dialogues with our civilization, and with our relation to particular ideological movements in history. Dialogues of this kind, however, should be in addition to and not take the place of our working with the more immediate aspects of our existence that involve our specific and personal life-connections.

An important aspect of the Dialogue with Society is that it enables us to draw ourselves into relationship with the historical sources of our life. The contents of this are more specific and also more subjective than our relation to the movements of political or social history in general; they are also more personal than our relation to the history of the particular people or nation from which we are descended. It is here that we work with whatever connection we subjectively feel between ourselves and any of our personal sources, or resources that lie in the past.

It may be, for example, that in the generations preceding us there lived an individual who made a particular contribution to the world around him, or who expressed a special wisdom, or sensitivity, or commitment in his life. He may have been related to us in a direct line of family descendance, or he may have been more loosely related to us by having been a member of the same nation or race, or perhaps only having lived in the same area. Whatever the actual physical connection, if that person's life has a stimulating or inspirational meaning for us which we feel in an intimate and personal way, it may be exceedingly valuable to explore the possibilities of an inner relationship with him by

257

means of the dialogue exercises. It is a means of establishing a working connection to the past in such a way as to make it accessible to us in the immediacy of our present situation.

There may be a particularly strong emotional factor involved when the individual is someone who lived directly in our line of ancestry. A personal charismatic element is present then and a great energy may be felt, as when the person is a known relative, as a grandfather, or a great aunt or uncle, or a kinsman, a member of the same clan or tribe or guild. Sometimes it is a person who is removed from us in time by more than a few generations so that blood ancestry cannot actually be traced. Or, where blood relationship is not involved, we may feel our kinship by virtue of being part of the same cultural tradition. Sometimes it reaches beyond the reality of a known person and is a culture hero of the distant past, a person whose life is meaningful not only to us but to many others as well. Such a person is of great inner importance to us, even though the actuality of his physical existence may be in doubt. His spiritual existence is nonetheless a fact for us, a fact that is essential for us to recognize and to work with in our Journal. Such individuals constitute a great inner resource for those who can understand the nature of their presence and can allow it to express itself without being falsified. They provide a personal connection for us to the traditions and the wisdom of the past, insofar as we have a means of contacting them via the depth of our Selves.

Our Dialogue with Society may serve not only to give us a means of deepened connection to the sources of the past in personal terms, but it may also enable us to maintain a continuing relationship with the political events of our time. We may be in dialogue with our country, with its leaders, and with the general issues that are at the fore of discussion. During periods of social tranquillity, these political issues may be only of moderate interest, except for those individuals who are involved in politics as their special area of lifework. During periods of social ferment or political crisis, however, these issues become the focus of intense personal involvement. At times of political turbulence, it becomes especially important to have an instrument like the *Intensive Journal* available to us as a means of clarifying our personal role in the events taking place around us, so that we can each determine individually where our social commitment lies, and so that we can act both creatively and responsibly.

In this regard, our experience at Journal Workshops over the years has been very instructive. At most of the basic workshops where there is a limitation on the time available to us and where the emphasis is necessarily on the personal aspects of the individual's life, Dialogue with Society is a section that is dealt with only briefly. It is described to the participants in the workshop, but its exercises are usually not carried out at length. At times of intense political excitation, however, like the Cambodian invasion, or the Kent State shootings, or the Watergate disclosures, political events become a major aspect of people's personal lives.

This fact is indicated clearly at an early point in the Journal Workshops when the participants read their Period Log entries. At times of social ferment, the Period Logs deal much less with the intimately personal areas and much more with the issues that were being discussed in the public press. At such times public issues become subjects for intimate and soul-searching decision, as when the young people had to decide each individually whether they wished to participate in protest marches and student strikes, and the adults had to determine what type of political action, if any, their personal integrity required of them. These questions are always present in the modern world, but in some circumstances they become more urgent. This section of the *Intensive Journal* is one private place to which individuals can go in making political decisions and commitments that will feel valid to them both personally and as members of their community.

Another subject of importance in our dialogue relationship with society, is our relation to the institutions and organizations with which we have an affiliation whether by belief or membership. As the pace of social change quickens in the modern era, the question arises for many persons of what they still require and desire from their old institutional affiliations. And the question arises equally from the other side of what these institutions require of them. Many important dialogues take place in this context, carrying the seeds of new social developments.

This is the section of the Journal where you can work out your relation to the institutional aspect of religion, to your labor union or business organization, or to the fraternal or cultural institutions in which you participate. It has been a very instructive experience for many persons in these dialogue exercises to discover that social institutions do indeed have a life of their own, that they may be understood as persons who have a seed-nature, a life-history, and purposes that carry them into the future where they may change, grow, or outlive their reason for existence.

An exceedingly fruitful, although less obvious, phase of our Dialogue with Society occurs in our relationship with the artworks that other people have created. The making of works of art, in literature, drama, music, or any of the other artforms, is inherently a social process. Some artforms, like the movies and the ballet, require the cooperation of a large number of persons, and thus they are obviously a product of society. However, even those fields of art, such as poetry and music where much of the creative work is carried through in lonely isolation, depend upon the social continuity of mankind. The artist in every field stands upon the shoulders of those who have gone before him; to the degree that his work is valuable, it provides a base and an inspiration for those who are to follow him. The artist is therefore always an intermediary of history. A question that is raised in one generation is inwardly experienced, responded to, transformed, and carried further, as the artwork gives the old issue a new aspect and suggests new possibilities for its further development. There is thus a social process of continuity that is inherent in the ongoing history of the arts, and this is the lifeline that supports and supplies the individual artworks of the future.

Ordinarily this social process is participated in and carried further only by those who are actively engaged in the creative process of art. For the most part, the exercises that these persons would carry through in building their dialogue relationship with the arts would be in the Dialogue with Works section. Here, in the Dialogue with Society section, however, we have a place and procedures that enable each of us to participate in the continuity of the arts and to contribute our psychic energies to their unfoldment. Whenever we read a book, see a painting, hear a symphony, or experience any other work of art that is deeply moving or significant to us, this is where we may record the feelings, perceptions, and other responses that have been awakened in us. We may then proceed to explore and expand them by means of the procedures that are used in this section of the Journal. As we deepen our own inner involvement in the artwork, we add our experience of it to the cumulative psychic process and social atmosphere by which the history of the creative arts moves forward.

With this as our background, we can now begin the basic exercises with which we work in the Dialogue with Society section.

Our first step is to draw together a list of those areas of interest or concern that will be meaningful for us to work on in this part of the Journal. Out of this list we shall choose one for our dialogue script exercise at the Journal Workshop.

It may be that as we have been describing them, a subject for dialogue has already come to the forefront of your mind and you have decided upon it. Often, as we continue our Journal work, we find that the leads into Dialogue with Society come from the exercises that we do in other sections of the Journal and especially our current experiences in the Daily Log. It is good, nonetheless, to have a reserve listing of the areas of social interest and involvement that are personally significant to us. To have them available in the Journal places them where we can see them and be reminded of them again. It may then be that one day after the workshop is over they will come to mind again and stimulate us to establish dialogue relationship with them. We make a list in order to prod ourselves to dig deeper inward and to loosen the soil of our lives.

In making this list, we have one major point of reference: our life. The place to look, therefore, to find our meaningful social interests is among our Steppingstones. Let us turn to that section now to review the Steppingstone Periods that we listed earlier in the workshop. Each of these periods covered a significant unit of time in our life and contained many different interests and beliefs and concerns. Now we reenter those periods of our life in order to refresh our memories with respect to the social factors that have had an impact on our lives. These may be in various forms.

They may be the recollection of specific events, as marching in a parade, voting for the Presidency, entering the Army, being tormented for being a minority person. It may be also a more general remembering of attitudes or continued experiences or group affiliations that lasted for a long period of time and then changed, like being a Socialist, or a Ku Klux Klanner, or an environmentalist. As you reconsider the Steppingstone periods from this special point of view, memories in this range of your life will come back to you.

As they arise in you, record these memories in the Dialogue with Society section. These entries can be brief, with only a few phrases to indicate the essential points. In some cases you will feel the desire to elaborate upon the memory and describe it at greater length. It is good to do so but, for the immediate purposes of our workshop experience, it is best to limit yourself to two or three sentences of description at this time. There will be opportunity to elaborate them after the workshop, but now we want to proceed with a single focusing experience. You may bear in mind, however, that most of the memories that stimulate you to expand upon them will very likely warrant your establishing a full dialogue relationship with them, following the essential model of our dialogue procedures.

To begin, we direct our attention back to the Steppingstone Periods as we listed and described them earlier. We reenter those earlier times in our life and draw out the memory-events that relate to this area of our inner and outer experience. At the workshops we have found it to be helpful if we speak these recollections aloud as they return to us. We do not elaborate them or explain them. We merely speak them out into the air of the workshop. As we say them aloud with no comment, we record them in our Journal. In this way we compile our list of memory-events related to the social aspects of our lives. Let us now do this together, as at a Journal Workshop.

"I was born in a working class Irish family. Friday night we expected our father to be drunk. I hid my books when he came home, and I resolved that knowledge would change my way of life. Later I discovered the history of Irish culture, and now I want to dialogue with the two sides of it."

"I am a black girl in the South. I know I had better not be on the sidewalk. I will dialogue with my blackness."

"Hearing Franklin Roosevelt give his Inauguration speech. My parents believed in him, and he became my idol. I wonder what he would say now."

"Being taught you had to use your fork a certain way, and dress and talk a certain way. I thought the whole world was like that. Then I found out that only a certain class was that way, and I didn't have to be the same if I didn't want to."

"Being in Parochial school. I believed in God, but I couldn't accept the way His representatives were treating us. I didn't know what to do about it, but I was going into revolt. I'll talk to the institution."

"When I came to America, I was shocked to see how different it is to be a woman here than in Egypt. It's so completely different. I'm not used to it yet, and I wonder what it means to have two such different ways of life."

"In college I believed in a social revolution. Then I gave it up and became a business man. I would like to dialogue with both systems."

"I listen to Bach and I think of when he wrote his music. I think he is deeper than civilization. Maybe he will tell me."

"I am an Arab in this country. I think a great deal about the history of my people, its glory in the past, and I wonder if it will return. I also wonder if it is relevant, considering the problems of modern civilization. I will dialogue with the Arab world."

"I am a woman and I never thought of myself that way before. It exhilarates and frightens me. I have to find out what to do with this new feeling of being a liberated person."

"I think of the evolution of the human species. I feel identified with mankind."

"I am an engineer and I have always taken science and technology for granted. I have always thought, if it works, it is good. Now I think I had better talk to both of them."

"I remember my mother covering her eyes when she lit the

candles on the Sabbath eve. Now that is irrelevant to me. Or I think it is. I could never do that myself. But there was something good and beautiful in it. Where has that world gone? I will dialogue with the Jewish world of the past."

"Pacifism. I believe in it. Several times in my life I have taken a stand for it. But I think the problems are more subtle than I have admitted. I'll talk to it."

"The Labor Unions. I have always supported them. And the working man, I have believed in him or the working class. Maybe they are not all the same, and I should talk to all of them."

"I went into the Army during the war. I will dialogue with both the army and the war."

"Sexual freedom. I found it. Now I'll talk to it."

"The earth. I love the earth and we depend on it, but we are spoiling it. I'll dialogue with the earth. Then maybe I'll dialogue with the people who spoil it."

"The Ghetto streets. They used to be the only world I knew. I remember those feelings. I have very different feelings now."

"I am an American and I am a Puerto Rican. I have studied here and I am part of Western civilization. But I also belong to the Puerto Rican people, and they need to be free. I will dialogue with them; then I will dialogue with America."

Many entries of different kinds drawn from all the time-units of our life will find their way onto our listing. Some will stretch over several units of time in our life. Others will drop away and then recur in a different form or in a further phase of development. One of the criteria by which we can select the memories, experiences, and concerns to extend and draw into a dialogue relationship is that they have returned to us in meaningful ways over a period of time. We may take that as an indication that, at least in some degree, they are an integral part of our life.

The listing that we make is open ended. As many items as we place on it now, we wish always to have room for others. When we are working in other sections of the Journal, additional realizations will come to us with respect to social factors in our lives that are or have been important to us. We shall always keep room on our list for these to be added. In that way we give them a place of recognition so that later, whenever the appropriate moment comes, we can establish a dialogue relationship with them. In order to keep our list open ended, it is a good idea also to leave a few pages blank before we begin the next phase of our exercise. Then we can maintain each as a separate sub-section.

When we feel that we have made sufficient entries on our list, we sit in quietness. Now our eyes are closed, and in the silence we contemplate the experiences we have mentioned. Taken together, they combine the movement of the social aspect of our life. Now we choose one of them to enter with us into a dialogue relationship.

When we have made our decision, we begin by writing a brief statement to draw into focus the essence of our experiences and our attitudes. This is simply to indicate the nature of our subject and the general direction in which we are going with it. It should not be a detailed statement, since the details of it are not necessary at this point. They will unfold of themselves as we proceed with our dialogue exercise. All we wish to do now is write a brief focusing statement. In fact, most of the examples of memory-experiences that were spoken aloud in the workshop a little earlier when we were each forming our basic list would be quite adequate for this purpose. Some of them could use a sentence or two for further clarification, but in general they would serve very well just as they are as focusing statements.

When we have written our statement, our next step is to begin establishing a personal relationship with our subject. We need to identify, and then to come into contact with, the *person within the process* of its life. To do this, we draw together the Steppingstones that mark the continuity of its development. As much as possible, we try to list the Steppingstones in chronological order, but that is not always necessary just as it is not always feasible. The best guideline to follow is to bear in mind that out of this listing a life history is to emerge.

We should list the Steppingstones in such a way as to help establish this life history. As much as possible, therefore, we try to place the Steppingstones in consecutive order; but we recognize that there is a great deal of overlap from time-unit to time-unit in this area of our experience.

When we list the Steppingstones here in the Dialogue with Society section, the criteria are very subjective. If we consider, for example, the young woman who was preparing to establish a dialogue relationship with her blackness, we recognize that she has a number of alternatives open to her when she goes to list the relevant Steppingstones. Since they are subjective, only she can choose among them.

One possibility is that she reconstruct those personal experiences in her life that relate to her being Negro. This may include the circumstances of her birth and early childhood, perhaps her playing with white children and only later realizing that society had marked off a difference between them. Her Steppingstones could then include other instances of discrimination and separateness, and other events that led her to identify her blackness as a fact of her life.

Another line of approach would have a non-personal emphasis. This might be in terms of the Negro people and Black civilization. She might list some of the main Steppingstones of Black history in Africa, in the slavery period of the United States, and recent world wide developments. Her dialogue would then be with the *person within the process* of Black civilization as a whole, and her personal situation of blackness would be an individual part of it.

In a similar way, the man who had been a social revolutionary in his earlier years and had then become a respectable business man would also have a number of alternatives before him. He could list the Steppingstones of the particular revolutionary movement with which he had been involved, and he could then dialogue with it. He could list the Steppingstones of the business ideology as a whole and dialogue with the business enterprise system. He could take a more personal approach and list the Steppingstones of his life as a businessman and make his contact through that channel. Or he could work out some combination of these that would express the movement seeking to unfold in his life.

It must be clear to us at this point in our workshop that there is no single correct way to draw the material of our life together. But we follow the guidelines of a basic, general format, and we improvise experimentally with the contents of our life until we find the combinations that speak to us most clearly in the dialogue relationship. We never assume that the Steppingstone list or the first dialogue script is just the absolute and final one. Rather we try it this way and see how it goes; then we come back from another direction and try it again.

Now, considering the various possibilities before us in listing these Steppingstones, let us return to quietness. We sit in stillness, our eyes closed, our breathing slow. In the silence we let the life of our subject present itself to us. Our mind is aware of the possibilities, but we do not make decisions on it at the mental level. We let it present itself to us in its own way and in its own format. We are open and receptive in the silence as the Steppingstones of its life take shape for us.

Presently the Steppingstones become clear to us, and as they do, we record them one by one. We write them briefly, only a sentence or two to describe them. At a later time we may elaborate some of them in great detail, but now we only describe them briefly. We continue listing the Steppingstones until they have taken us to the present moment in time. We read them back to ourselves in silence. Do we feel the continuity of a life-movement expressed in them? Are there any significant points where something important has been omitted? If so, can we fill it in with honesty by inserting another Steppingstone? We check the list, add to it whatever is necessary in order to make it feel right to us, and then we return to our quietness.

We sit in stillness preparing for our dialogue script. In our mind there may be many thoughts concerning the various things that both parties in the dialogue can say. Those thoughts are present, but we let them drop away. We do not encourage those thoughts. We do not think with them. We know that they are there, but we do not use them. Since we do not make use of them, they drop into disuse. They drop away.

We are sitting in silence. Our eyes are closed, and we are breathing softly, slowly. Thoughts are present but we are not using them, so they drop away.

We are sitting in silence, letting the self become still.

We are sitting in silence, letting the breath become slow—and slower.

We are sitting in silence, letting our thoughts come to rest.

Presently in the stillness we begin to feel ready to approach the dialogue script.

We read the Steppingstones again softly to ourselves. We let ourselves be especially sensitive to the inner continuity of its movement.

We let ourselves feel the process of its life moving within it. We become aware of the person within the process of its life. As that person becomes present to us, we acknowledge it. We speak to it. And it speaks to us. We speak, and it speaks. And we record in the Journal everything that is said. Thus the dialogue script begins and moves of itself. It continues through and beyond us. We allow it to go as it wishes to go, and we enable it to proceed as long as it wishes to continue. We are participating in the dialogue script, and we are also its instrument.

When our speaking and listening and recording have gone as far as they wish, we return to our stillness. There may have been strong and significant emotions stirring in us while the dialogue script was being written. We take note and add them to the entry. Presently we may feel quiet enough to read the dialogue script back to ourselves. As we do that, we take note once again of the feelings that arise in us as we read it. Record them, comparing them to the earlier feelings that arose in us while the dialogue script was being written.

It may be that when we read the dialogue script to ourselves a further dialogue is immediately stimulated. If so, let it resume and extend itself as much as it wishes and as much as feels right to you. When that is finished, let it come to rest, and let the dialogue have its own silence for awhile. After some days have passed, perhaps a week, you may wish to read it to yourself again. At that time it may resume once more. Then you will know that you have established an ongoing dialogue relationship with this aspect of your life in society.

Chapter 18

Inner Wisdom Dialogue

In this section of the Journal we turn our attention to the spiritual realm of our life experience. The word, "spiritual," as we use it in this context has a large and general meaning. It is not restricted to any particular metaphysical teaching or belief, but it refers to our fundamental human quest for understanding of the ultimate truths of existence. Some find this understanding in the terms of the traditional religions, others in the modern language of the technologist and scientist, and still others are working toward new personal syntheses that reach beyond the old dichotomies.

The categories, however, do not matter. The one thing that is certain about them is that they will pass through many changes for anyone who is actively engaged in a spiritual quest. The quest for abiding truth is the reality of the spiritual life, regardless of what particular metaphysic or doctrine is espoused at any moment. This ongoing quest in its permutations through each person's life history is the subject of the *Inner Wisdom Dialogue* section of the Journal.

We have learned from the history of depth psychology, and it is one of the principles of the *Intensive Journal*, that untapped capacities of awareness are contained latently at various levels of our being. Man does indeed know intuitively more than he rationally understands. The question, however, is how we can gain access to the potentials of knowledge contained in the depth of us, how we can achieve increased capacities of direct intuition and enlarged awareness.

We require a means of increasing our interior sensitivity to make an expansion of consciousness possible in personal terms. In a far reaching sense, the entire thrust of our work with the *Intensive Journal* has this as its goal. The process of *feedback interplay* that moves back and forth among the sections of the Journal achieves its results by moving on two levels simultaneously. On the one hand, it generates a movement within the person; on the other hand, it deepens the level on which all the contents of the psyche are experienced. It brings about this double effect by sending our inner attention and our psychic energies back and forth, up and down, in the inner space of our lives by means of the various exercises and sections of the *Intensive Journal.*

The movement of material in the Journal corresponds to the movement of the life contents within the psyche of the person. It generates a momentum of inner experiences within the individual, first on the personal, subjective level of the psyche, and increasingly on the deeper-than-personal, the generically human level of the psyche. As this momentum continues both on the surface and on the depth levels, it draws the psyche as a whole together, forming new integrations of personality. As it proceeds, progressive re-integrations take place, so that a series of changes is observable in the inner structure as well as in the outer aspect of the individual. These changes, which accompany the Journal work, are cumulative. As they continue, they bring about a new quality of being and especially a greater sensitivity to the interior dimension of life. In particular, as the work of *feedback interplay* multiplies its momentum, the subjective, personal contents of one's life are brought into closer relationship with the deeper, transpersonal levels. This progressive deepening enlarges the capacity of *inner knowing* with respect to the conduct and meaning of our human existence.

At this point in our Journal Workshop we are in a position to recognize how the process of *progressive deepening* takes place. We began our workshop experience at the rational surface of consciousness with our description in the Period Log of the recent unit of Life/Time. Following that, we had our first exercise in the use of Twilight Imagery.

Then, by the practice of *life correlation,* we drew out the relationship between our imagery and our outer experience. These last two steps began the process of drawing the focus of our awareness to a non-rational, an intuitive level beneath the surface of consciousness.

As we proceeded with our *Time-Stretching* exercises to reassemble our life histories, we combined the conscious use of memory with a cumulative prodding and prying open of the repressed levels of our unconscious psyche. This was the preparatory, ground-breaking work of loosening the soil of our lives which we carried through in the Life History Log, and to which we continuously add. Those entries activate our memory of repressed events, and our reentry into the Steppingstones and Intersections of our life further stimulates our nonconscious perceptions.

The data that we gathered in these Life/Time sections then provided the base for our dialogue experiences with specific contents of our lives. The dialogue work continues the process of deepening and serves as a bridge between the unconscious and conscious levels of our awareness. We see this mediating quality of the dialogue exercises in the fact that they frequently cause us to articulate a knowledge of things we did not know we knew. The dialogues reach into our unconscious knowledge and draw it up to conscious awareness in the form of language in the dialogue scripts.

We take a further step in our progressive deepening when we work with the procedures of Twilight Imaging and with our dreams. These enable us to move into the deeper-than-personal levels of symbolism and to experience our individual lives in larger contexts of meaning. This is especially so when we extend the seriality of our dream movement by Twilight Dreaming. Continuing beyond this, we find that our Twilight Imaging experiences enable us to move even more deeply than the dreams to the transpersonal level where the symbolism reflects a unitary wisdom of life. This takes us toward a direct knowing that is beyond intellect, but it does so in symbolic forms that are often ambiguous and difficult to understand. The symbolism that comes to us is often profound, but it is also obscure and thus liable to mislead us. It becomes essential, then, that we move back from our unconscious depths into consciousness again. We do this by following the feedback leads that have been given us by our dreams and our Twilight Imaging experiences, and by working with them in the dialogue sections which they suggest to us.

For this reason the exercises that we have carried out in our workshop so far have moved in two directions simultaneously. They have moved both down and up. The progressive deepening has taken us to a level where deeper-than-personal experiences become possible for us. And the dialogue work translates these experiences into the actualities of our life. Combining these is the specific role of our *Inner Wisdom Dialogues*. As we have worked in the context of our lives, we have cumulatively deepened our inward atmosphere and our level of depth contact. Now we take a further step. We hold ourselves at the deepest level to which our Journal work so far has taken us, and we now seek to establish a dialogue relationship with the quality of *knowledge beyond understanding* that becomes present to us at that depth. It is our attempt to enlarge our contact with wisdom and with the ultimates of meaning in life through the particular symbolic forms and contexts through which this may be accessible to each of us.

This section of the *Intensive Journal* thus becomes the place where we work to establish a dialogue relationship with all the possibilities of spiritual contact and larger philosophical awareness that reflect the *inner wisdom* of our deep human nature. Our first step in this direction is to go back over our life history and to recapitulate the main experiences, speculations and beliefs by which we have each sought in our own way to relate ourselves to the ultimate truths of human existence.

We sit in silence and reflect on the range of faith and doubt and seeking that we have experienced since childhood. We wish to draw together now what can be called the "Steppingstones of our spiritual life," understanding the word, "spiritual" in its broadest sense as our total inner quest for wisdom in life. To give ourselves a frame of reference for this, it may be helpful to turn back to the list of Steppingstones that we wrote earlier in the workshop. Here we can review the main points and periods that we marked off with respect to the movement of our life as a whole. Working within the large context of the Steppingstones of our life, we can take ourselves back in memory and ask ourselves specific questions regarding the content and quality of our spiritual life in each of those earlier periods.

Working within the Journal section of Inner Wisdom Dialogue, we set up a subheading for the *Steppingstones of inner experience* where we can reconstruct our private quest for truth and wisdom in whatever terms and to whatever degree we have pursued that quest. It may also enable us to recognize how our life has been carrying us toward a more profound knowledge, even though we were not consciously seeking the truth.

Sitting in quietness, moving back over our life history, we begin by recalling the Steppingstones of our spiritual life in all its forms and phases. We shall record these in our sub-section in the form of a list, each entry concisely stated, as we did earlier in listing the Steppingstones of our life. Here we shall be recalling and recording the striking events in our inner experience that involve a point of contact, or a moving-toward contact, with the ultimates of life and the wisdom within us. These may involve religious experiences of all kinds, or equally, they may be in the form of our search for truth through science, or through the arts, or through the evolution of society. There are many possible avenues along which we reach toward an inward experience of larger-than-personal truth, and we record now as many as we can recall and bring to our awareness.

Whether we are making these entries in our privacy or at a workshop, it seems to be helpful for many people to speak them out while writing them in the Journal. In any case, whether speaking them aloud feels comfortable or not, we record them as they come to our memories, without censorship, without judgment, without comment, and at this point without amplification. We are interested at this point in recording concise entries that will indicate the varieties of inner experiences that have been significant in our development. We are gathering the data for the later steps in our work.

As though we are at a Journal Workshop, let us now speak aloud the Steppingstones of our inner development, as the other participants also do, recording them as we speak them.

"Being told that God was watching so I'd better behave."

"Thunder clapping very loud one night while I was saying my prayers."

"The death of my mother. I prayed for an afterlife."

"I doubted God and all the stories of religion."

"On Yom Kippur seeing the rabbi in white robes lying prostrate before the Torah. There was a holy glow around him."

"My first communion experience. It was good but I thought it would be more."

"My call of vocation to the religious life."

"A conversion experience. It was so strong I thought it would never change."

"Realizing that Jesus loves me."

"Seeing my grandmother light the candles on the Sabbath. I have never done that."

"Feeling the presence of God."

"Entering religious life. A door closing and a door opening."

"Meditating on the Gospels and feeling the power of a truth grow stronger."

"Being transfixed when my minister spoke. He had a light around him."

"Reading Walt Whitman for the first time."

"Being at a funeral. Feeling awed by death and wondering about the afterlife."

"The presence of the Blessed Virgin. She was my mother too."

"My ordination."

"Reading Tom Dooley's books and wanting to live his life."

"Meeting a person who really felt God's presence. After that I knew I could recognize the real thing."

"Meditating in the Eastern way."

"Feeling the silence deepen by degrees."

"The waves in the ocean, the ocean in the waves. I wondered which was which. Then I gave up and felt it all wash over me. I was renewed."

"Being inside the vision of Isaiah."

"On a drug trip. I wouldn't go again, but I know it's there."

"Realizing there was spiritual truth before Jesus. That shook me, but my world opened."

"I fell in love with Socrates and I wished I were his wife. Poor Socrates, I thought."

"Realizing that I was creating my own misery. Scales fell off my eyes."

"One morning I suddenly knew what love is, and I felt connected to all things."

"I discovered philosophy and realized that my mind could be an instrument of truth. I admired it, but I began to worry about faith."

"I was walking into the ocean without hope. Suddenly something turned me around and here I am."

"With nothing and alone and walking in the shadow. Then seeing the light. Even when it's dark, it never goes away."

We record these experiences in the order in which we recall them. We shall very likely find, however, that we recollect our more recent experiences before we remember our earlier ones. The result is that our list does not reflect the actual sequence of steps and stages and changes by which our inner development has taken place. A main purpose in making this list, however, is to recapitulate not only the broad range of content but the specific style and tempo of movement of our inner life. We are seeking to assemble our spiritual life history so that we can establish an active dialogue relationship with the process within it. Toward this goal it is essential that we experience the events of our inner development in the sequence in which they took place.

Since we listed our spiritual Steppingstones spontaneously as they came to us, we can now set them in chronological order by numbering them in the sequence in which they took place. Even as we do this, we shall undoubtedly find situations of overlapping where we cannot tell clearly which came first. We can leave leeway for this irregular development since we realize that it is inherent in the spiritual and philosophic life. The continuities of inner growth do not lend themselves to sharp demarcation particularly because they frequently pass through long incubation periods when they are not visible on the surface. We shall bear this in mind, and later phases of our Journal work will enable us to draw out the details and nuances of this elusive timing in our inner life.

At this point, having listed the various phases of our experience, we number them in approximate chronological order. By drawing our list together in sequence we enable ourselves to see the unity of inner development that has underlain the many changes and uncertainties in the cycles of our life. With it we shall be able to identify the thread of integrity that has been seeking to establish itself beneath the variations of attitude that show on the surface.

We now read our list to ourselves in chronological sequence. We may read it aloud if it feels comfortable for us to do so. Especially we read it to ourselves silently, and reread it several times so that the feeling of its flow, including both its smoothness and its irregularities, can come to us. As we do this, we take note of the feeling and responses that arise in us as we read it, and we record these as an entry following our list.

After we have made the list and have read it back to ourselves, there is an important piece of data to be added. As we reread each of the entries and place ourselves back in that time of our lives, we think back to the persons who were of importance to us in a profoundly meaningful way during that time. These are not merely the persons who were with us at the time, or who were friendly to us, or in a personal relationship with us, but the persons who were of profound importance to us in specific relation to our inner experience and to the enlargement of our consciousness in that regard. As we become aware of such persons, we add them to each of the spiritual Steppingstones that we have listed wherever they apply.

The persons whose names we record in this way may possess a great variety of qualities. Their principal characteristic is that they are individuals who represent wisdom to us with respect to some particular area of our lives and who, at least in our perception of them, embody a capacity of deep and direct knowing. They need not be people who are well-educated, nor people who possess a great deal of information. That is not the kind of knowledge we are seeking here. They are, rather, individuals who personify wisdom for us because of the way that the quality of their inner being speaks to our own being. They may not represent wisdom to us in every aspect of their life; and the same individual may not carry the same deep relevance for us in all areas of our life. Although they embody wisdom for us, other people will not necessarily think of them as wise.

As we now go over our listing of the Steppingstones of our inner development, we realize that the persons who have been meaningful to us at one time in our life may be very different from those who have had an inner importance to us at other times. In our earlier years, for example, it may have been a grandfather or an uncle who represented truth to us. Or it may have been our image of God, or Christ, or the Virgin Mary, or our local priest or rabbi. In later years the wisdom figure may have been embodied in a Professor at college, in authors of books that influenced us greatly, Plato, Spinoza, or a contemporary author whose approach to life speaks to us. It may have become a missionary minister like Billy Graham or Mary Baker Eddy, a militant revolutionist like Che Guevera or Joan of Arc, political figures like Martin Luther King, John Kennedy, or Susan B. Anthony, depending on our areas of interest and commitment at particular times in our life.

As our experience proceeds and as our values change, the persons who personify wisdom to us will also change. They may be individuals whom we know personally and with whom we share an active interchange of ideas. Or they may be persons from history, St. Paul, Karl Marx, Gandhi, Paul Tillich, Van Gogh, Beethoven, and so on. Whoever has spoken to us in the depth of our being, whether through their spoken words, their books, their music, their paintings, or by their lives and the legends and symbolism that have grown around them, all of these may be wisdom figures for us in some areas of our life. Moses and the Prophets may have this role for us. So also may any of the Saints, different ones at different times in our life. Buddha or Krishna or any of the various pantheons of gods may have played this role for us, Zeus or Athene or Siegfried. Whoever they may be, living persons, persons who now live only through their works and words, historical personages, mythological figures, or divine beings, all may be among the persons who have served as wisdom figures for us at some point in our lives.

We can make a distinction here from a certain point of view regarding the two types of persons who have the capacity to personify wisdom for us in a dialogue relationship. We note the *personal* wisdom figures and the *transpersonal* wisdom figures. In the first group are the individuals who personify wisdom for us but who are part of the world in which we live, whether they are present with us physically or not. Included in this group may be such persons as a teacher who influenced us greatly at school, a grandparent, a public figure as a minister or an author. It may include an ancestor in our family or national line who lived long before we were born but whose reputation has drawn us to him or her as a figure of superior knowledge.

These are persons in whom we find wisdom, but whom we understand to be human beings, just as we are. The transpersonal wisdom figures, on the other hand, belong to history and the universe. They are persons whose lives, if they have indeed lived historically, have made them symbols for us of connection with the ultimate and encompassing truths of human existence. Among these are such figures as Jesus, Moses, Buddha, Socrates, whether or not we believe them to be actual human beings who have lived in times past or figures of legend and myth. They are transpersonal wisdom figures by virtue of what they represent in the universe, and because of the power of personal being that is identified with their names. It is in this sense that God, in one aspect, is a transpersonal wisdom figure with whom we can establish a dialogue relationship, God by whatever name and in whatever form He is recognizable to us.

Having made this distinction between personal and transpersonal wisdom figures, there is a further point for us to note. The personal wisdom figures are human beings as we are and share our realm of life, but the quality in them toward which we reach is more-than-personal. As human beings they have activated within themselves an aspect of the transpersonal depths of inner wisdom. They have lived it, and it is this level of the universe, which has been actualized and made real by their experience, that we now seek to bring into our own lives. We can do that by means of an ongoing dialogue relationship with them, including progressive dialogue scripts. As we proceed to this active phase of our exercises, we should realize, however, that we are not establishing contact by dialoguing with the personal side of these inner wisdom figures. We are reaching toward the transpersonal depth of wisdom within them seeking to establish a relationship between that and the corresponding depth of wisdom in ourselves. It is in this fundamental sense that all persons may be spoken of as *transpersonal* wisdom figures, including ultimately ourselves.

With this background and with these criteria, let us now go over our list again and add to each of our entries the names of those persons or beings who have personified wisdom for us. For each of the periods indicated in our spiritual Steppingstones, we jot down the names of the persons who were the focus of our deepened understanding and our beliefs at that time in our life. In our earlier years these persons will very likely be drawn from persons with whom we were in close contact, a grandparent, a priest or rabbi, a teacher. In many cases they will be persons in authority, but authority by itself is not the main criterion here. As the years proceed, our inner wisdom figures will tend to reflect the individual lines of our development. They will be authors or public figures, especially persons who embody major ideologies or lifestyles that drew our attention at the time. The personal wisdom figures who were of major importance to us will vary from period to period, but the transpersonal figures like God or Jesus or Moses or Mary will tend to remain the same for large segments of our life. What may change very significantly is the nature of our relation to them, and this will be reflected in our further entries and descriptions as the work proceeds.

For each of our spiritual Steppingstones we list the names of one or two or three wisdom figures, or as many as come to mind. We know that the entries we make in this regard will by no means be complete at this time. As our work in the Journal proceeds, however, we can add the names of others who are recalled to our memory. Many of our wisdom figures will overlap a number of periods in our life. Others will have been important to us only briefly, but remembering them now may lead us to reestablish our contact and draw forth what we had felt to be meaningful in them. We call them back out of our experiences of the past, but it is especially important that we give adequate attention to the wisdom figures of the present time in our life.

From the list of these various wisdom figures, we choose one to focus on for our dialogue experience at the workshop. At later times we shall work to build our dialogue relationship with others among the wisdom figures who have been meaningful to us, for each of them can help us reestablish contact with the deep sources of our life.

In deciding upon our first figure for inner wisdom dialogue, we should not necessarily choose one who is important to us at the present time, but we may choose a current figure. What can be most valuable for our first Inner Wisdom Dialogue is that it be with a person the very thought of whom, the mentioning of their name, causes us to become quiet and feel centered within ourselves. Let our first dialogue be with one whose presence we have experienced in an atmosphere of profound understanding, perhaps also of warmth and supportive love. Perhaps it will be one with whom we have been in contact in times of prayer or solitude. What is most important is that it be a person to whom we can open our hearts fully on any of our deepest concerns, and that we can do so with no reservation, knowing it will all be accepted.

We are now preparing to let a dialogue script be written to carry forward the inner relationship between ourselves and that other person, that other Being. This first dialogue is to reopen contact and to clear the way for successive dialogues that will take place afterwards in their own timing.

It is important for us to acknowledge to ourselves that this first Inner Wisdom Dialogue will not necessarily be profound, or poetic, or a great spiritual revelation. Dialogues in this section of the *Intensive Journal* have indeed been just that, but dialogues in any section of the Journal can have those powerful and transforming qualities *only unexpectedly.* If we are deliberately looking for them to be wise or inspiring, we tighten the channel and the passageway becomes too narrow. For this reason we approach our first Inner Wisdom Dialogue with the attitude that it is merely an introduction. We are merely saying hello, but in a deep sanctuary part of ourselves. In this relaxed way we make the experience of deep inner dialogue available as a continuing, open-ended contact with the transpersonal wisdom of life.

We may find also that as we prepare for an Inner Wisdom Dialogue, as we are doing at this moment, that we realize we are uncertain as to the person with whom we actually wish to speak. In practice it often happens that our conscious mind decides to set up the dialogue with one particular person whereas the intention of our deep psyche is quite different. In that case we suddenly recognize in the midst of a dialogue that we are speaking with someone other than the person with whom we had started. It is not uncommon for the script of an Inner Wisdom Dialogue to shift its cast of characters while it is taking place. What is important then is that you be open and receptive to the change, and that you be flexible enough to go with it. Let the dialogue lead itself and go where it wishes. When this is happening, it is an indication that you are allowing yourself to be drawn into the nonconscious depths of your self, and that it is indeed your *inner wisdom* with which you are speaking.

We are ready now to begin our dialogue script with the wisdom figure whom we have chosen. We sit in stillness. Our *Intensive Journal* is open and we have dated a new page. The sub-section in which we prepared for the Inner Wisdom Dialogue by listing the Steppingstones and the persons who were important in them, is left open-ended so that we can add to it from time to time. Now we are ready for our dialogue script. We are sitting in silence waiting for it to begin.

Our eyes are closed and we feel the presence of the wisdom figure with whom we wish to enter into dialogue. We feel their presence, but we do not think of them with conscious thoughts. We let our thoughts come to rest. Our breathing is slow. It becomes slower, softer. We are still.

In the stillness we feel the presence of this person, this wisdom figure, this being.

We are feeling their presence, feeling the inner quality of their being, feeling the deep wisdom, the unity and knowing of existence that is personified in them.

Sitting in quietness, we let images come to us. They may come to us visually upon our Twilight Imagery screen. More importantly, through our image of them we feel the quality of the person, their atmosphere, and especially their presence. We feel their life, their concern, their desires, and we speak to them. We greet them. We say what we feel of their life and of their quality of life. We say what we feel of our life, our concerns, and our questions. We speak of our relationship to them, why we come to them, why we call upon them and what we have to ask.

All that we say we write as our part of the dialogue script. We return to silence and wait. When they are ready, they speak to us, and it is written. Whatever they say, be it casual or profound, we record it. We let the dialogue move along its own path, make its own turns, cover its own subject matter. We speak and the other speaks, and we let the dialogue continue as long as it wishes.

We are sitting in stillness, waiting in openness. We feel the presence of the person and their quality of wisdom. We speak and we are spoken to. And we let it be written through our pen. Thus the dialogue script is written between ourselves and the person of wisdom. We sit in openness, enabling the dialogue to take form through us, in the silence, in the silence.

It seems to be more often true of the Inner Wisdom Dialogues than of other dialogue exercises in the Journal work that they come to points where they must stop although they are not actually finished. These stoppings are actually pauses during which the dialogue process seems to renew itself and gather new energy. It is as though the inner speakers are taking a second breath. When the dialogue script resumes its movement, it seems also as though it has moved to a deeper level. These pauses that occur in the Inner Wisdom Dialogues may therefore not be from fatigue or a diminution of energy in the dialogue process, but rather a deepening of the level. They are often the prelude to special profundities in awareness and expression.

When the pace of your dialogue slows, let it come to a stop if it wants to, but do not assume that it is finished. Let it rest. And while it is resting, let yourself become quiet. In the silence it will renew itself and continue when it is ready.

These pauses, renewals, and deepenings may take place three or four times during the writing of a single dialogue script. Each time you will move forward and then come to a stop. Eventually enough will have been said for the present, and you will know that by the way it feels to you. That will be the time to read what has been written. First you will read it silently; then, if the circumstances feel right, you will read it aloud, either at a workshop or in your privacy, perhaps into a cassette.

As you read, you take note of the feelings, the energies and emotional tone that become present in you. Compare these with the way you felt when the dialogue script was being written, and describe your observations. This is an additional entry to be made in the same section of the Journal. It is a further aspect of the Inner Wisdom Dialogue, extending the process now at a conscious level. All phases of the experience contribute to building the ongoing dialogue relationship.

With this entry the specific work with the dialogue script comes to a close for the present, but the dialogue relationship as a whole continues. In many additional ways it may be actively extended.

When you have recorded your observations regarding the side aspects of the experience, the dialogue script writing will come to rest. During that pause, while you are not deliberately trying to do anything further with this experience, a flow of additional thoughts, perceptions, insights, images, and awarenesses will very likely be activated within you. They will arise of themselves, and your role in the process at this point will merely be the neutral one of recognizing and recording them. As you write your descriptions a momentum will be generated, and a further stream of Journal entries will flow of their own accord. They may take the form of an inner monologue, but they will all be part of the ongoing dialogue relationship that builds and grows through many facets and phases. At a later time, in a week or a month, whenever its inner rhythm draws it to the fore again, the dialogue script also may spontaneously resume itself. All are part of the cyclic process by which a dialogue relationship continues and extends itself in the course of our life.

Each section of the Journal has its own style of approach to dialogue experience, but the inner relationships that we establish are not restricted to any one section. Quite the contrary, as they proceed they overflow their bounds and move in and out of the various sections and dimensions of Journal experience. At the close of each cycle of exercises in our Journal work, we ask ourselves the question: where else in the Journal can I go to explore and extend the material I have now recorded? What *feedback leads* do these entries give me? Do they lead me to memories that should be recorded in the Life History Log? Or to the realization of Intersections, of roads taken and roads not taken in our inner life? Or do they suggest to us connections to be pursued in other dialogue relationships in other sections of the Journal?

Most importantly, one Inner Wisdom Dialogue leads to another. Now that you have begun a dialogue relationship with a wisdom figure, you can initiate other dialogues of this kind as they are suggested to you by the further work you do in your Journal. Over a period of time we can establish a contact via dialogue with a number of individuals who personify for us a deep relationship to truth. As we extend our Inner Wisdom Dialogues, expanding their variety and their range, these become a major resource for the progressively deep experiencing of our lives.

Chapter 19

Now: The Open Moment

We come now to the closing experience of our workshop. We turn for it to the last section in the Journal, *Now: The Open Moment.*

When we began the workshop we took the last part of the past as our starting point. We marked off the unit of experience that immediately preceded the present moment in our lives. It was the contents of this period that we described with our first Journal entries in the Period Log.

Since that time we have no longer been in our past, but we have not yet entered our future. While we have participated in this workshop, we have been at a mid-point of time between our past and our future. Everything that has transpired in our life prior to the workshop is our past. Everything that will take place in it after the workshop is over is our future. Our Journal Workshop is the quiet place in between the two. Being here, we have been protected, at least temporarily, from the outer pressures of our life. We withdrew to it as a Sabbath in order to give ourselves an opportunity to reposition ourselves in the movement of our lives as a whole. In the terms of our metaphor, for the duration of the workshop we went down into the well of our lives to work in the deep places of the underground stream. And now, as our experience of the workshop comes to a close, we return to the surface of our life again. We come up from our well ready to go forth into the movement of our lives again.

As we prepare for this, we turn our attention to the first period of the future that we shall enter when we return to the world. This is the *Open Moment* dawning before us as we come to the close of the workshop and to the beginning of a new unit of time in our lives.

Let us sit in stillness now as we prepare to enter this Open Moment. With our eyes closed, we go back over the varied entries we have written in the Journal and the experiences we have had in the course of the workshop. Some of us may wish to go through the Journal pages quickly to remind ourselves of all that has taken place. For others it will be sufficient to take ourselves back mentally through the experiences we have had as we worked in the sections of the Journal. In either case, as we let it all come together within ourselves we can feel the wholeness of the perspective of our life that has been progressively crystallizing.

We can recall now how we thought of our life when we began by placing ourselves in the most recent unit of our experience and described it in the Period Log. We think back to the entries we made in the Daily Log recording the happenings and especially the inner phenomena of our minds and emotions. We began the discipline of recording them as they take place day by day.

Working on a larger canvas, we recall also how we began the Time-Stretching procedures, reaching down the track of inner time and recapitulating the cycles and continuity of our lives. As we listed our Steppingstones and elaborated the contents of the Steppingstone Periods, we took ourselves back over our childhood years, moved up through early adolescence and into physical and psychological maturity. Eventually, beginning with our birth and continuing to the present moment, we have reentered and explored as many units of Life/Time as we have individually experienced so far. Some of us who have lived through several decades, have recapitulated the cycles of later maturity leading to the ultimate transitions of life. Others of us, still in our early decades, have reflected in our Steppingstones the uncertain groping of life potentials that have not yet found their channel and are seeking a direction by which they can be fulfilled. For each of us, the continuity of our lives has moved toward a more unified focus and thus has taken a further step in its self-integration.

Our active work in the Life/Time dimension opened the way to dialogue with various important contents of our lives. We have begun what can now be ongoing inner relationships with the personal aspects of our life, with other individuals, with the artworks and activities in which we are engaged, with our body, and with the various events, situations, and circumstances of our life. We have also opened an avenue for expanding contact with the more-than-personal aspects of our experience, society, the arts, and especially those institutions and beings who embody the larger wisdom of life in our individual awareness. We have laid the foundation for continuous contact with all of these by means of dialogue as well as by the dynamic extension of our dreams and twilight imagery.

By working with all these procedures while using the *Intensive Journal* as our instrument, we have repositioned our life with respect to our past and our future. We have arrived at a new Now, and this is the Open Moment of our life. In the course of our experience at this Journal Workshop, an inner perspective has progressively formed in us, enabling us to *feel from within* the movement of our life as it proceeds through its cycles of difficulty and achievement. It brings us into intimate and ongoing contact with the elan vital of our life.

Beyond this perspective are the images of the future that form within us. They arise out of the depth of our continuing experience, and they reflect the results of the self-integrative process that has been taking place in the background of all our work. While we have been carrying out our exercises and making our entries in our Journal, a self-balancing and self-integrating principle has been progressively at work within us, recrystallizing the contents of our life at the deep level of knowing that is *behind our mind*. It has been working in the depth of us unseen, while we have been working in our lives on the visible level of our Journal. The process of Journal Integration has been stimulated and sustained by the entries we have fed into the Journal; and the Journal Feedback procedures have served as the medium by which the larger integrative process could establish itself and bring forth its new products of awareness and guidance for our life.

Out of this life-integrative process comes our vision of the Open

Moment which is our future. Let us now, therefore, close our eyes and turn our attention inward so that what has emerged from the integrative process in which we have been working can now reveal itself to us. Our eyes closed, we see again the varied experiences through which we have moved, the recapitulation of events of the past, our dreams, and our dialogues. Out of all of these as a new crystallization, a further flow of thought and imagery opens for us. Sometimes in symbolic form, this flow of consciousness presents to us the possibilities of the Open Moment of our future. It enables us to focus upon our future in the context of our life history as a whole.

In our silence we experience this present moment as the moment of our life history that opens into the future. Out of our nonconscious depth it presents itself in the variety of possibilities it holds for us. We let it express itself in whatever form it wishes to take so that we can be guided by it.

It may be that it comes as a fresh flow of twilight imagery. We behold this imagery, take note and record it as part of our open moment.

It may be that it takes the form of a conscious recapitulation of the experiences we have had during the workshop, and these then lead us to a projection of thoughts as to what the future may hold. We record these as they come to us.

It may take the form of a summary statement of the situation of our life as we have seen our life come into focus in the course of the workshop. Having repositioned ourselves between the past and the future, the possibilities of our Open Moment may now be clear enough to delineate and think about specifically.

In all the forms in which it presents itself now in our silence, we record it and describe it. Let it be as a conscious recapitulation, as a summary statement, as a refocusing, as a movement of imagery, as a stream of thoughts, as a hope that we project as a strong wish into the future, as a prayer for new conditions and a larger vista in our life, as a blessing offered by our deep self upon the movement of our life, and as a benediction that our whole soul places upon the open unfolding of our self. It may be a prayer that prays itself, a meditation that makes itself, a poem that writes itself, a vision that comes of itself, a brief focusing phrase that can give us a point of contact and a reminder through the continuity of our life. Whatever form it takes, we record it as the present expression of Now, our Open Moment.

We hold it in the silence. We do not speak aloud the statements that we write here. Rather we maintain our silence so that our newly generated energies can move inward, incubate, and multiply their power. At a later time we shall reread to ourselves in sequence the various Open Moment entries that we have written at successive workshop experiences. That, and other uses of this section, are part of the advanced Journal Feedback procedures that we shall practice at another time. Meanwhile we hold in the silence of prayerful focus the new intimations of purpose and meaning and life potential that have come to us.

Thus we draw our Journal Workshop to a close in peace. We reemerge from our well with the waters of life that we have found there, and we go forth again into the world.

Chapter 20

After a Journal Workshop

Now that we have completed our basic experience at a Journal Workshop, what shall our next step be?

When we began to use the *Intensive Journal* at the workshop, there were a few definite and attainable goals that we set for ourselves. One was that we would develop a perspective of the movement of our life history as a whole as it appears from the vantage point of the present moment. Secondly, we wished to *position* ourselves between the past and the future in such a way that we could refocus our current actions to support the unfoldment of new potentials in our life. And while we were working toward these two goals of *perspective* and *positioning*, we were learning the techniques for working with the various sections of the *Intensive Journal*. We were seeking to become familiar with their procedures so that we can feel comfortable in using them by ourselves in an ongoing way after the workshop is over. Now that time has come. How shall we work with the Journal in the future?

An important question that is often asked at workshops is, "How often should I make my entries in the *Intensive Journal?*"

There are no fixed rules or requirements. The purpose of the *Intensive Journal* is not to give us one more thing to feel guilty about not doing. We already have enough of that, and enough regulations for our life. But the purpose of working with the Journal is to give ourselves the means and the freedom of expressing the inner process of our lives when it wells up in us and desires expression. Writing your entries in your *Intensive Journal* should not be a chore. Once you have established a dialogue relationship with your Journal, your inner self will tell you when there are things to be written and it will become natural for you to do so. Recording Journal entries when they are there to be written will become an accepted part of your life.

We may recall in this regard a metaphor that is very indicative of the *Journal Feedback* process. It is a fact of nature that water finds its own level. This *self-balancing* principle is true of the entries that we make in the *Intensive Journal.*

What is most important is that the process be started, and that it be carried far enough so that it generates its own energy. Once that has been done, the *Journal Feedback* process will operate of itself. The material that has been fed into the Journal will be given back in new forms, stimulating additional experiences and thus calling forth a further continuity of entries. It is necessary, however, that we begin by feeding enough basic entries into the Journal so that the dynamic of the feedback process can build its momentum.

There is a larger context of time which we should bear in mind when we think of the *self-balancing* factor in the *Intensive Journal.* As we work with the Journal through the continuity of our lives, moving through one life period after another, the multiple interplay of the entries and exercises has a cumulative effect. It generates energies and movements of various kinds, and these balance one another. Over a period of time, as a person lives through more than one cycle or time-unit of his life, the self-balancing process becomes multiple. It works upon itself and thus it brings about a larger integration of the contents of the life as a whole. Beyond the self-balancing process which takes place within particular short range periods of our experience, there is a larger process of *life-integration* that builds and establishes itself over longer units of time.

As you continue your Journal work, it will be helpful to bear in mind the distinction between these two types of processes. The *self-balancing* process applies to the short run of our life experience. The *life-integration* process applies to the long run of our life movement, including within it and drawing together several short run time-units.

When we work in the *Intensive Journal* we are always engaged in situations that express the immediacy of the moment; but we are also working in the large encompassing context of our life as a whole. We therefore have two perspectives of time: the short run of the particular period in which we find ourselves and the long run of the total movement of our life. Each time-unit or individual period carries the possibility of coming into balance within itself. We experience this in the moment of its happening as a feeling that the problems of this period are being resolved and that its tensions have been harmonized. At such times, therefore, we feel that we can relax. We feel satisfied that a unit of our experience has been brought into balance within itself. A natural unit seems to have been completed. We thus feel free to enter a new period in our lives.

Each time-unit of our life passes through such a cycle of problems, tensions, and resolutions by a process that self-adjusts within the context of the period. Our Journal work serves as a vehicle for this self-balancing process in the short run. The long-run movement of our Journal work, however, includes a succession of such time-units in our life. Each achieves a degree of self-balancing within itself. As an individual continues to work with the *Intensive Journal* over a number of years, the succession of these self-balanced time-units builds a cumulative effect. The movement of the life as a whole restructures itself again and again to incorporate the meaning of new situations; each time this takes place our total life history is progressively recrystallized. This is the larger process of life-integration proceeding in the background of our Journal work.

The distinction between self-balancing within the short-run time-units of our life and life-integration in the ongoing movement and larger scope of our Journal work is important for the perspective it gives us in continuing our use of the Journal. Given the pressures of the modern world, it is fair to assume that most people who begin to use the *Intensive Journal* do so because there is a problem in their life that urgently needs to be resolved, an intense and difficult transition through which their life must pass, or a critical decision they must make. Because of the self-balancing process that underlies it, the Journal Feedback

procedures facilitate the solving of problems and the making of decisions. The approach of activating the depth of a person while maintaining the context of each unique life, stimulates the finding of answers
that are specific and relevant. In the short-run work, moreover, these
answers tend to be found sooner rather than later. As the needs of the
immediate situation are met, however, and as ideas begin to flow for the
next step in our life, there is a strong temptation to take these first fruits
and rush off with them before a fuller harvest can be gathered. Once you
have begun to use the *Intensive Journal* , however, it is a great waste not
to do the follow-up work that will give you the *accrued results* that come
from staying with the process.

Since the principle underlying Journal Feedback is that of cumulative movement, maintaining the Journal work has a multiplying effect if
it is allowed to continue over significant units of time. As we extend its
use, the scope of the *Intensive Journal* enables us to build a context for
decisions that encompasses our whole life-history. Beyond the factor of
self-balancing, the principle of life-integration is then able to operate on
the scale of the full movement of our life-history and reconstellate our
life for us in a perspective that neither our conscious minds nor our
imagination could conceive or create. We could not have figured it out
with our intelligence, but continuing the Journal process draws a
reintegrative factor into our experience. It progressively calls into play a
dynamic of inner direction that restructures our unfolding experience in
ever new contexts, opening new possibilities and meanings for our
future. Our rational thought processes would not by themselves be able
to envision these, and although it would contain them latently, our
nonconscious depth would not be able to give them form and bring
them to actuality. Neither consciousness nor the unconscious, but the
reintegrative factor which is brought into play by the continuity of
Journal work makes this possible. This carries the operation of the
life-integrative process and is the reason why we often find it to be true
in our Journal work that specific and immediate problems are most
meaningfully solved by Journal Feedback not when they are concentrated upon directly, but when they are allowed to take their place in
the movement of our whole life history. The Journal exercises carry this
movement, and our deliberately indirect way of working with them

makes it possible for solutions and new guidances to come to us *as though by themselves.* These new life-answers emerge as though they were merely by-products of our basic Journal work. And, in a sense, that is what they are. They are the by-products that emerge when the process of life-integration is given a broad range of time and experience in which to do its organic work using the *Intensive Journal* as its instrument.

The key to working with the *Intensive Journal* productively lies in the quality and quantity of the material that we feed into it in the continuity of our work. As we sustain our use of it, the Journal can feed back to us in self-transforming ways the n aterial that we have recorded in it. It is essential, however, that we supply it with sufficient data, and that we maintain this on a current basis. The longer we work with the Journal in continuity, the more we can reap the benefit of its progressive and cumulative feedback effect.

After a workshop, a primary means of building the continuity of the Journal work is with your entries in the Daily Log. It is not necessary to write in it everyday, but just often enough so that when you read the sequence of Daily Log entries back to yourself at a later time they will reflect the day-to-day movement of your life. In this way, the Daily Log can fulfill its basic function of supplying life–data that will become the starting point for further feedback extensions. This can ordinarily be achieved without writing in the Journal everyday. In the beginning, however, in order to gather a basic resource of life material and to set the Journal process into motion, it is good to make daily entries. At least for the first three or four weeks in which you are using the *Intensive Journal,* try to record at least some inner experience each day. This will establish your relationship to Journal work and make you secure in using it. Eventually, as it builds its own momentum, you will be able to continue it more flexibly and let it adjust itself to your life tempo.

In addition to our continuing entries in the Daily Log, a great deal of work remains for us to do in the Life/Time sections. The time at a workshop is sufficient only for us to begin the large task of filling in the details and elaborating the contents of each of the Steppingstone Periods. Extending the work of Time-Stretching as it leads to the progressive reconstruction of our autobiography, working in the Life History Log and exploring our Intersections: The Roads Taken and Not Taken, has the effect of feeding a great deal more life-data into our Journals. Thus the more we do here, the more we contribute to the self-balancing process and to the working out of the integrative principle in the background of our life.

In this same context it is important that we continue to make our entries in the Dream Log and the Twilight Imagery Log on a current basis. Whenever we recall a sleep dream it is important to record it so that, at a later time, we can work with the seriality of our dreaming and thus draw ourselves into contact with the energies and the meanings that are unfolding in us at an unconscious level. Whenever we become aware, also, that we are having a spontaneous Twilight Imagery experience, these are to be recorded and added to the flow of our depth material.

As we record our dream and Twilight Imagery experiences and while we are filling in and extending the Time-Stretching exercises, we find that we are building a large resource for the Journal Feedback work. We make our entries as they come to us without judgment and without analysis; but when we read them back to ourselves we become aware of the feedback leads they give us for working elsewhere in our life via the various sections of the Journal. We have learned in our Journal work that the question, "What is the *meaning* of this experience?" is not well answered when we turn back to look analytically at the events of our life. We find the *meaning* of our dreams and other life-experiences not by interpreting them but by following their feedback leads to other sections of the Journal. As we work with them in the Depth and Life/Time dimensions, whatever their specific content, they lead us toward a fuller dialogue relationship with a particular aspect of our life. The *feedback leads* direct us through a succession of Journal experiences, culminating eventually in a dialogue script. It is here that the meaning of our experience discloses itself, not in terms of an abstract or interpretive concept, but in the context and language of our own life as it is unfolding.

Following the feedback leads is the primary means of extending the Journal Feedback process in the continuity of our life. It makes possible the interplay among the sections, and this in turn builds the multiple and cumulative effects of self-balancing and life-integration. Thus we proceed in an open-ended way to extend the range of our inner experience and to find practical ways of expressing it in the outer world.

The concept that underlies the *Intensive Journal* approach is that the potential for growth in a human being is as infinite as the universe. This refers not to physical growth, of course, but to the qualitative growth of persons. It refers especially to the development of our inner capacities of awareness and our outer capacities for living as full human beings among our fellows.

In a profound sense, each human life has the potentiality of becoming an artwork. To that degree, each of us can become an artist-in-life with our finest creation being our own Self. Just as the true artist, like Casals or Einstein or Picasso among the recent generation, never ceases his creative work while he is alive, so we continue the creative development of the person within us. Whenever a phase of our life completes itself and we reach a particular level of integration or awareness and achievement, that in its turn becomes our new starting point. In this perspective, all those life difficulties that we might otherwise think of as problems or pathologies, become the raw material of our next development. When a phase of our life completes itself, only that phase is finished. We ourselves are not finished. Our life history continues to unfold.

A principle comparable to this is true of the process of evolution in the universe at large. When a season or a geologic period ends, when an individual animal or an entire species dies, that is not the termination of things. It is rather an event that feeds into the total process of evolution. From one point of view and on one level, it is an ending. From another point of view, it is the material for a new beginning. In the unfolding context of evolution, what appears as death and termination becomes on another level the occasion for a further renewal of life.

As this is true of the universe, it is also true of our lives as persons. On the qualitative level of our inner experience, our endings provide the material for new beginnings. In the midst of the everyday pressures of anxiety and pain, we often lose the perspective of knowing this and we forget that our individual lives are each an inner universe in which a process of evolution is seeking to unfold. Our Journal work seeks to give us a practical way of maintaining this large inner perspective.

A primary purpose of the *Intensive Journal* is to provide an instrument and method by which the qualitative evolution of life can take place within us as individuals. It seeks to maintain for the elusive subjectivities of our inner life an open space in which the processes of life-integration can proceed objectively in the context of each person's experience. The *Intensive Journal* becomes the outer embodiment of our inner life. It thus serves for many of us as the laboratory in which we explore experimentally the possibilities of our life. It also serves as the sanctuary to which we go for our most intimate and private, our most profound and universal experiences. But most fundamentally, the *Intensive Journal* is our inner workshop, the place where we do the creative shaping of the artwork of our life.

Appendix

The Registered Intensive Journal

The registered *Intensive Journal,* as it was originally published, has served as the cornerstone of the Dialogue House program for individual growth. Working with it is essential because it is the instrument that makes possible the method of Journal Feedback with its continuous and cumulative interplay of experiences. And it is this active interflow of Journal Feedback that enables the self-balancing process of life integration to establish itself in the course of our continuous and open-ended experience.

The indispensable function of the *Intensive Journal* is that its structure provides a tangible equivalent of the inner space in which the mini-processes of our life can move about until they find their appropriate level and form of self-integration. The *Intensive Journal* thus serves as the vehicle of our individual initiation into the larger process of existence. It enables us to draw our personal life into focus while opening an inner window to the transpersonal mysteries of human destiny. Since it serves so intimate and profound a role, it is inevitable that many people have found that over a period of years the *Intensive Journal* becomes a symbol to them of their contact with the larger meanings and possibilities of their life. It becomes the embodiment of the movement and the unfoldment of each person's unique existence. Its very presence thus becomes a token of the reality and the continuity of the inner person whom we each are and are progressively becoming. Small wonder, then, that many people like to carry their Journals with them even when they do not expect to write in them. Seeing their Journal reminds them that their inner process is real, and is continuing even when their outer life seems bleak and difficult. Beyond its functional value as an instrument for emergent growth, the *Intensive Journal* develops a symbolic value of inner life continuity that becomes even richer with its overtones of energy and meaning as it is used through the years.

This symbolic as well as functional role of the *Intensive Journal* is a major reason for working with it in the structured form that it has developed through its years of use. If, after carrying out the basic procedures that have been described in this book, you find the Journal Feedback method to be congenial to you, and if you feel it can help you focus and deepen your life in an ongoing way, your next step should be to have the actual experience of participating in a Dialogue House Journal Workshop. When you attend that, you will receive a registered and numbered copy of the *Intensive Journal*, and this will be yours to use permanently in your privacy as well as at successive workshops.

In the meanwhile, if you have not yet attended a Journal Workshop and are undertaking to learn the Journal Feedback procedures while working by yourself, you will need a model of the *Intensive Journal* to follow for your temporary use. With this in mind, the following pages contain a facsimile of the registered *Intensive Journal* as it is issued in numbered copies to participants taking part in their first Dialogue House Journal Workshop. It is reprinted here so that, even though you do not yet have your personal copy of the *Intensive Journal*, you can have at least a preliminary experience of working with it as a unit.

One of the important functions of Dialogue House as a public organization is its role in making Journal Workshops available in appropriate formats at various levels of society, in education, in religion, in the arts, in drug and urban tension areas, and especially for the general population. In supporting these programs, Dialogue House seeks to monitor the issuance of *Intensive Journals* as carefully as it is able so as to maintain professional standards of responsibility in the use of the *Intensive Journal* method. Consequently, only those who are approved as Journal Consultants on the basis of their training and experience in the Journal Feedback procedures as well as their other professional qualifications are authorized to issue these registered Dialogue House *Intensive Journals.*

When you come to participate in a Journal Workshop, one way that you can check the credentials of the leader is by his authorization to issue you a registered and numbered copy of the published Dialogue House *Intensive Journal.* This will be verification that you are not talking to a self-appointed Journal Consultant, but to a person who has studied the Journal Feedback procedures, whose basic competence has been recognized, and who is engaged in ongoing study. Such a qualified Journal Consultant will also have available to him new Dialogue House materials and procedures as they are developed, as well as whatever guidance and support he may require from Dialogue House staff consultants.

The facsimile copy of the *Intensive Journal* follows.

(white)

INTENSIVE JOURNAL

Your Registered Journal is   _____

This Journal is registered with and is part of
The Personal Growth and Creativity Program of:
Dialogue House Associates, Inc.: 45 West Tenth Street, New York, N.Y. 10011

(green)

PERIOD LOG

PERIOD LOG

(yellow)

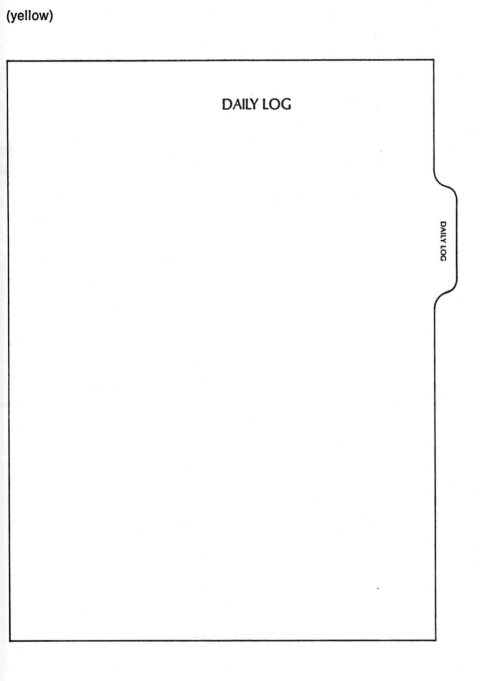

DAILY LOG

DAILY LOG

(orange)

DIALOGUE DIMENSION:
Special Personal Sections

DIALOGUE DIMENSION

(orange)

DIALOGUE WITH PERSONS

DIALOGUE WITH PERSONS

(orange)

DIALOGUE WITH WORKS

DIALOGUE WITH WORKS

(orange)

DIALOGUE WITH SOCIETY
Group Experiences

DIALOGUE WITH SOCIETY

(orange)

DIALOGUE WITH EVENTS
Situations and Circumstances

DIALOGUE WITH EVENTS

(orange)

DIALOGUE WITH THE BODY

DIALOGUE WITH THE BODY

(blue)

DEPTH DIMENSION:
Ways of Symbolic Contact

DEPTH DIMENSION

(blue)

DREAM LOG
Description, Context, Associations

DREAM LOG

(blue)

DREAM ENLARGEMENTS

DREAM ENLARGEMENTS

(blue)

TWILIGHT IMAGERY LOG

TWILIGHT IMAGERY LOG

(blue)

IMAGERY EXTENSIONS

IMAGERY EXTENSIONS

(blue)

INNER WISDOM DIALOGUE

INNER WISDOM DIALOGUE

(red)

LIFE / TIME DIMENSION:
Inner Perspectives

LIFE / TIME DIMENSION:

(red)

LIFE HISTORY LOG
Recapitulations and Rememberings

LIFE HISTORY LOG

(red)

STEPPING STONES

STEPPING STONES

(red)

INTERSECTIONS
Roads Taken and Not Taken

INTERSECTIONS

APPENDIX

(red)

NOW: The Open Moment

NOW:
The Open Moment